SUNDERLAND

By the same author:

Behind the Curtain

SUNDERLAND

A Club Transformed

Jonathan Wilson

Copyright © Jonathan Wilson 2007

The right of Jonathan Wilson to be identified as the
author of this work has been asserted by him in accordance
with the Copyright, Designs and Patents Act 1988.

First published in hardback in Great Britain in 2007 by
Orion Books
an imprint of the Orion Publishing Group Ltd
Orion House, 5 Upper St Martin's Lane,
London WC2H 9EA
An Hachette Livre UK Company

1 3 5 7 9 10 8 6 4 2

A CIP catalogue record for this book is
available from the British Library.

ISBN 978 0 7528 9117 0

Printed and bound in Great Britain by
Clays Ltd, St Ives plc

Every effort has been made to fulfil requirements with regard
to reproducing copyright material. The author and publisher
will be glad to rectify any omissions at the earliest opportunity.

www.orionbooks.co.uk

CONTENTS

At Orion, thanks are due to Ian Preece, for his constant support and many wise suggestions, to Tarda Davison-Aitkins for his copy-editing, and to Malcolm Edwards, for his vision in witnessing a worryingly sober rant at Jimmy Hill and seeing in it a book.

Thanks to my agent, David Luxton, for masterminding the seating-plan to ensure the rant was witnessed, and for concluding the subsequent negotiations so successfully.

A huge thank you to Jon Adams for producing the bridge designs at such short notice.

This is very much a personal book, but it nonetheless benefited from the input of Peter Daykin, Jeremy Robinson, Jeff Brown, Scott Wilson, Paul Fraser and Jason Burt. My thanks to them for their comments, anecdotes and suggestions of further areas of research.

Thanks also to Paul Howarth, for so regularly taking the time to explain in such detail how much better than Sunderland Ipswich were when they beat them in September.

For my dad, who first took me to Roker Park and made sure Saturday afternoons out ended always at twenty to five; and for my mam, who let him

hoc est adverso nixantem trudere monte
saxum, quod tamen summo iam vertice rusum
volvitur et plani raptim petit aequora campi.

(LUCRETIUS, *De Rerum Natura III*, 1000-1002)

INTRODUCTION

Once, it was the holiest of holies; now it is a housing estate. Sunderland had to move from Roker Park, and in almost every way the Stadium of Light has been a triumph, but to revisit the site of the old ground is to be devastated by the banality of what replaced it. Not that there is anything wrong with the houses; on the contrary, they are pleasant semi-detached properties that blend well with the surrounding terraces. Aesthetically, they are almost certainly an improvement on the dilapidated stands and the graffiti-scarred walls that once stood there, but still, there was a blandness about the place I hadn't expected.

That said, I don't really know what I'd expected. I hadn't been to that part of Roker since the summer of 1997, when I went with a few friends to watch the demolition, thinking we could maybe pick up a souvenir or two. We couldn't. All the good stuff had already been auctioned off so, unless you fancied an anonymous brick – it could perhaps sit on the mantelpiece next to that dubiously certified chunk of the Berlin Wall – all that was to be done was wander disconsolately around and wonder if going to matches would ever be the same again.

It was almost exactly ten years later that I went back. I live in London now, but was back in the Northeast reporting on the Test match. Partly because I had to make sure I was at Chester-le-Street for the first ball of the day, and partly because I didn't want anybody else around, I got a taxi through from Durham at a little after six in the morning. I was worried the driver might think it was a little odd, somebody going to visit an old football ground a decade after it had been knocked down, but Bobby from Chas's Cabs seemed not only to understand, but to be almost more enthused by the trip than me. He, it turned out, had missed only one home game since 1965, and that was because he was unavoidably hospitalised.

We turned left off Roker Avenue, down past the Cambridge, where the pub sign still shows an immaculate Roker Park gleaming in the floodlights, then swung right down Roker Baths Road, past where the Supporters Association and the Roker Pie Shop used to be. 'Yer can 'ear it,' Bobby insisted. 'Yer can still 'ear it, man. Listen to 'em.' Maybe he could, but I couldn't. I wanted to hear echoes of the past, the hubbub and the grousing, the chants and the roars, even the ageless programme seller with his shopping-trolley and his indecipherable sales pitch, but all I could hear were the coarse shrieks of the sea-gulls and the gentler twittering of the odd blackbird. I got out of the cab where Town Centre Garages had once stood, and tried to get my bearings. The New Derby, where in later years we'd go to clear out the quiz machines after night matches, was still there, and so was the newsagents at the end of Brandling Street, but nothing else was the same.

As Martin Chuzzlewit returns to England from America, Dickens has him rejoice 'at the sight of the old churches, roofs and darkened chimney stacks of Home'. His breast hums with 'life and exultation'. He and Mark Tapley, his travelling companion, have been away only a year and yet 'the distant roar that swelled up hoarsely from the busy streets, was music in their ears; the lines of people gazing from the wharves were friends held dear; the canopy of smoke that overhung the town was brighter and more beautiful to them than if the richest silks of Persia had been waving in the air.'

All exiles, perhaps, feel something similar as their feet traipse again the paths of their youth. Whatever has changed – in beholder or beheld – whatever previously unnoticed flaws, whatever previously neglected beauties, become apparent, it is, as Chuzzlewit reflects 'home. And though home is a name, a word, it is a strong one; stronger than magician ever spoke, or spirit answered to, in strongest conjuration.'

I haven't lived in Sunderland for eight years, and even then it was only temporary, as I worked in factories and data-entry centres for three months after university before blithely heading off to London to make my fortune. By working in a data-entry centre for an extra pound an hour, as it turned out, at least for the first six months. Really the break was made 13 years ago when, in what, looking back, appears an inexplicable whim, I headed off to India to teach in a Tibetan monastery.

Exile is probably too strong a term. It is, after all, my choice to live in London. I could return home – and 'home', I notice, is a term I use to refer not to my flat, the place where I actually live, but to Wearside – whenever I chose. I don't, for a variety of social and economic reasons, but I could. Still, there are occasions when I go back home, particularly when I've been away for a long time, when I find myself overwhelmed by an emotion. What it is, that feeling, I'm not entirely sure. Does everybody get it? Chuzzlewit certainly did, so I suppose it may be universal. It begins as a numbing warmth, a sense of heat behind the eyes, a pricking, then an ache in the throat, a slight tightening of the chest at times, and then, if you don't control it in time, a wobbling spasm of the jaw. Tears, I imagine, would follow if you allowed them to, although obviously if you're a Wearsider, you don't. (Gazza, who ranks alongside Diana and Dickie Bird as Britain's most notorious blubbers of the twentieth century, is characteristically Geordie in this regard: they're at it all the time. Booked in a World Cup semifinal, thus ruling you out of the final? Weep. Lost in the Cup final? Weep. Finished eighth in the league? Weep. Greggs out of sausage rolls? Weep. Cruel BBC bosses refuse to commission a fourth series of *Spender*? Weep. It's no wonder the Tyne's deeper than the Wear. When Roy Keane was booked in the semifinal of the Champions League in 1999 and knew he would miss the final, did he cry? No, he produced one of the great individual performances, as Manchester United overturned a two-goal deficit to beat Juventus 3-2 in Turin. Sir Alex Ferguson, his manager, called it the most selfless display he had ever seen.)

It is not a predictable feeling; there is no one thing that always sets it off. Perhaps it will be the sea gleaming as the sun rises over Roker Pier, or a ruddy-faced old man in a pub, the flattened whoops of a shop-assistant's banter perhaps, or even something as simple and seemingly universal as the scent of salt on the breeze. Roker Park, or rather, what had once been Roker Park, didn't do it for me that morning, though, which disappointed me, because the thing that is usually guaranteed to set me off is a bank of candy-striped fans, something, oddly, that is almost more potent outside of Sunderland.

Part of me knows my reaction to a mass of red-and-white shirts is ridiculous. Were I part of it, among the sweat and the beer-burps, the fag-smoke and the localised grumblings, I know I would feel no differently towards them than towards any other crowd. But from a short distance, when individuality disappears, and they become a red-and-white mass raucously bellowing their pride in what they are, pride wells also in me, because that is what I am. That was something I first really appreciated at the play-off final in 1998, by which time I'd already been away from home for four years, long enough for the process of romanticisation to be well underway. My seat at Wembley was above the corner-flag, slightly around the corner from the main bulk of Sunderland fans, so I was looking across them. I don't think I'd ever before been in such a position of being part of a crowd, and yet at the same time being detached from it. Certainly that was the first time I realised quite the emotional power, the sense of a unity of spirit, Sunderland fans emit. Other sets of fans probably do it too – I've no intention of turning this into one of those futile rants about whose fans are the 'best', as though such a thing were measurable or even interesting – but, naturally, the one that most appeals to me are my own. Even these days, watching from the press box, encased in a carapace of supposed professionalism, there are times when it gets to me. And yes, to those I pushed past, that was the reason for my rapid departure from the press box at the Hawthorns last season. Sorry. Something, I think, to do with the Trinidad and Tobago flag.

The Far Corner, Harry Pearson's hilarious and deceptively profound book detailing his year visiting football grounds across the Northeast, begins with his return home from London. Mockingly, he piles up the clichés – the rugged landscape, the idiosyncrasies of the accent, the smell of frying food – only to find himself strangely moved by it all. By the time I'd finished reading it for the first time, on a train home from the South, my hands were shaking, and it was all I could to croak an unconvincing 'aye' when a man sitting opposite me asked, 'Yis alreet, son?' It's not even as though Harry's home is my home – he's from Middlesbrough – but his evocation of a

mythic Northeast was enough to awake in me those same feelings. I suppose it's probably a form of nostalgia, but if it is, it's
nostalgia for a home that never existed. Home ceases to be an
actual place and becomes idealised. To go home is to look in a
mirror, and see stretching out behind you the narrative of your
life, the disappointments and the regrets, the opportunities
missed and the what-might-have-beens, and perhaps, if you're
lucky, even the odd triumph as well. It is more, though, than
that. It is also a return to a time that memory makes simpler
and rosier than it probably was, to our origins, to what we
were before time and circumstance intervened. That seems to
me a fundamental human urge, and it is surely significant that
so many great narratives, from *The Odyssey* to *The Wizard of
Oz*, detail the protagonist's efforts to return home.

The reason that sense of being home has a tendency in
Sunderland to sneak up and catch a returnee unawares, I suspect, is that there is no obvious trigger. Sunderland has no
defining landmark, unless you count Penshaw Monument, but
it's some way outside the town – and, from my point of view,
on the wrong side of town. Perhaps, if you approach by road
from the south, it serves as a sign that you're back, but I tend
to arrive by train and, anyway, it packs nothing of the impact
that the cathedral and the castle must have on those returning
to Durham. Nor, and I suppose I ought to say this through
clenched teeth, is it a patch on the Angel of the North and
Newcastle's awesome cityscape – the bridges, the cathedral,
the seahorse-flanked civic centre and, spit it not too bitterly, St
James' Park. Even the station in Newcastle, with its vast
Gothic arches, has a grandeur that announces the magnifi-
cence of its industrial past. Sunderland station, by contrast,
may be the grimmest place on earth, low-roofed, litter-strewn,
dark, and bleakly functional.

There are, admittedly, printed on pale plastic panels on the wall, images of the city crest, but even they are a dubious consolation. There is a crown on a blue field and lions rampant, but there is also the resolutely depressing motto, adopted in 1849, '*Nil desperandum, auspice deo*', which is usually translated as 'Don't despair, trust in God'. What on earth possessed them at the council meeting that decided that? Did they really think that the best way to present the town to the world was to try to caution visitors on arrival against desolation? And that was in the boom years, when Sunderland was one of the world's great shipbuilding centres.

The motto, in fairness, makes slightly more sense if you trace it back to its origins. It derives, via an admittedly winding route, from Horace's *Odes* and the description of Teucer setting out from Salamis to found a new city:

'*Nil desperandum Teucro duce et auspice Teucro:*
certus enim promisit Apollo ambiguam tellure noua
Salamina futuram'

(VII, 27-9)

('Despair not, while Teucer leads, of Teucer's omens:
For unerring Apollo surely promised
In the uncertain future a new Salamis')

Teucer had been forced from the state of Salamis after being disowned by his father following the suicide of his half-brother, Ajax, and fled to Cyprus, where he founded the city of Salamis. Given Sunderland's expansion from fishing village to major industrial town was prompted by merchants and shipbuilders forced out of Newcastle by restrictive guild-practices on the Tyne, you can just about see why the myth would have resonance, but the connection is tenuous and, anyway, why should anybody, particularly a casual outsider, trace the history that carefully?

And so, amid the subterranean darkness of the station, visitors are left, immediately, with the injunction not to despair, a message that seems unfortunately in keeping with the city's ready embrace of gloom. It's almost as though the council is looping a consoling arm around anybody arriving and murmuring, 'Don't worry, it's not *that* bad.' Sunderland, I was told by an elderly Geordie I once got talking to in a pub in West Jesmond, is what happened when they kicked the miserable people out of Newcastle. I thought perhaps that might be a hackneyed line I had somehow missed, but nobody else seems to have heard it. Nonetheless, it has a ring of truth. Geordies are madly, irrepressibly bubbly; Mackems rather more reserved. Pessimism feels a natural mode.

[1]

SOMEWHERE
OVER THE YO-YO

Cause and effect. Cause and effect. What is curious about certain events is not that they happened, how they happened or even why they happened, but why they happened when they happened. What concatenation of forces was it that brought that event to pass just then, not a week before or a month after, but there, bang, then, on that minute of that hour of that day?

Why was Mick McCarthy sacked on the morning of Monday 6 March 2006? As journalists and fans watched him drive off up the Shields Road, passing the old abattoir for the final time, nobody asked why, but everybody asked why then? The why was easy. Sunderland were bottom of the Premiership table and doomed to relegation, having collected a mere ten points all season. And yet the question remained: what was it about a 22nd defeat of a season that had persuaded the board that this was the time to take action? Was it really so much worse than the 21st? Why sack him in March with ten games of the season remaining? Why saddle some other poor sap with the burden of taking Sunderland down?

It wasn't as though – in context, at least – there had been anything particularly shameful about a 2-1 away defeat at

Manchester City the day before. Yes, Danny Collins attempting a drag-back on the corner of his own box to present Georgios Samaras with their first goal after nine minutes was unfortunate, and, yes, Gary Breen dawdling to play Trevor Sinclair onside as he set up a second for Samaras a minute later looked a little careless, but they weren't exactly uncharacteristic errors. And, it wasn't even as though anybody had really twigged at that stage just how ordinary Samaras was, that, at the end of the following season, those two goals would represent a quarter of his Premiership total. In the 80 minutes that remained, Sunderland had actually battled quite well. They even pulled one back through the improbable figure of Kevin Kyle – his first of a season ruined by a hip injury – and seemed to be mounting a late charge for an equaliser when Breen senselessly blocked a David James clearance with his arm, collected a second yellow card and was sent off with five minutes to go.

Perhaps the problem had been McCarthy's shoulder-shrugging response. 'What makes you do some things in games?' he had asked with the defeatist raise of the eyebrows that had become so familiar. 'There's no explanation. We ask them to play at the back, but then it's decision-making. When the ball's rolled back to you and you're under pressure you kick it as far away as possible.'

Other Premiership managers might have come up with something more sophisticated, but McCarthy's frustration was understandable. After all, other Premiership goalkeepers than Kelvin Davis might not have rolled a soft pass to their full-back to put him under pressure. Other full-backs than Danny Collins might have been alert to the danger and moved towards the ball. And other full-backs might certainly have realised that a team that has won two, drawn four and lost 22 of its games that season has no business pretending to be a reincarnation of Stefan Kovacs's Ajax. For better or for worse, most British defenders grew up under the mantra of 'if in doubt, boot it out', and Sunderland's defenders that season had more reason to adopt a safety-first mentality than most. If they had lost the ability even to lump it, what hope did McCarthy have?

At that stage, McCarthy's managerial career included 37 Premiership games, of which 31 had been lost. Whether that were his fault or not was a matter of some debate – the growing school of thought that sought to apply business models to sport suggested certain managers simply aren't cut out for the very top level, and McCarthy had done little to suggest he was – but even if you accepted that he, rather than circumstance, was to blame, that still didn't explain the timing of his dismissal. The season had long since degenerated from ignominy into numb farce. The reality that the club would be relegated had been recognised and accepted almost from the beginning of August. Fans weren't happy with it, but they had settled into their role with a certain gallows gusto, greeting every goal – there was a total of just 26 that season, four fewer than Kevin Phillips alone had managed in 1999-2000 – with manic abandon. When Daryl Murphy squeezed a last-minute equaliser past Paul Robinson to steal a draw against Tottenham in February, the celebrations had been such that, as Kyle said, 'you'd have thought we'd won the World Cup'.

So why? Why then? This wasn't like when Lawrie McMenemy had walked away in April 1987, seven games from the end of the season, so his record wouldn't be sullied by a relegation, leaving poor Bob Stokoe to carry the can. It wasn't even like March 2003, when getting rid of Howard Wilkinson and Steve Cotterill had served as a useful blood-letting, and an acknowledgement that their appointment had been a mistake. This, frankly, defied rational explanation.

There had been talk of a rift with the board the previous month, after McCarthy had blamed them and their transfer policy for the club's plight. 'There was a view taken that of course we wanted to stay up and do well but, if we didn't, then the group of players here will stay here and be a force to be reckoned with in the Championship,' he said. 'We have lacked experience, but if we had gone out and got experienced players on big salaries we might have had a real problem if we had gone down. If it turns out that we're not good enough and we go down, this team stays together unless any decide they don't want to.'

A summer that had seen only four players arrive for fees – and one of them the goalkeeper Joe Murphy, who fell behind the 18-year-old Ben Alnwick in the pecking order and joined Scunthorpe on a free transfer without playing a game – certainly seemed to suggest a policy of caution. But then the chairman Bob Murray responded with an interview in the *Sunderland Echo* that, as clinical deconstructions go, almost rivalled Roy Keane's demolition of McCarthy in Saipan, Japan ahead of the 2002 World Cup. Having spoken of being 'very angry', and of McCarthy's accusations as being 'blatantly untrue and insulting', he dismissed as 'ludicrous' the suggestion that Sunderland had approached the season 'just to make up the numbers or with a plan to come back down'. If Bolton failed to qualify for the Uefa Cup, he revealed, their players would receive the same total in wages as Sunderland's squad would if they stayed up.

'We did expect it to be a difficult and hard first season back, as Wigan and West Ham did, but we did not expect to be in the position we are today – and none of us are happy about that,' he went on. 'The policy was to acquire players to secure our position in the Premiership and certainly not a subsequent season in the Championship. The board did not dictate the number of players to buy or which targets to pursue. All our player contracts, like the majority of clubs' now, are much more performance-related and also reflect our status – wherever we finish in the league – but that's just sound business.

The facts are: we finished last season 21 points ahead of West Ham and seven points ahead of Wigan. 'In the summer [of 2005] we invested at least as much as both Wigan and West Ham and expected to be in there scrapping to the end of the season with the goal of retaining our Premiership status, so we could consolidate further in our second season. Wigan and West Ham have been able to invest again in the January window, as we would have done had we been in the same position with the comfort of knowing we too had all but secured our Premiership status. Unfortunately, the performances and results dictated otherwise. At our game against West Brom I was talking to their chairman and he confirmed that despite them being in their second successive season in the Premiership our wage bill is higher than theirs, so it's not a case of us lacking ambition, not being prepared to pay Premiership wages or not wanting to remain in the top flight.'

That was stinging enough, but he could have been harsher. He could have pointed out just how badly McCarthy's three biggest signings had done. Jon Stead (signed from Blackburn for £1.8million) had at that stage, after 27 appearances, still failed to score, while Andy Gray (£1.1million from Sheffield United), after scoring on his debut in the 3-1 home defeat to Charlton on the opening day, hadn't managed another goal before being offloaded on loan to Burnley at the beginning of the month. Even in money-go-round of the Premiership, £2.9million a goal seemed a little steep.

At the other end, Sunderland weren't charging the opposition anything like as much. The goalkeeper Kelvin Davis, brought in for £1.25million, had formed such a hilariously inept double-act with Gary Breen that they could be relied upon to concede corners from just about any aimless ball the opposition hoofed over the top. McCarthy had become disillusioned with Davis so quickly that as early as November he left him out for Alnwick. Davis, in fairness, had looked solid enough for Ipswich the previous season, but even at the time it had seemed odd to allow Mart Poom and Thomas Myhre, both internationals, to leave on free transfers. Hindsight showed it to be disastrous. By the time McCarthy was sacked, not only had Davis proved himself a significantly inferior goalkeeper to both, but the two forwards McCarthy had bought hadn't managed between them to surpass the number of goals that Poom had scored for the club.

And yet, for all that, nobody really blamed McCarthy. Crocodile tears are not uncommon at such times, but when Murray thanked McCarthy for his efforts and wished him all the best for the future, he seemed to mean it, particularly when he then admitted his own part in the failings. 'As chairman I take responsibility for what has proven to be an unsuccessful and heartbreaking season; despite the best intentions, efforts and expectations of every one at the club,' he said. 'I feel deeply sorry that the excitement, optimism and aspirations of all Sunderland fans looking forward to a return to the Premier League have been rewarded in this way and I apologise for this. It is especially tough on supporters who have turned out in numbers week in, week out; despite seeing so little to raise their spirits. It is hard to see such loyalty unrewarded and I am sorry that performances and results have not mirrored the tremendous level of support that the club has been given.'

As he left, McCarthy, lingering far longer than politeness demanded to chat to reporters in the car-park at the Academy of Light, seemed far from bitter. Perhaps he was simply relieved. 'It's been tough the last few months but I've enjoyed every single minute of it,' he said. 'It's been a pleasure and I've been very fortunate. As always, I've done my best and I can't do any more. I'll move on and eventually do something else. It's been brilliant and I've thoroughly enjoyed it and enjoyed the support of the fans. It was great last year with the championship but it's changed. I'm not going to dash away all aggressive and horrible, I'll leave you with a smile.' And so he did, before raising his car window, and pulling slowly away. It was all very restrained, all very dignified. This was less vicious boardroom putsch than regretful relatives turning off the life-support.

Fans had moaned and groaned, but there had been too much realism for them really to turn on McCarthy. His reiteration of the phrase 'What can you do?' after yet another defeat had begun to grate, but really, what could he do? What could he have done? Yes, his summer signings had been disappointing; yes, the goalkeeping issue represented a major error of judgement, but it was widely held that essentially he had been sacked for getting Sunderland promoted. His three years in charge had only shown what everybody already knew, that Sunderland were a terminal yo-yo club, too big for the second flight but not good enough for the top. People spoke of parachute payments for clubs relegated from the Premiership, but what Sunderland really needed was a mezzanine.

McCarthy had been appointed in March 2003, three years less six days before his dismissal, taking over a squad shattered by the disastrous dual reign of Wilkinson and Cotterill. With morale nonexistent, he presided over nine straight defeats as Sunderland were relegated from the Premiership with 19 points. Fans were split over whether Peter Reid – dismissed the previous October after a seven-and-a-half year reign gone stale after back-to-back seventh-place finishes – should have been given more time or been sacked earlier, but they were unanimous in concluding that the job should never have gone to the Wilkinson-Cotterill double-act. McCarthy, it was generally accepted, had been in an impossible position. That seemed then an unimaginable low, and Sunderland shuddered with the thought that they had set a record that would remain in the record books for all time. Three years later, 19 points would seem riches beyond the dreams of avarice.

Sunderland had also lost the six games before McCarthy took over, and when they were beaten by Nottingham Forest and Millwall in their opening two league games of the 2003-04 season, they found themselves within a match of equalling Darwen's 104-year-old record of eighteen straight defeats. Goals from Sean Thornton and Marcus Stewart, though, gave them a 2-0 win, sparking a recovery that carried them as far as the FA Cup semifinal and the play-offs, where they lost in a penalty shoot-out to Crystal Palace. The following year, despite severe debts that left McCarthy having to scour the lower divisions for bargains – Dean Whitehead arrived from Oxford for £150,000, Liam Lawrence from Mansfield for £175,000 – Sunderland won the Championship.

It was, without question, a remarkable achievement, and yet it was not greeted with any great joy. Crowds remained low, and largely despondent. There were 47,350 at the Stadium of Light to see the Championship trophy presented on the final day of the season – the largest post-War crowd for a game outside the top division – but the average remained a disappointing 28,821. It was the ninth promotion in Sunderland's history, and by some way the least satisfying. In their previous five seasons in the second flight, they had won the division three times, and been beaten in the play-offs twice, both times on penalties (being even more specific, both times in penalty shoot-outs that went on to the 14th kick). Going up had become routine, and almost everybody suspected – rightly – that this promotion would be the prelude to a savaging. That's the problem with yo-yos: when the bounce goes, they stick at the bottom, not at the top.

Statistics showed that of the 20 sides in the Premiership in 2005-06, Sunderland and Charlton Athletic had the worst records in their first game of the season, so when Charlton won 3-1 at the Stadium of Light on the opening day despite having Darren Ambrose sent off, it didn't take a pessimist to fear the worst – and Sunderland has never been short of pessimists.

By the time they finally won a point by drawing against West Brom on September 17 – having taken their run of consecutive Premiership defeats to a mighty 20 – relegation was regarded as a *fait accompli*. A freak April snowstorm that caused the match against Fulham to be abandoned after 20 minutes – with Fulham 1-0 up – delayed the inevitable, but relegation was finally achieved, with a fine sense of timing, on Good Friday, with a goalless draw away to Manchester United. That, as far as Sunderland fans were concerned, was the perfect result: it was relegation with a sliver of honour, and it was achieved before the derby on Easter Monday. The only thing that could have defiled the carcass of the season further would have been if the final indignity had been inflicted by Newcastle; as it was, the result of that game – and few expected anything other than a defeat – could safely be written off as a dead rubber. Even better, Sunderland went on to beat Fulham in the rearranged game; their only home victory of the season.

When McCarthy was sacked, though, relegation was still a month in the future. 'With ten games to go, to sack the manager – I don't see any point in it,' said Kevin Kyle. The giant striker's wholehearted but ineffective approach had come to embody Sunderland's haplessness. When he was ruled out of two games after suffering a scalded scrotum as his baby kicked over the pan of water he was warming to heat its bottle, his role as the club's malaise in human form was confirmed. It wasn't just the capacity for the ridiculous self-infliction of injury; the idea of team news in a paper listing the probable absentees as 'McCartney (knee), Wright (ankle), Kyle (bollocks)' seemed dreadfully apt, and not just for him. As the symbol of the club, he captured the attitude of fans perfectly. 'What's anybody coming in now going to achieve with ten games to go?' he asked. 'They are not going to save us; we're going down.'

Given part of the impact of a new manager often lies in the very fact of his novelty, it seemed senseless to waste that in a doomed campaign. Why inflict on anybody else something equivalent to the nine successive Premiership defeats McCarthy suffered when he had arrived? So Sunderland fans did what humankind has always done when presented with the inexplicable. They made stuff up.

The idea that McCarthy's sacking could simply be a snap decision made by a board reaching the end of its tether wasn't really explored. The fact that sacking a manager in early March gave the club two months to advertise the vacancy without running into the code of honour that states one manager should never tout for another manager's job was ignored. No, there had to be a higher purpose, a reason. Murray had said that the club would 'take its time about finding a replacement', but the rumour mill was not going to be distracted by that. It could only be that he had somebody already lined up, that a big name was about to step in, and had demanded the final weeks of the season to assess the squad so he could better exploit the transfer market in the summer.

Martin O'Neill, out of work since quitting Celtic to care for his sick wife, was mentioned, as always. He had, after all, as everybody was bored of hearing, been a Sunderland fan as a boy; and, even better, was at least to some extent a protégé of Brian Clough. Clough had for years been the fantasy candidate for Sunderland fans. He was a former player, scoring sixty-three goals in 74 games before being sacked in 1964 once it became apparent his knee was broken beyond repair, even though he had coached the youth team to the FA Youth Cup semifinal during his period of recuperation. He was even, at some point, supposed to have said that he would don a nappy and crawl over broken glass if he thought it would enable him to manage Sunderland, a phrase that was enshrined in the lore of the club in the late Eighties and early Nineties. The enduring popularity of O'Neill was, at least in part, a sentimental recognition of the fact that he was the nearest thing to Clough still available.

Graeme Souness had been sacked by Newcastle just a month earlier; had Murray been waiting for him? Souness had always been despised by Sunderland fans for a bad tackle on the great Shaun Elliott, but attitudes had been softened by the way he had led Newcastle so sure-footedly to mediocrity. Or Sam Allardyce, a former Sunderland player, who was known to feel he had taken Bolton about as far as they could go? Kevin Keegan? Glenn Hoddle? Alex McLeish? All were proposed, discussed, debated, and eventually dismissed. Besides, Kevin Ball had been appointed as caretaker until the end of the season, which hardly suggested a big name on the doorstep. Ball was immensely popular, a central defender-cum-midfielder of such commitment that he could hardly have failed to become a cult, but he wasn't what the fans were looking for. And then, somebody suggested Niall Quinn.

Quinn, it was true, had no managerial experience, but he had an undoubted affinity for the region, and it for him. As Ball's first game brought a 1-0 defeat to Wigan Athletic, and a few hundred fans demonstrated by the Murray Gates, calling for Murray to walk through them and never return, it became obvious that what was needed was a messiah-figure, somebody whose charisma could cut through the despondency and break the endless cycle of boom and bust, promotion and relegation. Sunderland looked back to 1992 and what had happened 13 miles up the road when Keegan, with no managerial experience, had arrived at a struggling Newcastle and dragged them towards the top of the Premiership. Quinn, it seemed, was Sunderland's Keegan. In fact, he was more than Keegan. He was just as charismatic, just as articulate, but Keegan had been at Newcastle for only two seasons as a player; Quinn had spent six years on Wearside, not merely scoring 61 league goals, but also doing great work for the local community. Most significantly, he had donated the proceeds of his testimonial to building a new children's wing at Sunderland General Hospital. Quinn became the favoured choice, but with the indicators from Ireland at best ambivalent, fans continued their campaign against Murray.

Murray hit back at the demonstrators, highlighting the mess the club had been in when he had taken over in 1986. In that, he had a point. When he had arrived to end Tom Cowie's acrimonious reign as chairman, it was financially crippled, staggering under the weight of the McMenemy farrago, and without his £750,000 loan the club would probably have slipped into bankruptcy. 'I am hurt that anyone suggests I am greedy,' he said. 'I was born in a Sunderland mining family and bought my local club. At the time it was a signature away from bankruptcy, on the way to the Third Division, with very poor attendances in the region of 12–14,000, ripped apart by conflict in the management and the boardroom and involved in numerous legal actions.'

His protestations cut little ice. That was then; this was now, and it doesn't take 20 years for gratitude to wither. A defeat to Blackburn, who, as was widely pointed out, seemed to thrive on gates of around half of Sunderland's, brought another demonstration, despite the efforts of the police to deny protestors access – the police's decision said the club, anxious not to be seen to be turning against the fans; a joint decision by police and club, said the police. Murray, his patience apparently exhausted, reiterated that he would leave if a suitable offer came in. That, though, seemed a distant prospect. Sunderland, after all, is not thick with millionaires, and who else but a local would invest in a club sinking under the weight of its own misery?

And then, three weeks after McCarthy's dismissal, came the news that Quinn, far from returning as manager, was attempting to put together a consortium to buy the club. Then there came another rumour, one whose grounding in fact rather than wishful thinking is doubtful but which proved weirdly prescient. It was said that Quinn had been planning his takeover for some time, and that when he arrived, he would install Roy Keane as manager. It was said that McCarthy had reacted furiously to the idea of being replaced by his nemesis, and that it was that that had led to his departure. Now, none of that made much sense. Quinn, after all, had felt the sting of Keane's wrath in Saipan almost as sharply as McCarthy had, being dubbed, among other things, 'a muppet' after his attempt to broker a peace. And McCarthy had been sacked rather than resigning. But then, Quinn and Keane did share an adviser in the lawyer Michael Kennedy. Perhaps it was possible. Keane looked like leaving Celtic that summer, bringing his playing career to a close, and he had been working on his coaching badges. Perhaps this was just the sort of challenge that would appeal to him. Then again, perhaps if Melanesians don headsets made of coconut, carry bamboo twigs like rifles and paint 'USA' on their bodies, the noisy winged beasts will descend once again from the skies and deliver more cargo. People have always invented theories to make the facts fit their own desires and prejudices.

The season dwindled on, bringing a 2-2 draw at Everton, the relegation-ensuring stalemate at Old Trafford and, then in the final home game of the season, a first home victory, as Fulham were beaten 2-1 in the replay of the match abandoned in the blizzard. Still 28,226 turned up, and celebrated with bitter-sweet gaiety. So what, if with two games remaining, they were already guaranteed to break their own record for the lowest points tally in Premiership history? So what if, even if they'd been allowed to carry over all their points from their previous Premiership season, Sunderland would still have been relegated by a distance? At least the last Premiership game at the Stadium of Light had brought a victory – and, at the time, that looked a record likely to stand for several years.

Almost as soon they had sprung up, the rumours of Keane's arrival disappeared. Stories of Quinn's consortium rumbled on in the background, but as spring drifted into summer and the

attention of the football world shifted to Germany and the
World Cup, even that seemed to be slipping away, just one
more hope unfulfilled, one more broken dream. Looking back,
although it turned out there had been a meeting between
Quinn and Keane, those stories of Keane's arrival have the
uncanny air of prophecy, as though Elijah himself had stood
by the banks of the Wear and proclaimed the coming of the
Messiah, but even when the season began the following
August, they lay forgotten.

Football, it seems to me, falls roughly into three phases. The
first can be described as self-validation. For people from
provincial industrial cities, achievement for their football team
– and that need not necessarily be winning trophies; it could
be simply having a large and passionate support, or playing in
a particular style – was a means of putting themselves on the
map, perhaps even of getting one over on the capital. In total-
itarian countries, sport had an obvious propaganda value:
Gusztav Sebes, the coach of the great Hungary side of the
Fifties, spoke of his side playing 'socialist football' and their
6-3 victory over England in 1953 was portrayed as the triumph
of Communism over empire. For less prominent nations, even
getting to a World Cup raises awareness – Senegal and
Slovenia, to take two very different examples – are far better
known now by the world at large than they were before 2002.
In each case football is a positive expression of identity.

The second phase is rather less healthy. It comes when a certain section of society feels itself disenfranchised, usually for
economic reasons. The disenfranchised, with little else to cling

to, turn to football clubs as a means of defining themselves. This process often goes hand-in-hand with a vague right-wing nihilism that lashes out against anything perceived as 'other' – be that other fans, other social classes, other nationalities, or other races. It happened in, for instance, Hungary in the Thirties as Ferencváros became a centre of support for the pro-Nazi Arrow Cross Party, it is happening in Hungary and Poland again today, and it in part explains the English football violence of the Seventies and Eighties.

English football, broadly speaking, is now in phase three. In a generally affluent – possibly even decadent – society, the great ideals of old hold little relevance, and football, filling the vacuum, takes on an absurdly inflated importance. People are on the whole relatively comfortable – or comfortable enough that they are not turning to religion or politics in huge numbers – and yet, in an increasingly transient society, they still seek something by which to root themselves. Football provides that. The notion of fandom gives a sense of permanence, even if, as it often is these days, it is ersatz.

This is not going to be a rant against the gentrification of the game, but it is true that the last 15 years have seen the arrival of the nouveau fan, as satirised by *The Fast Show* with their family in shining new Arsenal replica shirts ineptly copying chants and passing round the Pringles at half-time. Well, good luck to them: they have as much right to buy tickets and watch football as anyone else, and without their money English football would be a very different – and, to my mind, poorer – place, as our best players decamped to Spain or Italy and world stars barely gave us a thought. The point I'm making, though, is that the new wave of supporter consciously buys into football – they are, to use *The Observer*'s phrase, consumers rather than fans. For them it is an entertainment, and their adoption of club colours and attitudes is second-hand. It is an identity they have chosen, something they have adopted rather than something that is part of them. The result is that phase one and phase two fans feel a sense of alienation and resentment towards the new supporters, who are, by definition, other, and whose presence pushes up prices. A side effect is that success in phase three tends to be drawn more directly to money – that is, financial centres, or those traditional clubs who have successfully transformed themselves into global brands.

The cliché 'You can change your wife/job/friends but you can't change your football team' is often moronically uttered as some kind of ultimate truth (nouveau fans who take fandom too seriously, actually, do annoy me. If somebody who had previously had little interest in the game starts popping along to the Emirates to watch matches and buys an Arsenal scarf because they enjoy their style of play, then fine; it's if they then start berating Spurs fans for their underachievement that it grates). I've heard enough people talk about 'choosing' their team, a choice they then supposedly can't alter, to realise that that is what many, perhaps even most, people do. It is, of course, what the Maidenhead-born Nick Hornby does in adopting Arsenal – although for him it at least had a logic bound up in his relationship with his father. Still, the selection is often arbitrary. This was something else that surprised me when I left Sunderland; how common the idea of choosing was. I never chose. I just was. I am, in the terms of my theory, a phase one fan.

This, I suspect, is a common enough state of affairs in places like Sunderland and Newcastle where the distinction between club and city is minimal. I'm not making any special pleading here or prioritising one kind of fandom over another.

All I'm saying is that the Northeast – for Newcastle is just the other side of the same coin – retains a greater proportion of phase one fans than most places, and that as a result the emotional link between city and club is umbilical.

[2]

THE MAGIC CARPET

By the standards of the City, Niall Quinn's takeover of Sunderland was not particularly drawn out. By the standards of football, though, where everything is about instant gratification and a manager being booed by Middlesbrough fans can find himself head coach of England six months later, it was an agonisingly protracted affair.

It was towards the end of March that it was first confirmed that Quinn might be arriving not as manager but as chairman. He was, sources close to him revealed, 'actively seeking to put together a package'. With whom was not clear, although everybody seemed pretty sure it was not John Magnier or JP McManus, the Irish millionaires who had sold their shares in Manchester United to the Glazers. There was little of any substance for anyone to cling to, and although there was hope, the principal reaction was one of scepticism. By the time of the April Fool's Day draw at Everton, the initial excitement had subsided, with newspapers reporting that Quinn was 'quietly working in Ireland on a package to try to rescue his beloved former club, and is making progress'.

A fortnight later, as relegation was confirmed at Old Trafford, Quinn was 'poised to mount a takeover'. A week after that and Quinn was urging caution. 'It's not about putting money on the table and making an offer for a football club,' he explained. 'It's about proving ourselves, before we go near any fans or any club, that we are capable of running a football club. It's a jungle, as I have found out in the last three weeks. It's not a simple thing at all. I am making sure that myself and my group are capable of doing a job the club deserves and until we get to the bottom of that we can't possibly approach Sunderland.' That sounded typically honourable, but the sceptics wondered whether Quinn could really hack it in the business world, whether he might even be preparing the ground for a tactical retreat.

By April 28, though, Quinn was said to be within 48 hours of making a formal offer for the club, with solid financial details emerging for the first time. Everybody had known there was a £40million debt to be serviced, but it was now estimated that to buy three-quarters of the club's shares – of which Murray held 56.8 per cent – would cost an additional £20million, plus whatever was felt necessary for team-building. Fans, keen to welcome their saviour, planned a 'St Niall's Day' celebration for the May 1 meeting with Arsenal, which, it seems, would have looked much like St Patrick's Day, only with more Quinn-themed merchandise. Quinn himself, whether because he felt it would hamper negotiations, because he felt embarrassed, or because he recognised that May 1 is the feast day of St Joseph the Workman, asked for it to be postponed. 'Niall,' read a statement passed on to the organisers of the event, 'would prefer Monday to be a celebration of the club and its supporters rather than any of celebration of himself. Niall stresses he does not want this to be taken in any way as a sign of ingratitude to the club's supporters.'

This was generally taken as an example of Quinn's modesty, although inevitably there were doubters. Was this evidence he was getting cold feet; that negotiations between the consortium and Murray were dragging on for a worryingly long time? There were a number of green Ireland shirts at the Stadium of Light for the game, but Quinn, in the stands with a number of his potential investors, seemed not to mind; indeed, he later said the crowd that day had been instrumental in convincing his backers that Sunderland was a risk worth taking. For all that relegation had been confirmed several weeks earlier, there were 44,000 at the Stadium of Light, and even though Arsenal were 3-0 up by half-time, they were generous enough to give Thierry Henry a standing ovation as he was substituted. 'Arsenal were miles better,' Quinn said in an interview in *The Guardian*, 'but the investors saw the Sunderland crowd clapping Thierry Henry. Instead of going mad, these fans were showing they were pure football – Henry gave bows going off. My people saw that, and there are only a few places in the country where that could happen. Remember, Sunderland hadn't won at home all season.'

There are those who would dismiss that as only so much blarney, as Quinn saying what he had to say to get the fans on board, but even if that were true – it is, after all, far easier to be magnanimous when there is nothing left to play for – what a boon to have a chairman who said the right thing. Murray was almost certainly unfairly maligned, but he didn't help himself with his poor public relations. The recognition – and, indeed, the appreciation – of Quinn's abilities in that area, of course, are part of the curious knowingness of self-presentation in the media age. Sunderland fans wanted to believe in Quinn, wanted to believe in the myth of St Niall, and he wanted them to believe in him, and they wanted him to want them to believe in him. To call it a willing self-deception on both sides would be taking things too far, but there was, for the most part, a self-conscious lack of scepticism, almost as though to question the miracle would be to destroy it.

When Quinn beats the right drums, the reaction is partly visceral. What fan does not feel a warm glow in his gut when he is told of his own importance – whether it be for his commitment, his passion, or his graciousness? There is also, though, a secondary reaction. The idea of 'spin' in its political sense has entered the mainstream consciousness, and there was an awareness that Quinn may be, quite deliberately, saying the things that would provoke that sense of rosiness. Yet, because there was a desire that he should be the great leader, far from feeling cheapened, fans admired him for pressing the right buttons. Whatever else this past season has demonstrated, it is the way that chairman, manager, and fans can collude in generating a forward momentum – and that despite Wearside's pathological pessimism. Kevin McCarra, in discussing the weirdly inflated optimism with which Scotland went to the 1978 World Cup, spoke of the 'conspiracy of glee' between the manager Ally McLeod, sportswriters, and fans. Wearside last season was little different, as was demonstrated when the fanzine *A Love Supreme* (*ALS*) depicted Quinn on its front cover as Superman, swooping in over the Stadium of Light to save the day. This was not necessarily how it was, but it was how fans wanted it to be, and their desire somehow contributed to its own fulfilment. The same yearning was there, as there was for Scotland in 1978; but in this instance, there was substance behind the dream.

None of that was apparent, though, in the immediate aftermath of the Arsenal game. Quinn signed an exclusivity deal with Murray afterwards, meaning that he effectively controlled the process of any sale, and there were reports that the takeover should be complete 'by June', which did little to satisfy those desperate for instant change. Stock exchange rules prevented Quinn from saying too much, but he did his best to reassure supporters. 'The only thing I'll say is you don't play a game of poker by letting everybody know your hand,' he said, 'but my guys might have a good hand.'

Steve Cram, as devout a Sunderland fan is as likely to be found, echoed the general mood when he spoke of a change of leadership as 'timely and welcome'. He was, though, rather more generous than most to Murray. It wasn't just that he had saved the club in 1986, it was that, after threatening to leave towards the end of the lamentable Mick Buxton era, he had appointed Peter Reid, overseen the move to a new stadium and the period of success around the turn of the millennium. Crowds at that time were as high as they had been at any point in almost half a century, which must count for something. Although Murray presided over – statistically – the worst two seasons in Sunderland's history, in the final 11 years of his reign, Sunderland never finished lower than third in the Championship, which given the failures of the previous 40 years is some achievement. As a piece in *ALS* pointed out, for Sunderland fans to ask what Bob Murray had ever done for them was not entirely dissimilar to the Judeans asking the same question about the Romans. And yet there was a sense of opportunity missed. Those seventh-place finishes in the Premiership had hinted at what might have been, had dangled before fans the possibility of European qualification and more, and if Sunderland were incapable of building on a squad that had got them that far, coupled with regular gates of over 40,000, then it was hard to see how they could ever establish themselves as a meaningful Premiership club. Once the ambition had been fired and expectation raised, as Cram said, 'the inability of managers and players to meet it' was 'why he

[Murray] will leave feeling unfulfilled and unloved'.

There was also, it must be said, some pretty odd decision-making. Even Murray's greatest legacy involved more than a degree of serendipity. The Stadium of Light is magnificent, both in terms of design and location – right by the river in the heart of the city – and Murray deserves credit for that, but if his initial plan had come off, Sunderland would have been playing miles out of town down the A19. Fortunately Nissan, whose factory lies near the proposed site, objected, claiming match-day congestion would interfere with their production schedule, and when the Wearmouth Colliery site became available, Murray leapt at it, thus both avoiding a protracted planning dispute and winning the club European grant money for redeveloping former industrial land.

Hindsight has proved that emphatically the right decision, but Murray proved himself out of touch in the naming of the ground. Years of enduring the 'Blunderland' and 'Joker Park' jibes left Sunderland fans all too aware of how wearing unfunny rhyming insults could be; offering 'Stadium of Light', whatever Murray's bizarre post-hoc rationalisation that the name referred to the Davy Lamps miners had used on the site, was like stacking the fish in the barrel, and loading the gun themselves before handing it to the nearest Geordie. That said, one of the theories of the etymology of the term 'Geordie' – a local diminutive for George – to denote a Tynesider is that miners there preferred lamps made by George Stephenson rather than the Humphrey Davy model popular elsewhere. It seems unlikely, though, that Murray was really making a point about early nineteenth-century safety lamps.

The pretentiousness of the name, equally, was utterly out of keeping with the miserabilist ethos of the city. That in itself might not have been a bad thing, but it did make Murray look mystifyingly out of touch. Although not as much as the *Premier Passions* documentary about Sunderland's 1996-97 Premiership season which cruelly cut back and forth between footage of Reid stripping paint off the dressing-room walls at Roker Park with a furious half-time swearathon and Murray pondering the best design for the taps in the toilets at the new ground.

There was evidence of less than perfect planning on a more practical level too. The Academy of Light, opened at a cost of £10million in 2003, is by all accounts one of the finest complexes of its kind, and yet until Quinn arrived, players had to take their ice-baths in wheelie-bins. Murray, admittedly, made his fortune in kitchens rather than bathrooms, but surely he still should have been able to see that wasn't ideal.

Whatever the concerns about Quinn's progress, what was not in doubt by the beginning of May was Murray's willingness to sell. In interviews he gave the impression of being almost punch-drunk, beaten into submission by the constant defeats and the incessant criticism. 'I've been here twenty years and murderers don't get that long,' he said. 'I don't think there will be anyone happier if this deal goes through than me and my family. I really want to see it through.' He was adamant as well, that Quinn was the right person to whom to sell. 'The good thing about football is you meet people like Niall Quinn,' he said. 'He's awesome. I know he's the right man for this job. He'll do it justice. He'll do everything in his power to bring success to Sunderland.'

Slowly, details of the men who made up the consortium emerged. The major figure, at least in terms of shares held in the Drumaville consortium – 2,360 – was Paddy Kelly, the head of Kelland Homes, and a shareholder in the investment and property company Markland, and the building firm,

Rockbriar. His personal wealth in the summer of 2006 was estimated at around £50million.

Below him were five investors, each of whom held 1,180 shares. Patsy Byrne is the managing director of the Byrne Group, a project management and construction firm that was involved in both the renovation of Number One Court at Wimbledon and the building of Arsenal's Emirates Stadium. He also owns racehorses, and, through Byrne Bros, sponsors the Cleeve Hurdle at Cheltenham.

Jack Tierney is also involved in property and construction, and also has other links with sport, sponsoring the Gaelic football team Allenwood. He owns a number of hotels: the Stand House; Eyre Powell; and Killashee, an award-winning hotel and spa in which Quinn is believed to have a ten per cent stake. Some concern was raised when it emerged that his Faxhill Homes company had been fined for improper book-keeping in 2001, but the indiscretion appears to have been relatively minor, and the punishment imposed was nominal.

Charlie Chawke and Louis Fitzgerald made their fortunes in the more alcohol-related end of the hospitality industry. Chawke owns a number of iconic Dublin pubs, including the Old Orchard Inn complex in Rathfarnham, bought in 2005 for €20million. He is probably most famous, though, for having been the victim of a bungled robbery in 2003 in which he was shot in the leg.

Fitzgerald owns a chain of 24 Dublin pubs and, shortly after being named as an investor in Drumaville, he announced he was to open four further pubs around the O'Connell Street area, including the Baggot Inn, bought for £5.1million in 2000, but closed since because of planning complications. The 2006 Rich List ranked his fortune at £59million.

Quinn himself had 1,000 shares, with the remaining 738

belonging to Pat Beirne, another property developer.

There were early suggestions that Sean Mulryan, a joint owner of Markland, was also involved, but his name was absent from the list of consortium members published on 3 July.

All of that was of vague interest to Sunderland fans, but did little to reassure the eternal pessimists who saw a takeover as a potential vehicle for asset-strippers, with Quinn either as naïve patsy, or, even worse, as a willing fellow traveller intent on squeezing his former club for everything it had. The possibility of unscrupulous owners stripping the club to its bones seems to have been a particular fear for Sunderland fans – perhaps simply because of the club's centrality to the community – and it is notable how active they were in supporting York City after they had found themselves floundering following a takeover gone bad.

That was why the fifth member of the second tier of shareholders was of such interest: John Hays, a Seaham-born businessman who started out in a concession fitted out by his father in the back of his mother's babywear shop and built Hays Travel into the country's largest independent travel agent, employing over 600 people and, by 2006, turning over £200million a year. Not only was he local, the one non-Irish member of the consortium, but he was also a *bona fide* Sunderland fan. So committed was he – and his wife, fortunately – that he hired a double-decker bus to take 50 guests from his wedding reception to see Sunderland lose 1-0 at home to Norwich. 'Kevin Phillips hit the post,' he said, when asked to recall his wedding-day in *ALS*. He was at Roker Park on Boxing Day 1962 when Brian Clough suffered his career-ending knee injury against Bury; he was there on the final day when Sunderland lost for the first time at home that season, going down 1-0 to Chelsea to miss out on promotion; and he was able to reminisce with the best of them about Stan Anderson and George Herd, Johnny Crossan and Colin Todd. Put simply, nobody believed that somebody who had watched Sunderland regularly for over 40 years was suddenly going to rob it blind.

For all Drumaville's resources, though, the list of potential new managers bandied about by the papers remained mundane. After David O'Leary had denied all knowledge of an approach despite being 'a friend' of Quinn, and another client of Michael Kennedy, the *Daily Mirror* suggested the consortium wanted to restore Peter Reid to the club, a prospect that sent an icy tremor across Wearside, at least among those who felt his perhaps overly traditional approach to management had contributed to Sunderland's demise.

And, for about a month, that was it. History had taught caution, and as unease grew that this would prove just another false dawn, several fans announced they were refusing to renew their season-tickets until the takeover was complete. Murray responded by suggesting the doubters were hampering Sunderland's development, which only heightened suspicions. Finally, though, on 8 June, Murray led a four-man committee to Ireland to meet with Quinn and his partners in the Great Southern Hotel near Dublin airport. He resigned a week later, while making clear that that did not oblige him to accept Quinn's offer, if and when it eventually came. It was widely seen as an attempt to force Quinn's hand, but there were few who were too unhappy about that.

This, it was apparent, was the endgame, but there was to be a final twist, with the *Sunderland Echo* reporting on 19 June that four of Quinn's consortium had withdrawn from the deal and that the proposal was on the brink of collapse. The

hoteliers Tom Moran and Pat Power, who were named as leading the withdrawals, though, were never signed up members of
the consortium. Quinn flew to the Northeast the following day
for 'final talks', insisting his backers remained as committed as
ever. 'The idea that any of my consortium have withdrawn is
woefully inaccurate,' he said. 'Our finance is in place, our due
diligence is completed and I'm here to overcome the very last
obstacle.'

Finally, on 3 July, the deal was completed. When better to
silence the doubters than on the feast day of St Thomas?
Quinn had not said what that final obstacle had been, but the
assumption always was that it was price, something that
seemed to be confirmed when it emerged that Murray would
walk away with £6million, rather than the £16million for
which it had been reported he was holding out. The consortium undertook to buy 72.59 per cent of the club shares,
including Murray's 56.8 per cent, although the offer was con-
ditional on them achieving 90 per cent holding within three
weeks. Quinn's tone was one of relief. 'Over the last few
weeks,' he said, 'I've made it quite plain that I believe it's one
of the greatest football clubs in the world, that is in fantastic
shape everywhere but on the pitch. I hope that by being a former player here, by knowing what makes things tick at
Sunderland, that I will add something intriguing and new that
a chairman perhaps hasn't been in a position to do before here.
I really want to knit everybody back together again so the people of Sunderland will see what this club is all about, they will
see the passion again and the football team can be reunited to
the fans.'

He didn't formally become chairman until the 21-day period had elapsed, but nobody was too bothered about such
technicalities. Murray allowed him to take effective control

immediately and as a sense of liberation mingled with Quinn's ability to touch chord after chord with his talk of community and history, the mood was upbeat for the first time in about six years.

The issue then was to find a manager, a quest that dragged on, and on, and on through July. Whatever else could be said about Quinn and his consortium, they clearly weren't people to make snap decisions. Allardyce was quickly installed as favourite, despite denials from Bolton. There were further murmurings about David O'Leary, who, it was said, might bring Kevin Phillips with him from Aston Villa. The Martin O'Neill rumour refused to go away – but then, it had been hanging around, immortal as a cockroach, for the better part of a decade. Most intriguingly of all, though, the Roy Keane rumour resurfaced. 'I have to get a manager who really does stick his chest out and is passionate about driving this club back to where it should be, and who the fans can connect with,' Quinn said. 'What I can't have is someone who sees it as a stop-off point for another job. I need someone who wants the challenge of making Sunderland great again. I want to get everyone back on the magic carpet. None of my guys are in it for a quick buck. I firmly believe I can reconnect the club to the people.'

As if to emphasise how sincerely he meant that final point, he announced that season-ticket prices would be frozen. From another mouth the suggestion that there was even a possibility that a club that had just been relegated after losing twenty-nine of its thirty-eight games was considering raising prices would have seemed obscene, but this was St Niall, and so he was cheered to the rafters. The way he was talking, Quinn seemed not merely to want to return the glory to Sunderland, but to turn it into some sort of people's utopia as he did so. That, of course, only made him even more popular. Bob Murray's donations to the Labour Party were evidently forgotten; either that, or Blair's Labour doesn't quite set the socialist northern blood racing as Quinn's brand of compassionate populism does.

In terms of concrete developments, though, there was less to get excited about. Kenny Cunningham arrived on a free transfer from Birmingham, and the following day Gary Breen left on a free transfer for Wolves, which effectively meant that a ponderous 32-year-old centre-back with sixty-odd caps for the Republic of Ireland had been swapped for a ponderous 35-year-old centre-back with sixty-odd caps for the Republic of Ireland. Still, the general perception was that, while signing Cunningham wasn't necessarily a great leap forward, nothing that involved Breen leaving the club could ever be a step backwards. He had, in fairness, looked defensively sound and relatively composed on the ball for much of his first two seasons on Wearside, good enough anyway to make the title of Robert Banks's West Ham relegation memoir lamenting *The Legacy of Barry Green* – as the author's girlfriend spoonerised his name – seem unduly harsh. That third season, the only one in the Premiership, soon showed what Banks was on about.

Breen was only the start of the bloodletting. Kelvin Davis went to Southampton for £1million, which made either Quinn or McCarthy look like a business genius: how could his value have dropped by only £250,000 in a season in which his nerves had been shot, and his inadequacies exposed week after week? Christian Bassila was released to no great mourning, and Martin Woods, hailed as the brightest hope of the previous pre-season tour of the USA, went to Rotherham on a free. Most painful, though, was the departure of Julio Arca.

Arca was also a veteran of the two relegation campaigns, but he was more than that. For Sunderland fans, watching him leave was like watching the whale leap the wall into the ocean at the end of *Free Willy*. It was desperately sad, but everybody accepted it was for the best. Quinn called Arca a 'smashing player' and offered to match any contract he was offered else-where, but a player of his talent deserved his freedom, and it would have been unfair, whatever the mutual affection, to restrict him again to the shallow waters of the Championship. It had been, as the tagline for that film said, 'a friendship you could never imagine', a club with six decades of underachieve-ment to its name finding love with a shuffling, bush-haired winger-cum-full-back who had captained Argentina to victory in the World Youth Cup. That he was forced at times to play alongside Jeff Whitley and Paul Thirlwell seemed frankly bizarre, like a Rembrandt being exhibited alongside the finger paintings on a nursery wall; that Kevin Kilbane once kept him out of the side borders on the criminal.

True, he had only one foot, his left, but what a foot. The clip SkySports News showed on his arrival in July 2000 of him shambling through three Brazilians before pinging a right-foot drive into the top corner turned out to be misleading in fact, but not in spirit. Yes, on his worse days he could resemble a rowing-boat with only one oar, but even then his shoulders never slumped – figuratively, that is; physically they were never unslumped. He even insisted on playing, despite obvious injury, despite the fact Sunderland were already down, in that final derby on Easter Monday. He was that rarest of things: a gifted player who was also a trier; a winger with a full-back's temperament, or a full-back with a winger's ability. And then, on 26 July, after six years and a day at the club, he was gone, sold to Middlesbrough for £1.75million. There was no bitterness, merely a sense he probably deserved better. As Tim Rice, a Sunderland fan, had another Argentinian sing, he had to let it happen: he couldn't stay all his life down at heel.

O'Leary left Villa and McCarthy found another job at Wolves, but the Sunderland vacancy remained. By the end of July, having failed to attract any of the names on his shortlist, Quinn did what he had explicitly said he would not do, and appointed himself as manager. 'That would be all about ego,' he had said a fortnight earlier. 'I'm not good or experienced enough.' That would soon become painfully clear.

With members of the consortium concerned about the lack of transfer activity, though, Quinn felt obliged to fill the vacuum, at least in the short term. 'We could not have been more ambitious in our search for a manager,' he said, before admitting that the fact the club was in the Championship had proved the 'stumbling block'. 'We have a five-year plan which could not get off the ground because we could not get a top-class manager to come down a division,' he went on. 'We'll start the first phase in-house. We've got to stop the slide, turn the corner and gather momentum; then maybe we can attract a manager who I think is worthy – whether that takes three months, six months or longer.'

It was not, it is fair to say, a universally popular decision. This was the first big test of the new regime and, after all the talk of a 'world-class manager', they'd ended up appointing somebody who admitted he didn't want the job. Besides, it all seemed like a catch-22: a top manager was required to stop the slide, and yet until the slide had been stopped, Quinn didn't believe a top manager could be attracted. Besides, chairmen-managers were almost invariably disasters.

The most successful in recent memory was probably Ron Noades, whose 130 games in charge of Brentford between 1998 and 2000 brought 51 victories and 46 defeats. Noades said he believed Quinn could carry it off, but admitted that trying the dual role again 'would probably kill me'. It was one thing for Quinn to be hailed as a saint; nobody wanted a martyr.

Rather a martyr, though, than Michael Knighton. Eccentric and outspoken, he claimed to have seen a UFO in 1976, juggled a football on the pitch at Old Trafford when it looked as though he might buy them in 1989, and, most ludicrously of all, appointed himself to succeed the popular Mervyn Day as coach at Brunton Park in 1997, leading Carlisle to a predictable relegation.

It hardly calmed nerves that Quinn then decided to appoint Bobby Saxton as his number two. Saxton had the advantage of not being Peter Reid, whose return as a mentor for Quinn had been mooted, but the disadvantage of being the closest possible alternative. A former manager of Blackburn Rovers and York City, he looked like Inspector Morse gone to seed, had served as Reid's assistant for seven years, and on the *Premier Passions* documentary had achieved the dubious distinction of being the only person who made Reid look restrained and cerebral. There was a theory that Saxton had been the brains behind Sunderland's success under Reid – certainly it was after he had retired and been replaced as assistant manager by Adrian Heath that the slump began – but his appointment nonetheless seemed hard to square with Quinn's talk of 'modern methods', 'a more scientific approach' and 'getting an extra ten per cent'.

Still, when Quinn's first game as a coach ended with a 3-0 friendly victory away to Carlisle, meaning Sunderland's four-pre-season games had brought four wins, with ten goals scored and none conceded, there was a general sense of optimism. If Quinn showed his unfamiliarity with coaching etiquette by racing across the Carlisle technical area as he made a point to one of his players – 'I just forgot' he said – it was more than balanced by the rare sight of a Jon Stead goal, and a 25-yard drive at that.

Robbie Elliott arrived on a month-to-month contract from Newcastle and the goalkeeper Darren Ward was picked up on a free after being released by Norwich, but otherwise there was nothing but speculation. Quinn was expected to bid for his old strike-partner, Kevin Phillips, who seemed certain to leave Aston Villa; he insisted a deal to bring the Swiss midfielder Ricardo Cabanos from Cologne was 'not dead'; and there was talk of a loan move for Arsenal's teenage striker Anthony Stokes, but there was nothing of real substance, nothing likely to prompt street-parties around the Stadium of Light.

But those were mere details; there was still all of August to go before the close of the transfer window, and this was the most promising close season anybody could remember. 'When you come away from a game like this,' Quinn said after the Carlisle victory, 'no matter who you are or what type of year or two you've had, you feel good about yourself. I'm buzzing.'

I turned up alongside where the Main Stand had once been. Back when I lived in Sunderland, the route of my longest run would bring me down here, completing the loop off Fulwell Road before turning back for the long pull up alongside Roker Park – the park – and past St Andrew's church before dropping down to the sea-front. I probably ran it once a week on average for about four years, but now I barely recognised it. Along one side, where the garage used to be, runs a thick mesh fence, capped, about a third of the way along, by two flags, faded and fluttering forlornly. Below them, wedged into the fence, was the browning peel of a half-eaten banana.

On the other side of the road is the new Wimpey housing, protruding from what had been the stand into the old car park. It was there that you queued for tickets for games, there that you caught official buses to away games; there that Lawrie McMenemy was mobbed on his arrival in 1985. When it was built in 1929, the stand, designed by Archibald Leitch and featuring his trademark latticework, had once been one of the finest in the country – would have been finer too, if Rangers hadn't somehow managed to purloin his original design. By the nineties, though, it had begun to look shabby. The paintwork was faded, the concrete stained, and even the style of the lettering that spelt out 'SUNDERLAND AFC' looked dated, almost as though, as many Sunderland fans wished it had, time had stopped in 1973.

I wandered round, looking at the street-signs: Turnstile Mews, Midfield Drive, Clockstand Close … dullness appeared to have been adopted as a virtue. This surely, was a chance to pay tribute to the greats who had played on the spot, to celebrate Carter, Shackleton, and Hurley, but perhaps that would have been too much like showing off, and that, in the Northeast, is pretty much the unforgivable sin.

Wimpey also built the new houses on the site of the old Ayresome Park in Middlesbrough, and they too suffer from an uninspired naming policy. There, though, there are at least physical reminders of what the area used to be. A bronze ball marks a penalty spot, a child's coat hangs where the goalposts used to be and, most movingly, there is also a low, stud-scuffed bronze mound on the spot from which Pak Doo-Ik scored the goal with which North Korea beat Italy in the 1966 World Cup.

Local residents, 40 years on, looked out of their windows one morning to see half the North Korea squad standing to attention around the sculpture, singing their national anthem. Why couldn't Sunderland have similarly marked Jozsef Szabo's dramatic goal-line clearance for the USSR against Hungary in the quarterfinal of the same tournament? Or even a great Sunderland moment: Trevor Ford hitting a shot so powerfully on debut in 1950 that it uprooted a post, Vic Halom's screamer against Manchester City in 1973, or Gordon Armstrong's 20-yard header against Chelsea 19 years later?

Ringed by the new houses is a small, attractive patch of grass, in which someone has stuck a wonky sign. It reads, 'NO BALL GAMES'.

[3]

CHEATED BY THE GAME

'Coventry,' the notorious first line of John King's hoolie-lit classic *The Football Factory* has it, 'are fuck-all.'

If only. To Sunderland fans the existence of Coventry City serves as a continuing reminder that the world cheats you. No matter how bright, how bold, how full of youthful panache, you end up being cheated by the game. The injustice may be 30 years old, but if there's anything that keeps a fan going, it's a sense of moral outrage. Even the indignities and injustices Thatcher visited on the region have not obscured the memory of that particular affront. Most clubs have some kind of persecution complex – partly because it helps bolster the sense of us-against-the-world self-identification, and partly because it offers an excuse for mediocrity and failure – but it would be wrong to dismiss what happened in 1977 and Sunderland fans' on-going sense of grievance as mere paranoia. In the context of the seventies, when violence, bungs and alcoholism were rife, it would equally be ludicrous to speak of football losing its innocence, but something of the game's soul died at Highfield Road that day.

It took three seasons after the 1973 FA Cup win to secure promotion but, with Bob Stokoe in ill health, Sunderland's first top-flight season in seven years began atrociously. When

Stokoe was finally replaced by the youth team coach Jimmy Adamson in the October, Sunderland were still to win a game. Adamson, having effectively written the season off, began to promote young talent – most notably the central defender Shaun Elliott, the midfielder Kevin Arnott and the forward Gary Rowell – looking to case-harden them ahead of the following season.

Sunderland finally achieved their second win of the season on 11 February, beating Bristol City 1-0 at Roker Park. It hardly seemed to matter, but then something remarkable happened. A quirk of the calendar gave Sunderland three more home games in a row, and they won them all. And they didn't just win them; they did so playing irresistible attacking football. Middlesbrough were hammered 4-0, West Brom 6-1 and West Ham 6-0. What had begun as cackling in the dark, a team playing with the freedom of the damned, suddenly became a genuine survival bid. Ipswich, QPR, Manchester United, and Birmingham all succumbed at Roker Park. There was a fraught 3-2 win at West Brom, and when Sunderland drew their penultimate game of the season 2-2 away at Norwich, it meant that a point at Everton on the final day would be enough to complete a gloriously romantic escape. Their two rivals for the final relegation position, Coventry and Bristol City, met at Highfield Road, with the loser certain to go down. The only way Sunderland could be relegated was if they lost, and Coventry and Bristol City drew.

The match at Highfield Road, conveniently, kicked off several minutes late, supposedly because of the numbers making their way from Bristol, and almost as soon as they had, Sunderland fell behind to a Bob Latchford header at Goodison. It looked as though it wouldn't matter, as Coventry went 2-0 up through a Tommy Hutchison double, but Gerry

Gow and Don Gillies pulled it level with 11 minutes remaining. Pushing forward in search of a point, Sunderland conceded a second to Bruce Rioch in injury-time. A goal either way at Highfield Road would have saved Sunderland, but Jimmy Hill, then the Coventry chairman, in the words of the *Coventry Evening Telegraph*, 'raced up to the radio box to order the Goodison scoreline to be given'. Once it had been, the game became a sorry procession, with both sides content to play keep-ball, protecting the mutually beneficial draw. By the end, they were sitting down in the centre-circle, desultorily kicking the ball to each other.

'I do not feel guilty,' the Coventry manager Gordon Milne said. 'Both teams had given their all.' Sunderland were apoplectic, but Bristol City's manager Alan Dicks was equally unapologetic. 'A point was all we needed,' he said. 'When we realised we were safe there was no reason at all to push forward and look for another goal, and Coventry were in the same situation.'

The league censured Coventry, but did not punish them. Hill, who as regular viewers of his *Sunday Supplement* will know is not a man to change his views when he could say the same old thing over and over again (one of his regular rants is about managers who lose the ability to motivate their players because they run out of new things to say; seriously, Jimmy, does that ring no bells at all?), remains unrepentant. 'I had no sleepless nights at the time and none now,' he said in an interview in *FourFourTwo* magazine in January 2006. 'I can understand why Sunderland fans were upset, but we did not cheat. The reason the game was delayed was because so many supporters turned up to watch us and it was the ref's decision, not ours, to wait until everyone was in the ground for safety reasons. No one knew at the time that it would affect the situation.' Didn't they? Was it really so hard to predict given Sunderland losing and Coventry and Bristol City drawing was the only permutation that would have kept both of them up and sent Sunderland down? Nobody had thought of it? What a naive world the seventies must have been. And how many other games in that less-than-safety-conscious decade were delayed for crowd congestion? Go on: name six.

Perhaps Hill realised how ridiculous he sounded (although past record suggests not), because he then went on the offensive. 'Sunderland fans had to find someone to blame, as their team hadn't played well enough to stay in the division. If we'd lost, we wouldn't have complained about it.' Little wonder Sunderland have always reserved a special contempt for Coventry in general and for Hill in particular. It does, though, make you wonder whether his bizarre half-time defence of a blatant foul by Paul Bracewell on Ray Houghton that should have given Liverpool a penalty against Sunderland in the 1992 FA Cup final – 'if you look at the angle of the tackle, you'll see he's going down the line of the ball ...' – was some weird semi-conscious attempt to make amends. Either that or he'd say any old nonsense to generate controversy.

Some 20 years later, Coventry again overhauled Sunderland on the final day of the season, and again their game kicked off late because of supposed crowd congestion. On that occasion Coventry had to win away to Tottenham – they did, 2-1 – and hope Sunderland failed to win at Wimbledon – they lost 1-0 – so the delay was less meaningful, but it still left a sour taste. There were even wild suggestions it had been a deliberate ploy to invoke the memories of 1977.

Even leaving that aside, Sunderland's record at Coventry was dreadful. They hadn't beaten them there since 1985, although with the club having moved to the Ricoh Arena – a bracing reminder of the out-of-town soullessness Sunderland may have ended up with had the A19 proposal gone ahead – there was at least a vague hope that the Highfield Road curse might not carry over. So Coventry, certainly, was not the auspicious place Sunderland would have chosen to launch the revolution.

For all the talk of new eras, Kenny Cunningham was the only new face in a starting line-up that included four Irishmen, two of whom combined to give Sunderland the lead seven minutes after half-time, as Stephen Elliott hooked across goal for Daryl Murphy to prod in at the back post. There had been eyebrows raised the previous week when Murphy was offered a five-year contract – he had shown only flickers of quality since arriving from Waterford Town for £100,000 in the summer of 2005 – but Quinn's judgement suddenly looked superb.

It was perhaps a slightly fortuitous lead, but Sunderland seemed comfortable in it when, with 19 minutes remaining, from nothing, Stern John curled an 18-yarder in off the underside of the bar. Seven minutes later, Sunderland dozed as Don Hutchison took a quick free-kick, and Gary McSheffrey rattled in the winner. It wasn't quite the same old story, for Sunderland had at least been in the lead, but it all felt horribly familiar. Quinn blamed a 'losing mentality', speaking of how his players had lost the mental ability to see out a winning position. 'It is a tiny, tiny lack of professionalism, a little glitch I have to get out of this club – and quickly,' he said. 'It's about intelligence. We did it again today and a lot last season.' The most important thing, he insisted, was 'positivity', something he vowed to instil.

Sunday, 6 August, Championship

Coventry City	2-1	Sunderland
John 71		Murphy 52
McSheffrey 78		

Coventry: Marshall, McNamee, Heath, Ward, Hall, Birchall (Thornton 74), Hughes, Doyle, McSheffrey (Whing 86), Adebola (Hutchison 67), John
Subs Not Used: Steele, Tabb
Sunderland: Alnwick, Delap, Cunningham, Caldwell, D Collins, T Miller, Leadbitter (Kyle 80), Whitehead, Lawrence, S Elliott, Murphy (Stead 76)
Subs Not Used: Ward, Wright, R Elliott
Ref: C Foy (Merseyside)
Booked: Hughes (Coventry); Lawrence (Sunderland)
Att: 22,366
League position: 19

A setback certainly, but then Sunderland had lost 2-0 to Coventry on the opening day in 2005, and that was a season that had ended in promotion. There were the usual noises about Rome not being built in a day, but the classic excuse that new signings took time to settle didn't really fit because there hadn't been any. Still, they would come.

First, though, there was another departure as George McCartney, whose partnership down the left with Julio Arca had done so much to secure promotion two years earlier, joined West Ham in exchange for Clive Clarke and £600,000. Player of the year in 2005-06, McCartney had not played until February in the Premiership, the victim of a hamstring injury. To suggest his presence from the start of the season might have kept Sunderland up is to place too great a burden on a left-back, but the general feeling was that, had he been there to provide defensive shape and forward thrust, it might not have been quite so embarrassing. That said, McCartney had had the misfortune to make his league debut in Howard Wilkinson's second game in charge so that, by the time he left for West Ham, his Premiership record was played 37, won 3, drawn 6, lost 28. There weren't many at Upton Park who found their stats improved in 2006-07.

And then, finally, there was talk of a transfer that actually got people excited as Sunderland were linked with the Barcelona midfielder Arnau Riera. Now, admittedly, he was 25 and had never played for the first team, but he was captain of Barcelona B, and people who'd seen him – and Barcelona is one of those cities where everybody knows somebody – thought he had real class. With Arca gone, there was a vacancy for a Latin crowd favourite.

There was also a serious creative vacancy on the left, something Quinn was apparently trying to solve by signing the out-of-favour Andy Reid from Tottenham. For the visit of Birmingham, though, he had to continue with the policy of using the predominantly right-sided Liam Lawrence on the left of midfield, with Tommy Miller, ideally a central player, operating on the right. That shape, ungainly anyway, was further disrupted when Steve Caldwell hobbled off with a knee injury after 29 minutes to be replaced by Clive Clarke. The debutant slipped in at left-back, with Danny Collins moving into central defence, and, for the first few minutes there was encouragement to be found in his overlapping runs. But then, five minutes before half-time, he lunged at Damien Johnson in the box, and Mikael Forssell converted the resulting penalty. 'There are no excuses,' Clarke said. 'I'm an experienced player and it shouldn't have happened. I actually thought I got a clip on the ball, but the referee wasn't in a position to see it, and he gave the penalty.'

Sunderland had a goal ruled out for offside just before half-time as Murphy, in an offside position, touched in Lawrence's drive, but they rarely threatened an equaliser and looked pedestrian alongside Birmingham's trio of Arsenal loanees, Fabrice Muamba, Sebastian Larsson and Nicklas Bendtner. 'We haven't turned the corner yet but I really feel we're getting close,' Quinn said. 'We've played arguably the best team in the division and had a real go at them. We needed to be more creative but my players showed a lot of heart.'

The real worry, though, was a crowd of fewer than 27,000. Perhaps it was the absence of a 'world-class' manager, perhaps it was the lack of signings, perhaps it was the defeat at Coventry, but, for all Quinn's pleas for fans to play their part, cynicism evidently still prevailed. The magic-carpet ride Quinn had promised was looking distinctly bumpy.

Wednesday, 9 August, Championship

Sunderland   0-1   Birmingham City
Forssell 40 (pen)

Sunderland: Alnwick, Delap, Cunningham, Caldwell (Clarke 29), D Collins, T Miller, Whitehead, Leadbitter, Lawrence (Stead 74), Murphy, S Elliott
Subs Not Used: Wright, Ward, K Smith
Birmingham: Maik Taylor, Kelly, Tebily, N'Gotty, Sadler, Johnson, Nafti (Danns 84), Muamba (Clemence 71), Larsson, Bendtner, Forssell (Dunn 67)
Subs Not Used: Doyle, Martin Taylor
Ref: G Salisbury (Lancashire)
Booked: Kelly, Muamba (Birmingham)
Att: 26,668
League position: 22

It was to get worse before it got better – much worse. Quinn kept on talking about turning corners, but it felt as though Sunderland were stuck on a road built by the Romans, leading all the way to Ignominium. Still, at least that probably wasn't as far away as Plymouth. It is 412 miles from Home Park to the Stadium of Light, the longest distance between any two clubs in the same division in 2006-07. To the minds of Sunderland fans, the gap in prestige is even greater. Only once before had they lost at home to Plymouth, and that was in April 1992 in the midst of a ludicrous run of seven games in 16 days as Sunderland paid the price for reaching the FA Cup final. Under McCarthy, Sunderland had hammered them 5-1 at the Stadium of Light. Even if Plymouth had played Real Madrid in a pre-season friendly and taken four points from their opening two games, this, surely, was the sort of team Sunderland could overwhelm and finally get the revolution underway. This, though, was a day of ill-omen, weirdly cold for mid-August, so chilly that Plymouth fans chanted, 'Have you ever seen the sun?' It was meant as a meteorological taunt, but as boos rang out at the final whistle it felt metaphysical. Within a week goodwill had soured to discontent. Would this winter never end?

It looked as though spring might be on its way when, after 27 seconds, Daryl Murphy, further justifying his five-year contract, ran on to Tommy Miller's lofted pass and fired in from a narrow angle to give Sunderland the lead. Seven minutes later, though, Tony Capaldi's long diagonal ball embarrassingly evaded a square back-four, and David Norris levelled with a looping shot. Sunderland did not react well. 'There's a gremlin here to do with confidence,' Quinn said. 'Heads went down when they equalised, you could smell mistakes were in the air.'

The first came from Cunningham, taking his role as the new Gary Breen all too seriously. He fluffed what should have been a routine clearance wide on the right, allowing Barry Hayles to muscle by him before rounding a stranded Ben Alnwick to give Plymouth the lead six minutes before half-time. There were jeers as the players left the field at the break, which only added to Sunderland's edginess. They were much the better side for much of the second half, but nervousness always threatened to be their undoing. Stephen Elliott equalised from a Murphy cross midway through the half, Danny Collins had a header cleared off the line, Chris Brown struck the bar and Grant Leadbitter went close, but with the defence seemingly terrified of the ball, there was never a feeling of control. Another Cunningham gaffe was redeemed only as Alnwick saved from

Hayles, and the keeper also made a fine parry from Norris after he had burst through a static back four, but the writing was on the wall. Plymouth's third came against the balance of possession, but it was hardly unexpected. This time Danny Collins was the culprit, misjudging a long hoof into the Sunderland half, allowing Luke Chadwick in for the winner with eight minutes remaining.

'To press the self-destruct button twice was pretty hard to take,' Quinn went on. 'With a couple of exceptions the players haven't done themselves any favours out there.' More worrying was his acknowledgement that the longer Sunderland's poor form went on, the harder it would be to turn around. 'We really need that first victory,' he said. 'We have the money to bring new faces in, it's attracting people here that is the problem.' He was talking about players, but with the crowd over 2,000 down on the first game of the season, he could have been talking about fans.

Saturday, 12 August, Championship

Sunderland	2-3	Plymouth Argyle
Murphy 1		Norris 8
S Elliott 67		Hayles 39
		Chadwick 82

Sunderland: Alnwick, Delap, Cunningham, Clarke (Wright 20), D Collins; Lawrence (Stead 58), Whitehead, Leadbitter, T Miller (Brown 63); S Elliott, Murphy
Subs Not Used: Ward, N Collins
Plymouth: McCormick, Connolly, Doumbe, Aljofree, Capaldi, Norris, Wotton, Summerfield (Buzsaky 72), Hodges, Hayles, Ebanks-Blake (Chadwick 71)
Subs Not Used: Sawyer, Reid, Djordjic
Ref: R Olivier (W Midlands)
Booked:
Att: 24,377
League position: 21

As Quinn headed off to Tipperary to find some perspective with his family, he may have reflected that this wasn't the first time he'd had to win over the Sunderland fans. By 1999, they were releasing a single about his Disco Pants, but when he first arrived, the reaction was distinctly ambivalent. A transfer fee of £1.3million seemed an awful lot for Peter Reid to have paid for a player approaching 30 who had a history of knee problems. Quinn had a goal ruled out after coming off the bench to make his debut against Leicester, and then scored two in a 4-1 away win over Nottingham Forest. He did little against Liverpool or Newcastle, missed a sitter in a televised game at home to West Ham, was poor away at Derby, and then, at home to Coventry in September, snapped his cruciate ligament as his studs caught in the turf following a seemingly innocuous challenge from his Republic of Ireland team-mate Liam Daish. It was a fresh injury, unrelated to the cruciate problem he had suffered in his other knee at Manchester City, but that didn't prevent a general suspicion that, in signing him, Reid had done his old mate a pretty big favour.

Quinn returned the following April, but sluggish performances and no goals in the final five games of the season did little to change the perception of him as a waste of money whose time was past. He scored the first goal at the Stadium of Light as Sunderland beat Manchester City in the opening home game of the following season – an omen that went almost entirely unnoticed at the time – but it was clear something wasn't right. Sunderland lost both their opening away games and then lost 1-0 at home to Norwich, a game in which Quinn, set clean through against Andy Marshall, sent a weak shot trickling into the goalkeeper's arms. Boos rang around the stadium, and Quinn realised that there was still something badly wrong. It wasn't that he had mishit the shot; it was that there was no power in his leg. As he made his way to his car after the game, a fan ran up and spat at him. Four days later, when he was substituted in a 3-1 win over Oxford, the crowd roared their approval.

He contemplated retirement, but instead had exploratory surgery, which revealed two bones had fused together. He spent four weeks in plaster, and when he returned he was, in his own words, 'running like a foal'. The crowd mood changed too, forgetting their earlier hostility, 'cheering me on … as if one of us had been drunk at the time.' In a 1-0 away win over QPR, he was awesome, unplayable. He hit the bar three times, had two goals disallowed and scored the winner. By the end of the season he had managed 17 goals and was a hero. By the time he retired in November 2002, he stood at the highest level of the post-war pantheon, alongside Shackleton, Hurley, Montgomery, and Rowell. That was the kind of transformation he had to enact again.

In fairness, the anger after Plymouth wasn't really directed at Quinn. Football fans are notoriously fickle, but this wasn't quite a case of laying down the palms before his donkey on the Sunday, then crucifying him the following Friday. The booing was rather born from the frustration of watching a team slip from seventh place in the Premiership to abjection in five seasons. Before fans had had Murray to attack as a convenient scapegoat; now, although almost everything for which they'd asked had come to pass, the situation hadn't improved. To boo players scarred by that situation was self-evidently senseless, and so, for all the focus their disillusionment had, they may as well have been booing the air itself.

The easy short-term way for Quinn to reignite the optimism that had followed his takeover would have been a big signing, but transfer activity remained limited. Attempts to bring in Andy Reid from Tottenham had foundered, but Cabanos apparently still wasn't dead, there was said to be interest in the ageing Celtic full-back Didier Agathe, while the 23-year-old Hungary international defender Vilmos Vanczak had a trial at the club. Most of the attention, though, understandably focused on Kevin Phillips, with his potential signing dragging on like no deal since, well, since Quinn's consortium had bought the club. Whether he was really what was wanted was far from clear. Nobody disputed that Sunderland needed a goalscorer, and nobody could have denied that Phillips had been just that: he scored 132 goals in 234 starts for Sunderland, and won the European Golden Boot with 30 goals in the 1999-2000 season, but even towards the end of his six years at Sunderland, there had been suggestions that his pace was going. Three years later he was 33, and almost certainly not the player he had been. There was a concern than bringing him back might sully the memories, but the bigger worry was that Quinn, having already brought back Bobby Saxton, was revving up his time machine and setting the clock for 1999. By the eve of the fourth game of the season, away to Southend, Quinn was announcing that he had 'virtually agreed' a £2million deal with Aston Villa.

Southend should, in theory, be one of those clubs Sunderland hate visiting, but, historically, it is not. The basic rule goes that, at least in the Championship, the worse the ground, the worse Sunderland play, less because they are fancy-dans who need their luxuries than because, used to crowds of 20-odd thousand, they seem to find it hard to take it seriously if there's next to nobody there. At Roots Hall, though, Sunderland's record was excellent. Before 2006-07, Sunderland had won five of the six games they had played there. When things are going badly, though, that sort of record becomes less an inspiration than a millstone.

Sunderland held out anxiously until the stroke of half-time, when Freddy Eastwood crossed for Adam Barrett to thump a header past Ben Alnwick. He added a second midway through the second half, stooping to convert as Peter Clarke headed a Steve Hammell free-kick back across goal. Lee Bradbury, who knows a bit about ailing giants having joined Manchester City for £3million in the season they were relegated to the third flight, tucked in a Mark Gower cross to seal Sunderland's defeat late on. By the time Jon Stead scored his second for the club, in injury time, the away fans struggled to raise themselves to even ironic applause. Arnau Riera, the great Spanish hope, having been introduced for his debut ten minutes into the second half, must have wondered what on earth he had let himself in for.

'Rubbish,' said Kevin Kyle, once again demonstrating an accuracy in analysis he rarely showed with the ball at his feet and the goal gaping. Cunningham admitted he had been amazed by the atmosphere around the club, something Quinn had taken to calling 'shellshock'. 'There's a lot of tension around the club,' Cunningham said. 'The morale is low because there were big expectations going into the season. Nobody can wave a magic wand. Niall is working hard to bring in a few players, but it's important that we don't fall under the illusion that one or two new faces will suddenly transform our fortunes.'

Quinn, though, was done with being conciliatory. Sunderland fans had spent much of the second half chanting 'You're not fit to wear the shirt,' and Quinn, it turned out, agreed with them. He had tried 'positivity', he had tried cajoling, and now he simply told the truth. This was the day the good cop showed his claws. 'I feel for the fans who travelled down but the ones I feel most for are the players because I had to go in and tell some of them that they are not good enough,' he said. 'The levels of negativity are unprecedented. I've been involved in relegations as a player but there's something here that has crept in. The steeliness to win games is not in my dressing room now. On the training ground everything seems fine but in matches this fear, this losing mentality that is rampant undoes us all the time. The players are finding it hard, with all that went on last year, to stick their chests out and take things by the scruff of the neck.'

Saturday, 19 August, Championship

Southend United	3-1	Sunderland
Barrett 45, 68		Stead 90
Bradbury 89		

Southend: Flahavan, Francis, Prior (Clarke 38), Barrett, Hammell, Campbell-Ryce (Lawson 73), Guttridge, Maher, Gower, Bradbury, Eastwood (Hunt 84)
Subs Not Used: Cole, Collis
Sunderland: Alnwick, Wright, N Collins, Cunningham, R Elliott, S Elliott, Leadbitter (Riera 55), Whitehead, Delap (Kyle 70), Stead, Murphy
Subs Not Used: Lawrence, Ward, D Collins
Ref: J Singh (Middlesex)
Booked: Whitehead, Wright (Sunderland)
Att: 9,848
League position: 24

The defeat left Sunderland as one of only four clubs in the entire league without a point after four games. With a hideous inevitability they faced one of them in the Carling Cup the following Tuesday – the worst of them, Bury, last of all 92 league clubs. There comes a time when a club suffers a defeat so bad, so shameful, that it is almost a relief, because you *know* it has to be the nadir. Gigg Lane, 22 August 2007: the date after which it couldn't get any worse. This was Sunderland's harrowing.

The day began badly as Kevin Phillips opted to join West Brom rather than return to Sunderland. As though to compensate, Quinn did sign the 23-year-old winger William Mocquet from Le Havre, while revealing that he was in talks with the Swedish club Djurgården over a possible deal for Tobias Hysen, a left winger and the son of the former Liverpool centre-back Glenn Hysen. Width certainly was an area where Sunderland needed strengthening, but then, they'd been found wanting in pretty much every department.

What little hope remained at that stage centred around Riera, who had been built up as a player of far greater technical ability than anybody else at the club, and had been one of the few to emerge from the Southend debacle with even the slightest credit. He was the only change to the team that had lost at Roots Hall, which made what happened at Bury even more desperate. Quinn wasn't resting anyone: this was what he saw as his strongest team. As Bobby Saxton had said, this was a team desperate for a win, any win, even if it came in a practice match. The problem was, it looked as though it would never arrive. The old Tommy Docherty line came to mind: 'I had my players practising by dribbling round dustbins. They lost 4-2.' Sunderland wouldn't have got the two.

Within four minutes of kick-off at Gigg Lane, things had already begun to go wrong. Perhaps Riera could have been one of Sunderland's all-time greats – although his subsequent form when on loan at Southend suggests not – but his *Sliding Doors* moment came as he jumped with Richie Baker, catching the midfielder with a flailing arm. He protested his innocence, but Michael Jones, the referee, saw it as a deliberate elbow, and Riera was sent off. By the time he returned from his suspension, the situation had changed, and he never played for the club again. 'I'd barely sat down,' Quinn said in disbelief. 'I was still looking at my notes. I looked up and he was walking off the pitch.' The great Spanish hope's Sunderland career totalled 38 minutes spread over defeats to Southend and Bury.

As is customary in such circumstances, Quinn went on to praise the 'character' of his players, sticking it out for almost 80 minutes before conceding, but however you dress it up, a defeat to the team 92nd in the pyramid is a humiliation. Even being taken to extra-time would have been embarrassing, and that was where the game seemed to be heading before John Fitzgerald met Brian Barry-Murphy's corner with a firm header. In his glee, the defender leapt into the crowd, collected a second yellow card and was himself sent off, but on this night that seemed less a sliver of hope for Sunderland than a further dose of disgrace: they couldn't even beat the worst team in the country when they were down to ten men. Chasing an equaliser, Sunderland were caught on the break, and Andy Bishop added a second with two minutes remaining.

Quinn's tone was valedictory. 'It sums up the past four weeks,' he said. 'We weren't able to appoint a manager then, so I stepped into the breach to try and help but obviously it's not been successful. I cannot legislate for the things happening at this moment. I stepped into this role because I didn't think we got the quality of applicant I thought we would. I cannot name the manager but we think we have somebody who will give the players the real lift they need, and we will give him the budget he deserves. We are now getting very close to doing that. We've tracked a would-be manager for the last four weeks and we're getting closer. I would hope by Monday, I can say 70-30, that we will have a world-class manager in place.'

Tuesday, 22 August, Carling Cup first round

Bury   2-0   Sunderland
Fitzgerald 82
Bishop 88

Bury: Fettis, Scott, Fitzgerald, Woodthorpe, Brass (Parrish 81), Baker, Adams,
  Buchanan, Mattis (Barry-Murphy 82), Pittman (Youngs 57), Bishop
Subs Not Used: Collinge, Flitcroft
Sunderland: Alnwick, Wright (Lawrence 38), Cunningham, N Collins, R Elliott (Stead
  86), Whitehead, Leadbitter, Riera, Delap (D Collins 70), S Elliott, Murphy
Subs Not Used: Ward, Smith
Ref: M Jones (W Yorkshire)
Sent Off: Fitzgerald 83 (Bury); Riera 4 (Sunderland)
Booked: Fitzgerald, Brass (Bury); Cunningham (Sunderland)
Att: 2,930

There were, it must be said, sceptics. Quinn had always said he would step aside, that he was just keeping the seat warm for the right man, but if he couldn't attract that man in the summer, how on earth was going to bring him in after five straight defeats, one of them to Bury? Who but a masochist would do the job? By now the rumour mill was as baffled as anyone else, spewing out the names of just about anybody who had ever managed a club in England: Alan Curbishley? David O'Leary? Steve Bruce? Glenn Hoddle? Claudio Ranieri? Or, most likely and most feared, Peter Reid?

The motto wrought into the Murray Gates reads 'Into the light', echoing the slogan that had been written at the top of the lift-shaft at Wearmouth Colliery. This was certainly as dark as the pit; but the club, to everyone's surprise, was about to step forth into the sunshine.

It was in India that I first realised how much football meant home. This was, objectively speaking, ridiculous. I lived in an idyllic Himalayan monastery, with a stream babbling by my door and monkeys swinging from tree to tree outside, where the only thing to worry about was that leopards might come in the night and attack the rabbits, and yet hearing of a 2-2 draw at home to Grimsby got me yearning for the grubby concrete of the Fulwell End.

Perhaps that is only natural, because for the exile, football is the readiest point of contact with home. For the vast majority of provincial towns, the football results represent the one moment on national television or radio when they can guarantee they will be mentioned (a corollary of this, incidentally, is how much better, in general, a football fan's sense of geography is than a non-football fan's). I don't think I heard Sunderland mentioned at all in India apart from during the reading of the football results (although the crossword in the *Hindustan Times* did once carry a clue that read: 'Separate land from N-E town (6)', which filled me with undue pride).

It was August 1994 when I went out there, which sounds recent enough, but in terms of the gap year it was a different age. Himalayan tourist traps were not awash with Internet cafes in those days, and with the postal service intermittent and telephone calls prohibitively expensive, my main interaction with home came through a shortwave radio and the World Service. I spent most evenings either giving private tuition to villagers or out with teachers based at other local monasteries, but on Saturdays I would always be back in my room by 9 p.m., ready for the start of the second-half commentary when the World Service took coverage from Radio 5.

I don't know what the situation is now, but back then the coverage couldn't have been more frustrating. At 10.15 – 4.45 British time – the World Service would switch to *South-East Asia Report*, which – 10.15 being very late when the horns in the temple start bellowing at dawn – meant you were never quite sure of the final scores until the following morning. A 2-2 draw at Middlesbrough after Sunderland had been 2-0 up when I'd gone to bed was particularly galling – because, of course, being as mindlessly superstitious as the next fan, I partly blamed myself. If only I'd stayed sitting in the lucky chair, hadn't turned off the lucky radio, hadn't brushed the lucky plaque off my teeth and washed the lucky sweat off my face, and hadn't taken off the lucky T-shirt to get into the unlucky bed, we might just have been all right.

I even took the radio with me when I went climbing with a couple of monks one weekend. We spent the night in a cave on the coll where Triund meets the mighty Ilaqa. It was shaded from the sun and very, very cold, but after a quick breakfast on the Sunday, as the howls of wolves mingled with the low groaning of the wind, I made them wait, shivering, until I'd found out that we'd beaten Barnsley 2-0 at home. In retrospect, that was probably a wasted effort: Sunderland always beat Barnsley at home.

[4]

THE COMING

New dawn turned false dawn in five straight defeats? Sunderland had been there before. After relegation to the second division in 1985, Sunderland, uncharacteristically proactive, turned to Lawrie McMenemy. The Gateshead-born former guardsman seemed a bold, even inspired choice. With limited means he had achieved great things in his 12 years at Southampton, leading them to an FA Cup triumph as a second-division side, before guiding them to promotion and, in 1984, a club-record second place in the First Division. When it emerged that Sunderland had made McMenemy the highest-paid manager in the country, the scale of the club's ambition – after years of moans about under-investment – staggered Wearside. McMenemy was mobbed by fans when he arrived at Roker Park to begin work on 6 June – and the symbolism of the date did not go unremarked – while just about every window in the town seemed to be adorned by a banner or sticker promising 'We're on our way back with Big Mac.'

It was close: Sunderland were on their way backwards with Big Mac. As the joke of the late Eighties had it, McMenemy – or 'Mackem-enemy', as he became known – was like the *Titanic*: he should never have left Southampton. Even now, there is sufficient bitterness over the gulf between his salary and his achievements that when Sunderland fanzines refer to him, they asterisk out the middle letters of his name as though it were a swear-word.

If the optimism sparked by his arrival hadn't disappeared by the end of his first game, a flaccid 2-0 defeat at home to Blackburn Rovers, it had by the end of his second, a 3-0 capitulation at Portsmouth. Then came a 1-0 reverse at Crystal Palace, a 3-0 home embarrassment against Oldham, and a 1-0 defeat at Millwall. Sunderland rallied towards the end of the season, three wins in their final four games seeing them escape relegation by four points, but by the time McMenemy slunk away in the middle of April the following year, they were on their way to the third division for the first time in their history.

To try to isolate what went wrong would be impossible: everything did. Explaining why he'd bought Peter Shilton for Southampton, McMenemy had said that a team should be built around its goalkeeper; at Sunderland he used six. At Southampton, McMenemy had achieved success by coaxing an extra season or two out of ageing players; Sunderland he turned into a retirement home, and a debt-ridden one at that. At least under Quinn Sunderland had scored, had actually held out the possibility of victory; but, then, McMenemy's side had never lost to a side as bad as Bury. As connoisseurs of bleakness bickered over which had been the greater let-down, others wondered why it had to be this way. It was hardly surprising board after board had stifled ambition with caution (in the classic – and possibly apocryphal – formulation of the trope, falling £10,000 short of Newport County's valuation of John Aldridge shortly before he moved to Oxford United) when the slightest sign of ambition brought such pain. If Icarus had been a Mackem, you feel, he would never have crashed to earth after flying too close to the sun, but only because he'd have dislocated his shoulders putting the wings on in the first place.

The difference with 20 years earlier, though, was that in Quinn, Sunderland had a chairman prepared to accept he had made a mistake and effectively sack his manager, even if that happened to be himself. Even better, they had somebody of the requisite stature ready to step in: Roy Keane.

Wherever that odd, isolated rumour had sprung from six months earlier, it turned out to be right. There were those who quibbled that Keane, with no experience whatsoever, was not technically a 'world-class manager', but they were in the minority. Keane's qualities as a player and a captain were hardly in doubt and, in world terms, he was probably the biggest figure to associate himself with the club since Raich Carter was allowed to leave after the war. Quinn's revision of his earlier comment, that Keane 'is a leading figure in world football who will bring steel and a winning mentality to Sunderland', was beyond dispute. And even if he did fail, there was at least a sense of adventure, of fun: as every fan knows, that is the next best thing – perhaps even preferable – to silverware and success.

Amid all the excitement, though, one huge question remained. Trace any of the threads of Sunderland's revival back far enough, and you arrive in Saipan. The narrative of Sunderland's season was set in motion by an argument between three Irishmen – one of them admittedly born in Yorkshire – in Japan. Football is an enclosed world with a limited cast, and has a habit of offering up quirks and coincidences, but even by those standards this was something extraordinary on the part of the fates. What scriptwriter would have dared have those three men – McCarthy, Quinn and Keane – succeed each other as manager of the same football club? When Keane, later in the season, took disciplinary action against three players who had missed the bus to an away game at Barnsley – by another coincidence, McCarthy's birth-place – and condemned the 'complacency' that pervaded the club, who did not see it as the continuation of a five-year-old attack on McCarthy's methods?

The first sign of tension ahead of the 2002 World Cup came when Keane failed to turn out for the Republic of Ireland against Sunderland in Quinn's testimonial match. Keane was still feeling the effects of the knee injury that had – controver-sially – kept him out of the second leg of Ireland's World Cup qualifying play off in Iran and told Quinn he was struggling. Quinn said he understood, but asked Keane to sign a message for the programme. Keane was happy to do so, until he discov-ered that the programme notes were being written by Cathal Dervan, a friend of McCarthy and the journalist who had urged the Lansdowne Road crowd to boo Keane during a game against Iceland because of his supposed lack of commitment to his country. As Keane stayed in Manchester to receive treat-ment on his knee, the newspapers interpreted the story as 'Keane Snubs Charity Benefit'. Or, as Keane thought people would read it, 'Keane Snubs Sick Kids'.

When he met up with the Republic of Ireland squad in Dublin, Keane was angered by the travel arrangements. He had protested at the 'package tour' mentality before, and here it was again, players lugging a month's-worth of kit through a crowded airport. Then, on the flight, Keane watched the Michael Mann film *Ali*. In the mood he was in, there probably couldn't have been a worse film for him to see. In his autobi-ography, Keane speaks of how moved he was by Muhammad Ali's decision, even when all his friends and family urged him to back down, to refuse the draft. It confirmed in Keane's mind the importance of sticking to your principles.

There is, of course, an unavoidable sense of bathos in all this. Stripped to the marrow, Keane's arguments were essentially trivial. While Ali was protesting about going off to fight the 'white man's war' in Vietnam, Keane was protesting because the Ireland squad was being provided with cheese sandwiches rather than pasta and cereals before training. Still, a principle is a principle, and whatever the difference of scale, that revelation does at least help to explain why Keane made the stand he did. The cheese sandwich incident, which occurred before a qualifier against Holland, was in itself not especially important – or at least not beyond the confines of football – but extrapolate it as some did, and you find Keane speaking up for a new, more aggressive and assertive Ireland against a culture of complacency. 'We did it our way,' as he put it in his autobiography. 'The world loved us, we told ourselves. Weren't we the cabaret act, there to get the party going before leaving when the tournament got serious?' He was talking about the football team, but there was a resonance through other spheres of Irish life.

Quinn's autobiography also speaks of his frustration at the disorganisation of the FAI, but whereas Keane's inclination was to attack their inadequacies, he merely laughed. When he is sent an itinerary for the 2002 World Cup, for instance, he mocks 'one small step for mankind, but one big step for the FAI.' He notes the difference in mood between his first World Cup, in 1990, and his second, in 2002, after the economic boom, lamenting the absence of the 'old excited innocence'. He suggests the haphazard approach 'suits us'; not Roy Keane it didn't.

Things only got worse when the Irish squad arrived in Saipan. The training gear, the footballs, the medical supplies, even a drink to aid with acclimatisation hadn't turned up. The first day's training was spent running in tracksuits wholly ill-suited to the conditions. The training pitch was hard, littered with loose stones and unwatered because nobody had told the local authorities that they wanted to use it that day. The next day the equipment arrived, and the pitch had been watered, but so inefficiently that a 20-yard strip was flooded, while the rest remained like concrete. Steve Finnan turned his ankle in a pothole.

It wasn't just the conditions. Keane was unhappy with the way training went, felt that it was badly organised and that the areas for the possession drills were either too big or too small – technical details, but further straws adding to the burden he was already bearing. In his autobiography Quinn is sympathetic, recognising the travails of genius, of being, as he puts it, 'a twitching twenty-four hour a day obsessive': 'Roy is more driven and more obsessed by success than the rest of us … He rails against failure and rages for success … he might even despise us for not having the same brooding, obsessive passion that he has.'

Training ended with a game, but without goalkeepers. Keane was furious. Had there been any five-a-side nets, he says he would have accepted it, but a game with full-size goals and no goalkeepers was farcical. He protested. The goalkeepers, he was told, had had a hard session and were tired – another example, as Keane saw it, of the 'happy camper' approach. So he approached McCarthy and told him he wanted to go home. McCarthy agreed, with, it seems, a measure of relief, and rang Colin Healy to fly out as a replacement. Then, after a conversation with Mick Byrne, the experienced physio, Keane agreed to stick it out until the end of the tournament. When he told McCarthy he had changed his mind, though, the manager did not respond as warmly as he'd have liked and expressed a concern about people having to 'walk on eggshells' around Keane. So Keane again decided to leave. That evening, after a telephone conversation with Sir Alex Ferguson, he changed his mind again.

Keane did an interview with the *Irish Times*, in which he refused to bow to 'PR crap' and said exactly what he thought: 'You've seen the training pitch and I'm not being a prima donna. Training pitch, travel arrangements, getting through the bloody airport when we were leaving, it's the combination of things.' The piece appeared on the Thursday morning, and that evening McCarthy approached him about it as the squad ate their evening meal, accusing him of 'going against your team-mates'. As the argument escalated, McCarthy attacked Keane for having missed the second leg in Iran, of 'faking an injury'. Keane later claimed it was a set-up, that McCarthy had been provoking him, looking for a reaction. He got one.

'Suddenly I snapped,' Keane wrote. 'All the fuck-ups and bullshit I and every other Irish player had put up with for ten years flashed through my mind.' It all came spewing out. 'Mick, you're a liar ...,' Keane raged. 'You're a fucking wanker. I didn't rate you as a player, I don't rate you as a manager, and I don't rate you as a person. You're a fucking wanker and you can stick your World Cup up your arse. The only reason I have any dealings with you is that somehow you are the manager of my country. You can stick it up your bollocks.' That was the bit that made the papers, anyway, but Quinn later described Keane as dismantling McCarthy from A–Z, 'his personality, his play, his style, his tactics, his contribution ... Spineless. Useless. Stupid. Gutless ... Incompetent. Ignorant. Backward. Conman.' It went on for nine minutes, and nobody intervened because they were all, as Quinn put it, 'mesmerised ... transfixed': 'People talk about Irish patriot Robert Emmet's speech from the dock. They talk about the oratory of Brendan Behan, Eamon de Valera, Michael Collins. But Roy Keane's ten-minute oration can be mentioned in the same breath. It was clinical, fierce, earth-shattering to the person on the end of it.'

After he had left the room, Keane relates, Quinn stood up and spoke of the need for everyone to stick together. Quinn says it was Gary Kelly. There was a round of applause that only two players – Gary Breen and David Connolly – did not join. A press conference was held in a small Chinese restaurant around the corner from the hotel at which McCarthy, flanked by Quinn and two other senior players, the goalkeeper Alan Kelly and the defender Steve Staunton, announced that Keane had been expelled from the squad. Connolly asked what would happen if Keane were to say sorry, at which Quinn set about canvassing opinion among the other members of the squad, and Michael Kennedy looked into the possibility of getting Keane to apologise.

As the saga dragged on, McCarthy eventually decided enough was enough, that the players had to decide whether they backed him or not. A statement was drawn up saying Keane's return would be a distraction. It was intended to be released after a McCarthy press conference, as evidence that the players supported him. The press conference was delayed, but the release of the statement was not. It came out first and so, rather than serving as a message of support for McCarthy, it looked like the players had themselves taken the decision to veto Keane's return. It was just the sort of incompetence against which Keane had campaigned that led to the final severing of relations. 'I can only guess – as I'm sure you can – who drafted that statement,' Keane said. Quinn insisted it was a combination of himself, Kenny Cunningham, Alan Kelly and Steve Staunton.

The sniping continued. Quinn is only five years older than Keane, but they straddled a gulf in the culture of the game. Quinn, when he retired, spoke of how football had lost its spark for him because the club no longer stopped off at country pubs on the way back from away games to drink themselves stupid in celebration. The problem, he said, was that the foreign lads had to get back to their yoga teachers. It was, many believed, the mishandling of that transition from the drinking-together-winning-together mentality to the era of Prozone and the intensive statistical analysis of diet and fitness that had led to Sunderland's decline under Peter Reid. Possibly slightly ahead of his time, Keane was of the new age, and, according to Lee Sharpe, having cut back on his drinking in 1996, he became an obsessive trainer convinced above all else of the value of preparation. 'Human beings are not an exact science,' Quinn maintained. 'It doesn't have to be dead solid perfect. There's an intangible called spirit.' Keane preferred to think of how much further that spirit would go if it were allied to proper diet and full intensity in every training session.

It was only in 1998 when Arsenal, in their first full season under Arsène Wenger, won the Premiership with a late surge that football became convinced of the value of eating broccoli. By 2002, it had become impossible to ignore science. Sunderland finished fourth-bottom of the Premiership in May that year, then came Keane's outburst at the backwardness of Ireland's preparation, and that October, after a 3-1 defeat at Arsenal had exposed just how far behind Sunderland were, Reid was sacked. As Quinn pointed out in the wake of Keane's walk-out, though, training is not the only part of being a footballer. 'How do you measure professionalism?' he asked. 'By how much pasta you eat? Bleep tests? Abstinence? The ability to get on with it no matter what the circumstances? Walking out on your team before the greatest games of their lives? We all take responsibility for ourselves. Roy left us in Saipan, not the other way round. And he punished himself more than any of us by not coming back.'

Keane, meanwhile, saw Quinn as a 'coward' for his refusal to stand up against the inadequacy of the preparations, and later dismissed him as a 'muppet'. The most damning line, though, is one that is often taken out of context, his comparison of Quinn to 'Mother Teresa'. Had he just been saying that Quinn was whiter-than-white, too-good-to-be-true, that would have been easy enough to laugh off, but what he actually said was much worse: 'He's sitting on TV pretending to wipe a tear from his eye. He deserves an Oscar that fella, making out to be Mother Teresa. People don't know half of it.' Keane wasn't saying that Quinn was a goody-two-shoes, he was accusing him of pretending to be. He was saying, in other words, that he was a hypocrite.

Four years passed after Saipan before the two spoke to each other again.

If the personal jousting could be put aside, the issue became whether you saw Keane's actions as evidence of a dangerous unreliability, or whether you appreciated his frustration and applauded his refusal to accept anything but the highest of standards – both from himself and his team-mates. Such an uncompromising nature might not make him an easy man to deal with, but it might just be the quality that led him to excel as a manager.

Quinn described Keane's rant 'the most articulate, the most surgical slaughtering I've ever heard … a feat of oratory, intelligence and some wit', all valuable skills for a manager to have. A dressing-room is no place for democracy. As the great

Hungarian coach Béla Guttmann said, a manager is like a lion tamer: 'He dominates the animals, in whose cage he performs his show, as long as he deals with them with self-confidence and without fear. But the moment he becomes unsure of his hypnotic energy, and the first hint of fear appears in his eyes, he is lost.' It was hard to believe Keane, with his quick brain and his quick mouth, his self-confidence and his self-possession, would ever show that fear. Quinn described McCarthy facing Keane as looking like he'd turned up at the gunfight at the OK Corral without his gun. It seemed inconceivable that Keane should ever find an opponent wielding superior weaponry.

Keane, after all, had grown up under two of football's most celebrated angry men. Brian Clough was unpredictable and might have been better known for his one-liners, but he, just as much as Sir Alex Ferguson, ruled his dressing-room with a rod of iron. In his autobiography, Keane recalled an incident at Forest after he had made a mistake that cost a goal. 'When I walked into the dressing room after the game, Clough punched me straight in the face,' he wrote. 'I was too shocked to do anything but nod in agreement.'

The endless Clough comparisons clearly came to rile Keane, but it was hard to dispute their relevance. 'I was very lucky to play under Clough,' he acknowledged. 'He kept things very simple and he was a genius with it.' Like Clough, he had a philosophy of how the game should be played – 'pass the ball and move it; pass the ball and move it'. Like Clough, 'one look from those eyes' – as Dwight Yorke later put it – was enough to command respect. Like Clough, he named his dog after a character in *Only Fools and Horses*. Clough's golden retriever was called Dell – short for Del Boy; Keane's Triggs – short for Trigger.

Keane clearly revered Clough, and, particularly, his theory of the 'Law of Cumulation'. 'If you weren't doing your stuff,' he wrote, 'Clough would spot it. A seemingly innocuous mistake that resulted in a goal conceded three or four minutes later, a tackle missed, or a failure to make the right run or pass would be correctly identified.' That, in Keane's eyes, was what marked out the true managers from what he regularly dismissed as 'the bluffers and bullshitters'. 'Every football match is made up of a thousand little things which, added together, amount to the final score,' he explained. 'The manager who can't spot the details in the forensic detail Clough could is simply bluffing.'

Martin O'Neill had been seen by Sunderland fans as the next best thing to Clough, but Keane, perhaps, was even better. Quite apart from anything else, he was available, without experience and so a far more plausible candidate. With no history, he could be shaped. He could be adopted, assimilated, made Mackem.

The possibility of Keane made Sunderland mainstream news again, with columnists and pundits falling over themselves to offer an opinion on whether Keane would make a successful manager. The old saw about great players not necessarily making great managers was trotted out again and again, with only the most astute adding the proviso that there are different kinds of great players. Keane was not, by his own admission, a Pelé or a Maradona or even a Bobby Charlton, blessed with an instinctive genius. He was very good technically, of course he was, or he would never have climbed as high as he did, but what really marked him out was his intelligence, his charisma and his determination. He analysed a game and led his team-mates so effectively that Ferguson spoke of him as his manager on the field – and seemed at times to use him as an enforcer off it – and his was a talent from which every last drop was wrung. If he could read the game as effectively from the bench and instil a semblance of his own desire in his players, then there was no reason to believe he would not be hugely effective as a manager.

Most focused on Keane's ability to inspire fear. The reaction of Gary Pallister, once Keane's team-mate at United, was typical. 'If I was a player, I wouldn't want to play under him,' he said. 'I reckon he would dish out bigger rollickings than Sir Alex.' The Republic of Ireland goalkeeper Dean Kiely spoke of how vocal Keane was in a dressing-room even as a player. 'He commands respect and has an aura about him,' he said. 'Players will respond to passionate people.'

Two potential pitfalls were foreseen. Would he be able to control his temper, which was perceived as volatile to the extent of being self-destructive, as had been seen, most notoriously, in the horrific retributive foul on Alf-Inge Haaland? And would he be able to work with players of lesser ability? This, after all, was a man whose United career had come to an end after an extraordinary outburst on a programme recorded for MUTV following a 4-1 defeat at Middlesbrough. First he addressed Rio Ferdinand – 'Just because you are paid £120,000-a-week and play well for 20 minutes against Tottenham, you think you are a superstar' – before broadening his target area: 'The younger players have been let down by some of the more experienced players. They are just not leading. There is a shortage of characters in this team. It seems to be in this club that you have to play badly to be rewarded. Maybe that is what I should do when I come back. Play badly.' The programme, on Ferguson's orders, was never broadcast, but Keane still made sure he got his message across, reputedly looking his team-mates in the eye and telling them exactly in person what he had wanted to say on television. There have been allusions throughout his career to Keane's shyness, but that spoke of an astonishing ruthlessness, everything else being subsumed by his belief in the value of saying what he felt needed to be said. Keane had said he had never made a friend in football, something presumably resulting from a combination of that shyness and his demanding nature. Whether that is healthy is doubtful, but for somebody in management the advantages are obvious. Keane had no vested interests, no emotional ties, no Falstaff to shake off; he could get on with the task of dragging the club in the direction in which he felt it should be going.

That said, hammering a United player for supposed laziness or complacency is all very well, because at Old Trafford an expectation of a certain ability is realistic, but at Sunderland he might run into players who couldn't do something not because they weren't trying, but because they weren't good enough. 'The one thing Roy has to get into his head straight away is that he will be working with lesser players,' the former United full-back Paul Parker said. 'People will have nowhere near the quality he had as a player or his team-mates had. He will have to restrain himself because Sunderland's players won't be able to do what David Beckham, Eric Cantona or Ruud Van Nistelrooy were capable of.'

It was Lee Sharpe in *The Guardian* who summed it up most presciently. He spoke of Keane being 'quick-witted, in a cutting, merciless, kind of way', and so invoked the memory of Clough, before drawing the obvious conclusions from Saipan. 'At Sunderland, as long as he is in control, Roy will make sure it is all top-class: the training facilities, coaching, preparation. He won't ask for skills the players haven't got, he'll demand absolute professionalism. Roy will want the players to give their best, not hide, keep wanting the ball, play it simply in possession. If I were a Sunderland player, waiting for him to take charge for the first time, I'd think this is a great opportunity. They're working for somebody who really knows football, who has played and won the biggest games at the highest level. I wouldn't want to cross him, obviously – but then all good managers have that steel. If the players give everything and do their best, they'll learn a huge amount, and, more importantly, they'll be safe with Roy.'

Before any of that became relevant, though, there was the matter of getting Keane actually to sign the deal. Sunderland had, after all, had lost several battles they'd have backed themselves as 70–30 to win before, and Keane was said to be unhappy at the way the news had broken before the contract had been signed. The remarkable thing, though, if negotiations really had been ongoing for four weeks, was that it had not leaked out earlier. Quinn had initially said he wanted Keane in charge for the bank holiday Monday game at home to West Brom, but as the weekend approached, it became apparent that that wasn't going to happen.

He did, though, appear at the training ground on the Sunday morning to meet the players, on the understanding that he would sign a contract after the game. From the ranks of those greeting their new boss, there was one large absentee: Kevin Kyle. The thought of the lumbering Scottish striker doing anything surreptitiously is laughable, but amid the furore surrounding Keane's imminent arrival, he had slipped away almost unnoticed, sold to Coventry. Their manager Micky Adams claimed Kyle was 'a proven goalscorer at this level', which seemed a little generous for a man whose 91 league appearances for Sunderland (many of them admittedly as a substitute) had brought a meagre 11 goals, at least two of which were involuntary. His real skills seemed rather to be an admirable forthrightness after defeats, and an ability to injure himself in increasingly comical ways. With characteristic lucklessness, when he scored his first goal for Coventry, his father was not there to see it, having been told it was not worth making the journey from Scotland because Kyle had a tight thigh and a back spasm. 'Stranraer's only a small town and there's nothing better to do on a Saturday, so they travel down to watch me play and have a good day out,' Kyle said. 'My dad was a wee bit annoyed because he'd filled the car up with petrol and had no money left to go out with.'

Aside from raising spirits with his genial haplessness, Kyle had, in fairness, played a useful part in promotion under McCarthy, but his best days probably came the following season, as he languished with a hip injury. Somehow the thought took hold that what Sunderland were lacking was a physical presence up front and that things would improve as soon as Kyle could get himself fit. By the time he returned for the FA Cup fourth-round game at Brentford in late January, he had come to loom as some great hybrid of Quinn, Nat Lofthouse, the Incredible Hulk, and Pelé. He was not, and £600,000 seemed pretty generous. Happily, his knack for getting into avoidable scrapes was undiminished, and the following April he was sentenced to 120 hours of community service for brawling in the street while celebrating Scotland's victory over France the previous October. 'They are making an example of me,' he protested. 'It's only because of who I am.' Yes, among the world's put-upon peoples, there are few so wronged as the fringe Coventry target-man.

By the time Sunderland's game with West Brom kicked off, Sunderland were bottom of the table, Colchester having jumped above them on the Saturday with a 4-3 win over Derby.

If it were not an ideal position from which to relaunch the revolution, it was at least appropriate. It certainly felt like rock-bottom, something reflected in the fact that, despite Keane's imminence, only 24,242 turned up. It would be easy, given what followed, to dismiss the dismal start as teething, to suggest there had always been a belief that things would turn round. It wasn't, there wasn't and the sense of hopelessness was genuine.

Poor West Brom. Somebody had to play the part of sacrificial lambs, cut down by Sunderland's renewed belief, and it was them. A week earlier, a month later, and they might have had a chance; on that day they were the unwilling patsies in someone else's story of redemption. Sunderland had won only five of their previous 47 games, but Keane's presence in the stands, glowering, bestubbled, clad all in black, was sufficient to change them out of all recognition. Quinn, in his final game, had his first victory, although he may have reflected that it would have come sooner if only he'd enjoyed from the start the sort of luck that gifted Sunderland their opener. Dean Whitehead swept in a corner from the right and, after the goalkeeper Pascal Zuberbuhler had missed it, Paul Robinson could not prevent it crossing the line.

Sunderland had played West Brom in the sixth game of their previous season – having lost their first five – and, having dominated, would have collected their first win had they not permitted Zoltan Gera a soft equaliser from a last-minute corner. This season, though, it was West Brom who were struggling to defend dead balls, and Neill Collins headed a second from Tobias Hysen's free-kick two minutes after half-time. The relief was palpable, which probably spared Kevin Phillips, jeered after his introduction as a half-time substitute, a more uncomfortable afternoon.

Keane's previous appearance on Wearside, in August 2002, had ended in ignominy, sent off in the final minute of a 1-1 draw for an elbow on his former Republic of Ireland teammate Jason McAteer. It was not hard to read into that clash echoes of Saipan, particularly when McAteer then mimed writing in an imaginary book. What must have made that gesture, a mocking reference to the disrepute charges Keane was facing over his controversial autobiography, all the more infuriating was the sense of surprise: who'd have thought McAteer – a man who once asked for a takeaway pizza to be cut into four rather than eight because he wasn't that hungry – knew how to write?

Quinn, still a Sunderland player, attempted to shake hands with Keane as he left the field, a gesture misinterpreted by Sir Alex Ferguson, who intervened, further poisoning the atmosphere. Five years later, Keane was serenaded by the same fans who had then howled in derision. With victory secured, as if to show they had not forgotten the old messiah, they chanted Quinn's name as well. If not forgotten, the traumas of the previous five games were at least forgiven.

Quinn, though, had no illusions as to what had inspired the victory. 'Roy played his part,' he said. 'I think there was a buzz at the end, suggesting those at the match will say to their mates: "You should have come." I'd be pretty confident of that. He brought a buzz to the place and my players responded. I'm glad he has seen that the team has character.'

Monday, 28 August, Championship

Sunderland   2-0   West Bromwich Albion
Whitehead 33
N Collins 47

Sunderland: Alnwick, Delap, Cunningham, N Collins, R Elliott, Lawrence, Whitehead, Leadbitter (Nosworthy 90), Hysen (Murphy 78), Brown (Stead 89), S Elliott

Subs Not Used: Ward, D Collins
West Brom: Zuberbuhler, Watson, C Davies, Perry, Robinson, Gera, Chaplow (Wallwork 58), Quashie, Greening (Carter 58), Hartson, Ellington (Phillips 46)
Subs Not Used: Steele, Albrechtsen
Ref: P Joslin (Nottinghamshire)
Booked: Leadbitter, Brown (Sunderland); Perry, Wallwork (West Brom)
Att: 24,242
League position: 23

The timing did not quite fit, but it turned out those initial rumours had had a little substance. Late in May 2006, Keane had received a call from Michael Kennedy, inviting him to a meeting in County Kildare at the house of one of the Drumaville investors. Before the main discussions, though, he had to clear the air with Quinn. The two had not spoken since Saipan, but, in a private room, the two put their differences behind them. Neither have revealed details of what was said, although Quinn has admitted that when he walked into the room he was unsure whether he should have his hands raised to protect his face, or outstretched to offer a hug. 'A lot of people are making a big issue of the past but we sorted it out a few months ago,' a freshly shaved Keane said, sitting alongside Quinn at a press conference the day after the West Brom game. 'It's important to move on. I apologise if I've done something wrong but I really don't see a problem. That's the kind of character I am.'

The Kildare meeting had been broadly positive, with Keane agreeing that Sunderland had potential, something that helped convince wavering members of the consortium that this was a risk worth taking. He was unwilling at that stage, though, to be considered as a manager because, in his phrase, he 'had a bee in my bonnet' about completing his UEFA 'A' coaching licence. Quinn was convinced enough that Keane had not 'shut the door entirely' that as things started to go wrong for him, he got Kennedy to approach Keane again. By then Keane was coming to the end of a coaching course which, he said, had restored his feeling for the game after the disillusionment that had crept in during his final days at Celtic. 'Sunderland ticked all the boxes for me and the family,' Keane said. 'I just thought why not? I had to give it a go.' Better, as Yeats said, to have strife than loneliness.

Still, nobody was quite sure what to make of the new cordiality, a confusion best summed up by an anecdote that did the rounds at the time. It is almost certainly apocryphal, but it has at least an emotional truth. A relative of Keane's, it is said, rang him up after the Bury game and told him to take the job because it looked like Quinn was about to have a heart attack. 'I'll give it a week, then,' Keane is supposed to have replied.

The welcome press conference, it turned out, did not merely confirm Keane's arrival with the usual clichés of intent. Keane does not do banality, and this was him offering another side of himself: assured, witty, and self-deprecating as his questioners probed around the issue of his temperament and how he would cope working with less able players. 'All I expected from my team-mates was a hundred per cent,' he said. 'I never criticised people for having bad games, I criticised people for slacking off and not being focused on the job. I've already reassured the players here that if they give a hundred per cent there won't be a problem. But if the staff or players take their eye off the ball and are not prepared to give a hundred per cent, then there will be a problem. It's very, very straightforward.'

Although he insisted he was 'too young to be wise' this was Keane settling his accounts, admitting his faults as though to start a fresh page. 'I haven't helped myself over the years with the image,' he said. 'That was part of my scene I had at United and maybe with Ireland, that I was football mad. Psycho's probably too strong a word, but football means a hell of a lot to me. It was like an acting job, I used to feel that when I drove up to Old Trafford that I would turn into this kind of mean machine. When I was going to work or to games it was like going to war. That was the only way I could describe it. But afterwards you switch off and go home to your family. The reputation didn't help with one or two sendings-off – I didn't help myself. Maybe that was part of the picture I had to paint for the opposition, sometimes you can play with people's minds and that was part of my game. I'm aware as a manager I can't go off the handle as much as I did, but if I feel something is not right and it is affecting the football club, I will look to nail it – just with a bit more subtlety.'

Reflective as his tone was, though, there was no apology for Saipan. 'Did I say I regretted what went on at the World Cup?' he asked. 'I said there were things that went on in the past that I regretted and it has cost me a lot, but what happened in the World Cup I would do again tomorrow. I hope I won't be going around accusing my players of faking injuries, I know that.' McCarthy's jibe about Keane's absence from Iran clearly still stung.

The only thing tempering the euphoria on Wearside was the knowledge that Keane had only three days before the transfer deadline. There were other practicalities to be taken care of as well. Brian Kidd, highly respected as a coach while Ferguson's number two at United, had been approached to become Keane's assistant, but family commitments meant he could not move to the Northeast, and he ended up at Sheffield United. The role eventually went to Tony Loughlan, a former team-mate of Keane at Nottingham Forest, who had initially been offered a coaching role.

Signings, though, were what the fans really cared about, and although Keane pulled out of a deal for the Odd Grenland defender Per Nilsson, on deadline day they arrived in their droves. First, there was the 34-year-old Dwight Yorke, brought in from Sydney FC for £200,000. It was a move that shocked many, given Yorke's playboy reputation – in Sydney he was nicknamed 'All-Night Dwight' – but he has always insisted that was exaggerated. If even half the stories are true, for him still to be playing at the level he is would take some constitution. 'There is one reason that I am here and that is purely down to Roy Keane,' Yorke said. 'I was playing for Sydney and I had no desire to leave the lifestyle or the weather. The gaffer and I had maybe spoken once since I left United, but then the call came through from him. He just said, "I'd love you to come and brighten up the place and bring your experience." And because it's Roy Keane, that is very flattering.' Or at least that is what he told *The Times* the following spring. At the time, at least in the *Sydney Morning Telegraph*, he sounded far less convinced. 'I'm gutted and completely devastated to be leaving,' he said. 'I sat by the phone waiting for someone from Sydney FC to say they didn't want me to go. But that call never came and I'm very emotional about it.' That didn't sound good, particularly not when Keane revealed that Yorke had been brought in as much for reasons of morale as for what he could offer on the pitch. 'You've got to have a good dressing room – a bubbly, happy dressing room,' the manager said. 'Results have not been great and hopefully he'll help lift the other players.'

Within a couple of hours, Yorke was followed by the left-back-cum-left-winger Ross Wallace and the former Sunderland centre-back Stanislav Varga from Celtic. The Irish midfielder Liam Miller arrived from Manchester United – the real Roy Keane signing the man who had singularly failed to live up to his billing as the next one. Then, from Wigan came another Irish midfielder, Graham Kavanagh, and the forward David Connolly, Keane's most ardent supporter among the other players in Saipan. Keane's policy, it seemed, was to sign only players with whom he'd shared a dressing-room. As the club lurched closer to the SundIreland stereotype, it was easily mockable as some sort of sub-Kitchener recruitment drive – have you, at any time in the past five years, been on the same pitch as this man? Then Sunderland needs you – but given the lack of time available for scouting, it made sense.

An international break at least gave some breathing space before Keane's first fixture, an away game at Derby, which, inevitably, conjured up the ghost of Clough. There was anticipation, sufficient that Derby had to increase Sunderland's allocation of tickets from 3,600 to 4,600, but there was also fear. In so much as it existed at all, the possibility of relegation lingered no more, a distant bogeyman somewhere near the horizon of the perception and, while most fans would probably have accepted a comfortable mid-table finish with the promise of greater things to come, there was a real dread that Derby 2006 would prove just as big a let-down as Blackburn 1985 or, well, Coventry 2006.

My initial intention had been to walk directly from Roker Park to the Stadium of Light, but I decided first on a little diversion. I retraced my steps, and turned left by the newsagents down Givens Street. The streets here are typical of the early twentieth century, imposing and sturdy, unwaveringly respectable, with between them the back lanes that allowed for coal and such-like to be delivered out of sight without offending anyone's sense of decency. I passed Cooper Street, where George Reynolds, the notorious safecracker and former Darlington chairman grew up, and then the back lane where, between the walls topped with shards of broken glass, my dad taught me to ride a bike. Then I came to Appley Terrace, where my dad grew up and where my gran lived until her death.

From her back garden – even from inside the house if the crowd was big enough or the wind was right – you could hear the roars from Roker Park so clearly that there was no need to check the final score. In the old days, as she would regularly tell me, she'd open the doors of the garage so fans could park their bikes inside, leaving a box on a shelf for them to drop sixpence into as a fee. We'd regularly go up there for tea on a Saturday, and after a while my dad started taking me to watch the last 20 minutes of games, sneaking in when they opened the gates to let people leave. The first piece of action I saw live in a football ground was Steve Williams stroking in an equaliser for Southampton, Ally McCoist having put Sunderland ahead with an overhead kick in the first half. I had a vague sense that it was a long time before I saw a Sunderland goal, which I remember vividly as a plunging Gary Rowell header to equalise 1-1 against Leicester, but I hadn't realised quite how long. Checking through Bill Simmons and Bob Graham's statistical history of the club, I see the Southampton game happened on 9 October 1982; the Leicester game not until 18 December the following year. In that time I must have gone to at least a dozen games, maybe more. If my dad had dismissed me as bad luck and never taken me again, I could hardly have blamed him.

Fortunately he didn't, and even after I started going to

games with mates – and so reawakening the old Fulwell End-Roker End debate – we'd still meet up at my gran's afterwards. A match wouldn't have been a match without an over-milky coffee and some home-made ginger biscuits to follow.

My gran died shortly after Christmas 1995. She was cremated on 6 January, the day Sunderland played away at Manchester United in the third round of the FA Cup. In the afternoon following the funeral, my dad drove me back to university. As we passed the Harbour View at the far end of Givens Street, Nicky Butt gave United the lead. There was, I think, almost a sense of relief. Neither of us would have said it, but I suspect we had both dreamed of some kind of send-off; this at least punctured those hopes early, and let them gently deflate. But then, in quick succession, Steve Agnew and Craig Russell scored. There may have been a snort at the ridiculousness of it all, but otherwise we were silent, recognising what this could mean. But there are, of course, no fates; there is no guiding force. Football does not hand out sentimental favours. Eric Cantona equalised with a late header and United won the replay.

As we lingered on the terraces following the 3-0 victory over Everton 18 months later, my dad in the Roker and me in the Fulwell, it wasn't just a football ground to which we were saying goodbye.

[5]

BEGINNINGS

Keane himself seemed relatively unconcerned by the specifics of that first fixture. His focus in the days leading up to it was far more about the bigger picture, and, although he did not go as far as Quinn in tapping the history reflex, he did show a pleasing awareness of the club's traditions. When Gary Megson took over at Nottingham Forest, he had ordered the photographs of the club's past successes to be taken off the walls. Constantly seeing John McGovern lifting the European Cup or Kenny Burns clattering Kevin Keegan, he decided, was having a deleterious effect, burdening players with the memories of a past to which they could never live up.

Keane, though, saw the positive side, despite the regular claims in his autobiography that history means nothing. He seemingly drew a distinction between the sort of recent history that could distract players, and sort that could inspire them. 'These are very good facilities,' Keane said of the Academy, 'but you've got to make it a good environment. It's well and good having the nicest building in the world but you have to make it a football environment, you've got to know you're at Sunderland. The building, nice as it is, it's a bit cold. Someone could drop you in here and you wouldn't know it's Sunderland Football Club. In a sense it's cold, you want pictures up, past players, past teams, whatever, different sports people that might inspire, the history of the club, so that you know what you belong to, where you're at, that you are attached to something.'

That, of course, rather glossed over the fact there weren't that many images of the glory-days to be had, sports photography not having been particularly advanced in the 1890s. Even the one indelible triumph of the post-War years, the 1973 FA Cup final victory, has a certain ambivalence, given it ranks in the country's collective memory as highly as it does only because it was such a shock; because, in other words, Sunderland were so inferior to the Leeds team they beat. It celebrated, in a sense, the idea of Sunderland as jolly but essentially harmless underdogs, with their passionate, easily patronised salt-of-the-earth fans and their manager in his comical attire of trilby, mac and red tracksuit bottoms. The parallel may not have been exact, but the need to discover a more professional ruthlessness was no less acute for Sunderland than it was for Ireland.

Generally that first pre-match press conference confirmed the impression Keane had made at his unveiling. He was direct, authoritative, and even a little playful as he parried questions with a dead-pan wit, only the vaguest hint of a smile playing around his eyes. How often had he called Sir Alex Ferguson? 'I didn't call him that often, Jesus.' How did he think he would behave in the dug-out? 'Cool and calm, that's the plan.' Did he anticipate many rucks with match officials? 'I've never really had a problem with referees over the years.'

Of Keane's six signings, only Dwight Yorke did not start at Pride Park, having not arrived on Wearside from Sydney until three days before the game. There were five Irishmen in the team – a quotient that remained steady as Stephen Elliott replaced Connolly late on – while seven of the starting 11 had played with Keane at some stage of his career. It was the manager, though, who remained the centre of attention, as everybody waited for his first explosion of rage. There were a couple of mild harangues of the officials, but nothing to get overly excited by, until, deep into first-half injury-time, Steve Howard nodded down Mo Camara's cross for Matt Oakley to sweep Derby into the lead. The stroke of half-time is supposed to be the worst time to concede a goal; with Keane as your manager, it was feared it could be cataclysmic.

Keane, though, remained calm in the dressing-room. 'There were no tea cups flying around,' Robbie Elliott insisted. Keane, he said, had merely encouraged them to 'keep passing'. Whatever he did, it worked. Graham Kavanagh, having gathered a raking Liam Miller pass wide on the left, held the ball up, played a one-two with Miller as he charged to the corner of the box and then chipped in a cross that Chris Brown, bundling through defenders, took on his chest and poked past Stephen Bywater.

Keane had demanded links to the past, and he got them, as the first goal of his reign was scored by a player whose father had overseen the beginnings of the modern age of yo-yoing. Brown's father, Alan, had been the Sunderland manager in 1958 when they'd suffered their first relegation. He made amends by leading them to their first promotion six years later, immediately left the club for Sheffield Wednesday, and then returned to take Sunderland down for the second time in 1970. Alan Brown also provided yet another link with Clough, having signed him for Sunderland from Middlesbrough, and been a major influence in forming his abrasive managerial style. To complete the cat's-cradle of interconnection, he was also the manager who forged the link between Sunderland and Ireland by signing Charlie Hurley.

It is hard to believe Sunderland will ever have another player so deeply and universally loved. Even in the Nineties, three decades after his heyday, Hurley's name would roll around Roker Park as the Fulwell End, bereft of any more modern heroes, continued to affirm he was 'the greatest centre-half the world has ever seen'. He is certainly the greatest centre-half Sunderland has ever seen, and possibly the greatest Ireland has as well. He was a huge man, physically and morally, with a forehead the custom of ages dictates must be described as being hewn of granite. 'Constructed of pre-cast concrete,' a fans' guide to Sunderland legends once claimed, 'he often played when fatally wounded, like with his head missing.'

Born in Cork, he moved to Essex when a few months old, grew up there and signed for Millwall, before, on 26 September 1957, at the age of 20, joining Sunderland for £18,000. 'I can remember driving up to Sunderland,' Hurley said, 'and wondering just how far north I had to go. I had thought I was driving to the end of the world.' His first game was hardly auspicious, a 7-0 defeat at Blackpool. A week later, things got better, but only just: a 6-0 defeat at Burnley. 'Seven and six,' local bingo-callers took to shouting when they drew out the number 76, 'Charlie Hurley.' Fans, understandably, were unimpressed. 'They must have thought they'd signed a colander, not a centre-half,' Hurley said, but his home debut, against Preston, brought a clean sheet in a goalless draw.

Sunderland were relegated that season – for the first time in their history – and, as promotion was again and again snatched from their grasp at the last, it took them six years to return to the top flight. When they finally did, it was Hurley who took most of the credit, finishing second to Bobby Moore as Footballer of the Year. Not only was he an immense presence defensively, but by then he was captain, and also managed seven goals that season. More than that, he had come, in his gentle dignity, to embody the club's best image of itself. Like Quinn, he once played in goal for the club, and he also, as so many Sunderland greats, had a penchant for own-goals, scoring one not merely on his debut, but also in the epic 3-3 draw away to Manchester United in the FA Cup in 1964.

He was a popular, humble champion, a man who even now seems bemused by his own popularity. In almost every interview he has given since he finished playing, it seems, Hurley has spoken about fans desperate to shake his hand, and again and again the same image occurs – that of miners, their hands blackened by the coal dust embedded in their skin.

He seems fascinated by the quotidian heroism of manual labour, and to have demanded a similar physical courage from himself. Perhaps for that reason, there are few photographs of him in his playing days when that granite forehead was not grimed with mud. Although it took him until his fourth season to score for Sunderland, his headed goals from set-plays became such a regular feature that every corner at Roker would be greeted by chants of 'Charlie! Charlie!' as he rumbled menacingly forward. Nine thousand once turned out for a reserve game against South Shields to witness his return from a rare injury, and it came as little surprise in 1979, when, at a dinner to mark the club's centenary, Hurley was voted Sunderland's greatest ever player. 'Every time I get up in the morning and feel my arthritic joints,' he said, 'I think of Roker Park.'

Sunderland's old training ground on Moor Lane, just outside Whitburn – abandoned since the move to the Academy – was named after Hurley, but Quinn was aware of his greatness long before that. Hurley won 40 caps for the Republic of Ireland, and Quinn, noting the span of his international career

links Liam Whelan to Johnny Giles, speaks of him as reverent-
ly as any Sunderland fan. 'I know now,' Quinn said on his
retirement, 'the truth of something Charlie Hurley said to me
a long to me ago: "You can leave the area but you never leave
Sunderland. It seeps into you. The people. The landscape. The
passion."'

Quinn goes on, in his autobiography, while commenting further on his feeling for the region, to admit that 'I won't be
remembered like Charlie Hurley is remembered.' Well, maybe
he will. Not as a player, perhaps, but if things carry on as they
did in 2006-07, in terms of all-round popularity, he won't be
far behind. Sunderland were founded by a Scot, James Allan,
and their first golden age was founded on Scots; the second,
perhaps, will be rooted in Ireland, and Hurley will stand, as
Allan did, as a precursor.

Not that anybody at Pride Park had time to reflect on such
things. Two minutes after the equaliser, Connolly glanced on a
high ball, Wallace took it in his stride and thudded a shot
across Bywater and into the bottom corner. Second-half fight-
backs were to become a familiar theme, as was Wallace's celebration, his shirt coming off as he ran into the fans, earning
himself a pointless booking.

This time, the optimism had caught and been given suste-
nance by a performance. As the candy-striped hordes celebrated, Robbie Elliott was reminded by the reaction to Keane of
the atmosphere 12 years earlier when he had been breaking
through at a Newcastle side galvanised by the arrival of Kevin
Keegan. 'The buzz he's brought to the city is the same,' he said.
'He's lifted the whole club and the whole area. When Kevin
came there was a sense of amazement and it's the same at the
minute.' The comparison may have made Sunderland fans
uncomfortable, but few questioned its validity.

Saturday, 9 September, Championship

Derby County	1-2	Sunderland
Oakley 45		Brown 62
		Wallace 64

Derby: Bywater, Edworthy (Bolder 88), Leacock, M Johnson, Camara, Barnes, Oakley, Smith, Peschisolido (S Johnson 56), Howard, Lupoli
Subs Not Used: Grant, Malcolm, Nyatanga
Sunderland: Alnwick, Delap, Cunningham, Varga, R Elliott, L Miller, Kavanagh, Whitehead, Wallace, Connolly (S Elliott 84), Brown
Subs Not Used: Ward, Hysen, Leadbitter, N Collins
Ref: A Bates (Staffordshire)
Booked: Edworthy (Derby); Varga, Brown, Delap, Wallace, Kavanagh (Sunderland)
Att: 26,502
League position: 21

The second leg of the Clough memorial tour came at Leeds four days later. Thanks to his past as the most successful captain of Manchester United ever, Keane was never going to be a popular figure at Elland Road, but what cemented his position as a hate-figure to Leeds fans was the incident with Alf-Inge Haaland. Keane had been made United captain at the start of the 1997-98 season, succeeding Eric Cantona on his retirement. In the middle of September, they drew 2-2 at home to Chelsea, and a frustrated Keane, seeing the draw as two points dropped, went out drinking after the game with some friends from Cork, celebrating the birth of his nephew. In the bar of his hotel, he became involved in an argument with some United fans from Dublin. It became a brawl.

By his own admission, Keane was in no shape for the match at Leeds that Saturday. United trailed 1-0 to a David Wetherall goal and Keane was having 'the nightmare game I deserved' when, with five minutes remaining, sick of being niggled by Haaland, he lunged at him. As Keane slid in, his studs caught in the turf, tearing his cruciate ligament. He made the foul, but was left, prone in agony, with Haaland standing over him, screaming at him to stop faking it. As he left the field, he was booked. Four years later, when Haaland was playing for Manchester City, Keane took his revenge. 'I fucking hit him hard,' as he famously put it in his autobiography, the suggestion that there had been a level of premeditation earning him a five-game ban. Leeds fans, eager to show Keane they had not forgotten, spent the final minutes of their defeat to Wolves the previous Sunday chanting Haaland's name. Keane's response when asked about the reception he was likely to receive was characteristically wry. 'I'm sure they're going to give me a nice round of applause,' he said.

There was, at that stage of the season, a curious sense that everything was part of a vast nexus of interconnection. Football does this. Perhaps it is simply the law of averages, that there are a limited number of personalities, a limited number of clubs and a limited number of things that can happen, but the effect of the webs of coincidence is to offer a sense of something profound, of a meaning that refuses ever quite to crystallise. That is why the word 'ironic' is so overused in football, usually for things that are not ironic at all, merely coincidental. Umberto Eco makes just that point about history as a whole in *Foucault's Pendulum*: seek connections assiduously enough, and they will be found. Still, given the way the memory of Clough had haunted Keane's first days at the club, this was some coincidence. Clough, like Keane, had been taunted by a defender as he lay, racked by the agony of ruptured ligaments, and Liam Daish had similarly accused Quinn of faking it. Quinn had consoled himself by thinking how bad Daish would feel when he found out the truth, but Clough, like Keane, had fostered a terrible resentment.

The winter of 1962 was ferociously cold. It was a winter of

so many postponements it necessitated the invention of the pools panel. Sunderland did not play a league match between 29 December and 23 February. They played on 26 December, but they probably shouldn't have. The pitch was bone-hard, rendered treacherous by hail. Middlesbrough's game at Ayresome Park was called off but, at Roker Park, Sunderland against Bury went ahead. Clough chased a misplaced pass into the penalty area at the Fulwell End. He had already scored 28 goals that season, and sniffed the chance of a 29th. It would never come. He collided with the goalkeeper, Chris Harker, his body sagged, and he collapsed onto the frozen mud. He tried to stand, but fell again, the ligaments ripped. 'He's only fuckin' coddin', ref,' shouted the Bury centre-back. Clough claimed later he kept a photograph of him permanently pinned to a dart-board at home. Weirdly, that centre-back was Bob Stokoe.

How strange that every time Keane arrived at the Stadium of Light, he should pass a statue of a local hero who happened also to be a man his great mentor despised. Strange, too, that Clough and Stokoe should come to be united in their loathing of the Leeds manager Don Revie, another former Sunderland player, who led Leeds against Sunderland in that 1973 Cup final. Stranger, when Clough and Revie teams first met on a football pitch, Leeds beat Derby thanks to a penalty conceded by Bobby Saxton. Stranger still, the momentous Charity Shield meeting between Leeds and Liverpool, when the dismissals of Kevin Keegan and Billy Bremner soured Clough's first competitive game after replacing Revie at Leeds, took place on 10 August 1974, Roy Keane's third birthday.

Not that Keane was a man to be drawn into such cabbalistic wondering. With hindsight, he admitted, he regarded the Haaland incident as a turning point. 'It was probably a good thing that happened to me,' he explained. 'I had to look at the bigger picture, what I was doing on and off the pitch. I was taking everything for granted and I wasn't preparing properly, I wasn't leading the right lifestyle. When I was out I had to step back and take a look at where I was going wrong. So as much as there was a down side, there was a plus as well. I learned a lot about myself, about what I was doing right and wrong, the diet side of things.' It was after that injury that he cut back on the booze, and, recognising its precariousness, began really to appreciate his time in football.

Even without the Keane factor, Leeds was always a special game for Sunderland. For one thing, it evoked memories of 1973 and all that, and for another, it was the nearest they got to a derby in 2006-07, even though 99 miles separate Elland Road and the Stadium of Light. On that September evening, they were close in no other regard.

In the cold light of day, the Derby result looked a little for-tuitous, a victory snatched in 120 seconds of frenzy. Not that there was anything wrong with that – it demonstrated charac-ter and self-belief if nothing else – but beyond the emotion of the occasion there had been little evidence to suggest the side was about to mount the sort of sustained run they would need if they were to make the play offs. Leeds, though, was a differ-ent matter. Time would show the poverty of their opponents, but this was, by any measure, a superb display. Only when two disgruntled Leeds fans tried to attack Keane as he left the pitch at half-time did Sunderland seem even remotely threatened. *ALS* suggested it was probably the best performance since the 4-1 win over Chelsea – remember Quinn and Phillips's aerial one-two before Quinn volleyed against the post late on? – in 1999-2000. The following day a tornado tore through Leeds city centre, closing the railway station and ripping the roofs from a number of buildings; the analogy didn't need spelling out.

This was Sunderland playing with verve and class, two wins seemingly having flooded them with confidence. Miller, who had spent part of the previous season on loan at Leeds, got the first, finishing off a flowing move with a low drive, and the game was settled by two goals in a three-minute spell straddling half-time. First Miller's pass set up Kavanagh for a screaming volley, then Stephen Elliott, on for the injured Connolly, smashed a third from Murphy's flick. Almost more encouraging than the performance was a story that emerged a couple of days later. When the players returned to the dressing-room at full-time, it was said, one of them asked what had happened in that night's Champions League match between Manchester United and Celtic. Keane, having played for both, might have been expected to show some interest, but instead he turned on the player. 'Don't worry about that,' he is supposed to have said. 'That'll be us in two years' time.' Now perhaps that is a ridiculous dream, but it is the sort of single-mindedness of ambition Sunderland had lacked for far too long. Perhaps at Leeds, a club whose present struggles stand as a morality fable of the dangers of over-reaching, thoughts of 'living the dream' were inappropriate, but still, there are ways of progressing without mortgaging the future on a flimsy present.

'It was a fantastic performance from all of the lads,' Kavanagh said, although most agreed that it was his domination of central midfield that had been critical. 'We felt we could open Leeds up at any time. You have to give credit to the gaffer. He has given us confidence – told us we're good players who need to have faith and belief in each other. It's been a good start, but there's a hell of a long way to go.' Was that really all it took? Somebody credible telling players they were good enough? Perhaps it is, for, as Ljupko Petrović, the Serbian coach who led Red Star Belgrade to the 1991 European Cup once said, 'only the believable is achievable'. Certainly, as Leeds fans chanted for the head of their manager, Kevin Blackwell – he was eventually sacked a week later – Sunderland fans began to believe. 'I've spoken about character, desire and spirit,' Keane said, 'but on top of that you need good players and talent. They showed that tonight. I'm very proud of them.'

Wednesday, 13 September, Championship

Leeds United   **0-3**   **Sunderland**
                                L Miller 28
                                Kavanagh 45
                                S Elliott 48

Leeds: Warner, Kelly, Butler, Kilgallon, Crainey, Stone (Carole 54), Douglas, Westlake, Lewis (Nicholls 46), Horsfield, Healy (Blake 63)
Subs Not Used: Gregan, Moore
Sunderland: Alnwick, N Collins, Varga, Cunningham, R Elliott, L Miller, Whitehead (Lawrence 80), Kavanagh, Wallace, Murphy, Connolly (S Elliott 43, Leadbitter 60)
Subs Not Used: Ward, D Collins.
Ref: A Marriner (West Midlands)
Booked: Westlake, Butler, Nicholls, Kelly, Douglas (Leeds); Kavanagh, L Miller (Sunderland)
Att: 23,037
League position: 14

Proud he may have been, but Keane was still looking ahead to further transfers, and, if the *Daily Mirror* was to be believed – and they had, they said, got the story from a man called Bob, who had heard it from the vet who had wormed Triggs – he was looking to bring Paul Scholes in from Manchester United. But it was another member of United's Treble-winners everybody was looking at the following Saturday. With Connolly suffering a thigh injury and Stephen Elliott turning his ankle against Leeds, Keane confirmed that Dwight Yorke would make his debut against Leicester.

Keane had been highly critical of the way Yorke lost his focus after the Treble success, and the forward admitted he had allowed his social life to take over. Certainly his diligent performances deep in midfield at the World Cup had suggested a reformed player enjoying an Indian summer to his career. 'We all get to a certain age and we see things differently,' Yorke said, the day before the game. 'I'm not saying I'm a completely changed man but I have calmed down a wee bit as an individual and I understand more about the importance of being a footballer. The most significant thing for me is that I have my appetite back.'

That, he said, had gone in his final season at Blackburn and his year at Birmingham as he struggled to come to terms with the sudden death of his sister, Verline. 'In that period I didn't do very well and things didn't go particularly great,' he said. 'But then I sat back and thought that my sister would want me to do what I am good at which is to play the game with a smile on my face. Going to Sydney got that energy and the vibes back and the feeling again for football. And, of course, Trinidad and Tobago qualifying for the World Cup brought back the feel-good factor as far as football is concerned. Even though the legs are not quite as fast as they used to be, the brain is pretty much as sharp as it can be.'

Keane had done his best amid the euphoria at Elland Road to dampen expectations, but where his words had failed, the game against Leicester succeeded. The match itself was rather overshadowed anyway by tabloid reports of comments Keane had made in an interview to be published in a Sunday magazine. There was 'respect' but no 'affection' between him and Ferguson, Wayne Rooney had 'achieved nothing' and Michael

Owen had been sucked into the celebrity culture, Keane was quoted as saying. And, unsurprisingly, Keane was riled by the WAGs and all they stood for. None of it was particularly earth-shattering, and none of it was directly related to Sunderland – in fact, its football-centric earthiness probably played well on Wearside – but it was hard to avoid the feeling that it was a distraction.

There were more than 35,000 there for Keane's first home game in charge, many of them sporting Irish tricolours, but what they saw was a performance as flat as the Leeds game had been exhilarating. Yorke began on the bench, but he made his introduction after 15 minutes, as Daryl Murphy hobbled off. He later admitted that, after three weeks without a game, he was well short of match fitness.

Leicester took the lead three minutes after half-time, as Andy Johnson picked up on an error by Liam Miller, and slipped the ball through the legs of Stanislav Varga for Matty Fryatt, who cut inside Neill Collins and clipped a low finish past Ben Alnwick. There had been a feeling that Tobias Hysen, impressive against West Brom in Quinn's final game had been a little unfortunate to be immediately supplanted by Ross Wallace, and he strengthened his case within a minute of replacing Liam Miller midway though the half. Gathering the loose ball after an Alnwick clearance had been half-cleared, he burst in unchallenged from the right, before guiding an elegant left-foot strike into the bottom corner from just outside the box. Minds went back to Derby, but there was little sign that Sunderland might find a winner, and there was possibly even a trace of relief in Keane's smile as he shook the hand of Rob Kelly, the Leicester manager, at the final whistle. 'It's a good reality check for everyone at the club, especially the players,' Keane said. 'Any team has got to work its socks off, tackle people, close people down. We didn't do that in the first half. It was a tired performance and I should have freshened things up. I take responsibility for that. Three games a week is a lot for any player, but that's my job, I should have freshened things up.'

Saturday, 16 September, Championship

Sunderland   **1-1**   **Leicester City**
Hysen 66   Fryatt 48

Sunderland: Alnwick, N Collins (Leadbitter 55), Cunningham, Varga, R Elliott, L Miller (Hysen 65), Whitehead, Kavanagh, Wallace, Brown, Murphy (Yorke 15)
Subs Not Used: Ward, D Collins
Leicester: Henderson, Kenton, Kisnorbo, McCarthy, Johansson, Wesolowski, Johnson, Hughes, Porter, Fryatt, O'Grady
Subs Not Used: Logan, Maybury, Hume, Tiatto, McAuley
Ref: M Pike (Cumbria)
Booked: Fryatt (Leicester)
Att: 35,104
League position: 14

Keane did change things the following week, bringing in Steve Smith, the 1996 Olympic high jump bronze medallist and an Everton season-ticket holder, to give a motivational talk to his players. 'He was different class,' said Kavanagh. 'It was about setting your goals further than what you hope to achieve. If you set them high you might come a little bit lower than you wanted but it will still be further than you previously set. It was very interesting and when you left the room you wanted to achieve more for yourself and the team. It shows that the gaffer is not going to leave any stone unturned to make us a better club and a better bunch of individuals.'

At least in the short term, though, it didn't really work. Smith's intervention seemed to have turned Sunderland into some dreadful parody of Everton's 'dogs of war' midfield of the mid-Nineties. If they weren't as flat away at Ipswich as they had been against Leicester, it was only because they had adopted a policy of unedifying aggression. The class they had shown at Elland Road was nowhere to be seen. Ross Wallace was eventually sent off after collecting a second yellow card for cynically checking Billy Clarke with four minutes remaining, but Sunderland were lucky not to have been reduced to ten men before that. Aside from Wallace, they had three players booked, there were three mass brawls and Chris Brown got away with what seemed to be an elbow on Castro Sito. Jim Magilton, the Ipswich manager, was less than impressed, but Keane was unrepentant. 'Listen,' he said to one accuser. 'It's a game of football. You've got to tackle people. Jim used to tackle people, I used to tackle people and sometimes you are late. You've come to watch a game of football, but maybe you're better off watching snooker.'

A Jason de Vos own goal, slicing Wallace's free-kick into his own net, had presented Sunderland with the lead just before the half-hour, but Ipswich were level within three minutes as Darren Currie's free-kick skipped above Alnwick's dive. What followed showed that the defensive neuroses that had plagued Quinn's spell as manager had merely been disguised, not eradicated. First, Neill Collins failed to get proper purchase on a clearing header from Currie's right-wing cross and Alan Lee looped a clever finish across Alnwick, then Stanislav Varga misjudged a De Vos ball over the top, allowing Lee to run on, round Alnwick and roll the ball home. 'The honeymoon is over,' admitted Robbie Elliott. 'It was a very disappointing result and a very upset dressing-room. We know we weren't at the races the way we had been against Leeds and West Brom. We've got our ideas about why it didn't happen for us and we've got to rectify things.'

Keane spoke of his 'hurt' after his first defeat as a manager, but his mood remained largely positive; he had, after all, been warning since he arrived that patience was required. 'When you're a player, sometimes you are in your own little world,' he said. 'You're looking after yourself, making sure you're playing well and you are fit. As a manager you're obviously taking responsibility for the fans and the general feeling of the club. That's my responsibility and that's why it is harder to take. There's a lot of work to be done but Rome wasn't built in a day. I've been saying since I took the job that one or two results probably covered over the cracks. People on the outside were maybe getting carried away but the staff, myself, and the players know there's a lot of hard work ahead. We never thought we were the finished article, far from it.'

Saturday, 23 September, Championship

Ipswich Town 3-1 **Sunderland**
Currie 32   De Vos (og) 29
Lee 63, 66

Ipswich: Price, Richards (Moore 90), De Vos, Naylor, Harding, Noble, Williams (Bowditch 87), Sito, Currie, Macken (Clarke 73), Lee
Subs Not Used: Supple, Wilnis
Sunderland: Alnwick, N Collins (Lawrence 70), Cunningham, Varga, R Elliott, L Miller, Whitehead (Leadbitter 45), Kavanagh, Wallace, Brown (Hysen 45), Yorke
Subs Not Used: Ward, D Collins
Ref: M Russell (Hertfordshire)
Sent off: Wallace 86 (Sunderland)
Booked: De Vos, Noble, Williams, Sito (Ipswich); Varga, Brown, Wallace, Whitehead (Sunderland)
Att: 23,311
League position: 17

James Allan founded the club that would become Sunderland, in 1879. It was initially a club for schoolteachers, but, finding it difficult to recruit sufficient members, the following year it opened its doors to all professions. It entered the Northumberland and Durham Challenge Cup in 1880-81 and, despite being beaten 5-0 by the Newcastle side Rangers – at St James' Park, meaning Sunderland played there before Newcastle United did – quickly came to represent the city as a whole. This is something that makes Sunderland almost unique. The only other one-club cities of comparable size in England are Newcastle and Leeds, but even Leeds has a major rugby league club to dilute the attention – not to mention being the headquarters of the most successful county in English cricketing history. (Leeds, incidentally, is the biggest exception to my three-phase theory of football; they missed the early boom of the provincial industrial cities and only began to achieve their successes in the Sixties. That may be to do with the dissolution of Leeds City in 1919 for financial irregularities, but I suspect it is probably related to the way the area's emotional energy was invested in other sports.)

For those who haven't lived in Sunderland or Newcastle, I think it's very hard to grasp the way the form of the club can affect the general mood. There is nowhere else in Britain, I suspect – or nowhere else of similar size – where the gaze is so intently focused, the collective will so firmly behind one entity. This was something I first became aware of in reverse, when, having left Sunderland, I realised that the conversation on buses, in pubs and in shops, was not always dominated by debates over whether Derek Ferguson was a sideways-looking waste-of-space or an elegant facilitator who needed better players around him. Harry Pearson, in *The Far Corner*, says that what alerted him to the Northeast's obsession with football on his return from London was that nobody ever made facile comments about how violent fans could be. All people were fans, and some people were violent, which was obvious, so nobody bothered commenting on it.

Approach Sunderland north along the A19 and you come to the offices of the *Sunderland Echo*. Mounted prominently near the roof is the image of a football with arms, legs, a face and a cap. On matchdays, he is lit up and, if Sunderland have won, he smiles; if they have lost, he frowns; and if they have drawn, his mouth remains a flat line. In the days of car radios and mobile phones it is probably redundant, but what other city felt the need to install such an early-warning system?

So inseparable are club and city in Sunderland these days, that when a new badge was adopted in 1997 to coincide with the move to the new stadium, the design incorporated two local landmarks: the arch of the Wearmouth Bridge and Penshaw Monument, the strange replica of the Parthenon that stands on Penshaw Hill. The lions rampant reflect a similar design on the city crest, but there is an odd sense now in which the badge of the football club relates to Sunderland more recognisably than the city's crest.

[6]

DOUBTS

Two wins, a draw and a defeat from his opening four games. It was neither as good as fans had hoped nor as bad as they had feared; seven points, in fact, was what Keegan had taken from his first four games at Newcastle. Keegan, though, having taken over from Ossie Ardiles in the February, had an immediate brief merely to avoid relegation; it was the following season when Newcastle, bolstered by their new signings, surged to promotion. Keane had been given 41 games, and that dangled the possibility of a play-off place. After the defeat at Ipswich, it all felt rather anti-climactic. The bubble hadn't lasted as long as people had hoped – although there had at least been a bubble – and neither had there really been any ructions. By Keane's standards a few home truths about former colleagues hardly counted.

At least on the outside, he remained wryly detached. The defeat, he insisted, had done nothing to make him doubt the wisdom of taking up what he acknowledged was 'a massive challenge'. 'I'm really enjoying it,' he insisted. 'Over the weekend, after the defeat, I was back in my place and I thought I wouldn't want to be anywhere else than Sunderland.' With others that might have sounded like populist cant, but Keane had shown no previous inclination to cloak his true feelings in what he thought he ought to say.

What, everybody wanted to know, was he like in training? Brian Clough, certainly towards the end of his career, had often gone a whole week without seeing his players, occasionally wandering by the training ground with his dog, but essentially leaving the coaching to the coaches and turning up only at the last minute before games to rattle the cages of those players whose cages needed rattling, or more subtly encourage those who needed a sympathetic approach. Sir Alex Ferguson, it was known, involved himself on the training pitch only when he felt there was a danger of standards slipping. Keane, similarly, kept his distance, as a photograph in the *Sunderland Echo* proved. As the players worked with the coaches, he sat on a hillock by the side of the pitch, perched on a ball and surrounded by saplings, eyes narrowed in thought, looking for all the world like a Sioux elder contemplating the field of battle. 'We all respect him,' Nyron Nosworthy said diplomatically, when asked if the players feared their manager. The defender had worked under Peter Taylor at Gillingham, as well as under McCarthy at Sunderland, and found Keane's approach quite different. 'At Gillingham, Peter was very much involved in training and always having a laugh with you,' he said. 'And, on and off the pitch, Mick was much more vocal.'

Keane also, like Clough, saw the importance of making everybody feel involved. When, on the final day, he made a point of thanking everybody behind the scenes, they were not empty words. In his first week, the story was told, Keane walked in on the groundsman and three assistants eating their sandwiches in a hut at the training ground. 'This is no good,' he's supposed to have said. 'We can't have this.' The groundsman, intimidated by Keane's reputation, apologised, wondering where he was supposed to eat his lunch. 'Tomorrow,' said Keane, 'you eat in the canteen with everybody else.' Given it was only a little over three years earlier that Michael Gray had witlessly turned up at the club in a new Ferrari on the day one third of the club's staff was made redundant, this was progress indeed.

Keane's relationship with Quinn was also a source of fascination, but the manager was forthcoming only in his evasiveness. How had Quinn reacted to the defeat? 'We have a perfect relationship,' he said with a typical twinkle. 'We hardly speak to each other. I think he might have gone on holiday or something.' A more likely explanation was that he was still working on the final details of the takeover. Drumaville's stake in the club reached 90 per cent on 28 September, allowing them compulsorily to purchase the remaining shares.

The sense of calm, though, Keane later admitted, had been in that instance illusory. He claimed in May to have lost his temper only three times over the course of the season: the Ipswich game was the first, which explained some elliptical comments from Robbie Elliott about 'what was said in the dressing room' and players knowing 'we have to improve if we want to stay at the club'. Ferguson had always maintained after a defeat that what was important was not the result itself, but the response to it, and Keane offered a similar line. 'Where we are trying to go, there are going to be a lot of disappointments ahead,' he said. 'You only find out about certain individuals after a setback. I gave one or two the benefit of the doubt after the Leicester game but on Saturday one or two disappointed. I'm looking for reactions and characters.'

The result, for all Keane's calls for patience, was six changes for the following Saturday's home game against Sheffield Wednesday, two of them, admittedly, enforced, with Wallace suspended and Kavanagh facing surgery on an injured knee. Nyron Nosworthy was brought in at right-back, his only previous appearance of the season having been against West Brom as an 89th-minute substitute for Grant Leadbitter, who was also recalled. The 20 year old had been one of the few bright spots of the previous season, a Sunderland native and a product of the academy who, as all about him had collapsed, had proved himself a pleasingly tenacious midfielder. It was also rumoured that he could shoot, although given how few chances Sunderland had created in the Premiership, that was hard to assess. He proved it against Wednesday, though, meeting a Liam Lawrence cross with a smart half-volley after 58 minutes to score his first goal for the club and to give Sunderland their first home victory under Keane. The parallels with his manager were obvious, as Leadbitter acknowledged. 'He was a hero of mine when I was a kid,' he said. 'You always watch players in your position and I watched him a lot because he was one of the best central midfielders in the world.'

Keane repaid the compliment, calling Leadbitter 'a clever player who gets in good positions', but he was just as effusive about the overall display. A crowd of over 36,000 suggested the defeat at Ipswich had not caused any lapse back into cynicism, and their faith was justified with what Keane described as 'an outstanding performance'. The composure in possession was back, and Daryl Murphy and Dean Whitehead both struck the woodwork before Leadbitter's goal. Although Alnwick was called on to make late saves from Marcus Tudgay and Brunton O'Brien, Sunderland's superiority was clear.

Saturday, 30 September, Championship

Sunderland   1-0   **Sheffield Wednesday**
Leadbitter 58

Sunderland: Alnwick, Nosworthy, Cunningham, Varga, D Collins, Lawrence, Leadbitter, Whitehead, Hysen (L Miller 74), Murphy (Brown 84), Yorke (Connolly 89)
Subs not used: Ward, R Elliott

Sheff Wed: Jones, Simek, Bougherra, Coughlan, Spurr, Brunt, Folly (MacLean 76),
   Tudgay, O'Brien, Burton (Small 65), Talbot (Adams 76)
Subs not used: Bullen, Lunt
Ref: S Mathieson (Cheshire)
Booked: Whitehead (Sunderland); Coughlan (Sheff Wed)
Att: 36,764
League position: 14

'The good times are coming back, and you get the feeling after a win like this that they are not too far away,' Leadbitter enthused. 'Speaking as a Sunderland fan I would say the manager has given the club a tremendous lift. I want to go out and impress him at every opportunity. The crowd was an indication of how people feel. They're coming back. I used to come in the Reidy era when the place was full. It was a fantastic place to watch football and the atmosphere feels the same now.'

Perhaps that was the problem, the sense that, to use Quinn's phrase, the corner had been turned. Perhaps relief set in, prompting a lessening in intensity. Perhaps there was a sense that once a bandwagon has started rolling, it careers on of its own accord. Leadbitter, certainly, wasn't the only one who felt the good times were close at hand, but the darkest weeks of Keane's reign were just ahead.

Keane spoke bullishly about the advantages of an international week to freshen his players up with a three-day break in Portugal, but having seemingly regained their momentum, a fortnight without a game was probably the last thing Sunderland needed. Dwight Yorke posed a particular problem, with Trinidad and Tobago scheduled to play friendlies in Port of Spain against Nicaragua and Panama. Yorke wanted to go, Keane wanted him to stay, and in the end they compromised that he would play just the first game before returning, giving him five days to recover from the 9,000-mile round trip.

Those negotiations were one distraction, but a more serious one came in the wake of the BBC *Panorama* investigation into bungs in football. Although the programme proved nothing other than that some agents will say anything to make themselves seem important, which was hardly a revelation, the FA – coincidentally they said – did take action in the days that followed. Sunderland were involved only tangentially – and there was never a suggestion that the club itself had done anything wrong – but the Northeast-based agent, Ian Elliott was warned as to his future conduct after admitting a charge of failing to lodge with the FA his representation contract with Grant Leadbitter. It shouldn't have, but it did seem to take the gloss off what had been the midfielder's best performance for the club to date.

In the absence of matches, Keane got on with restructuring his squad. Rory Delap negotiated a loan move to Stoke, while Jon Stead (35 appearances, two goals) went to Derby. It was another less than prolific former Sunderland forward, though, who was to exercise the minds of the 6,000 fans who made the journey south to Preston: Danny Dichio. Given he started only 21 of his 76 league appearances for Sunderland, perhaps a haul of 11 goals isn't too bad, but what aggravated fans was what happened at the end of the 1998 play-off final.

That was the season when Sunderland began slowly as they readjusted to life in the second flight after relegation, and gradually improved as the season went on, to clamber into contention for promotion. Admittedly, that doesn't narrow it down particularly, but after losing 4-0 at Reading in October, they began playing extraordinary attacking football, and lost only twice more before the end of the season. With two ball-playing centre-backs in Jody Craddock and Darren Williams, Allan Johnston and Nicky Summerbee on the wings and the

Niall Quinn–Kevin Phillips partnership clicking, they scored 86 goals – comfortably more than anyone else in the division, and gathered 90 points. Dichio had arrived from Sampdoria in the January, and proved a useful back-up, a paler version of Quinn, as Michael Bridges deputised for Phillips. The trouble was that the two teams relegated with them the previous season, Nottingham Forest and Middlesbrough, were also playing great football, and had not had such a ropey start. Going into the final game of the season, Sunderland needed a better result away to Swindon than Middlesbrough achieved at home to Oxford to squeeze past them into the second automatic promotion place. At half-time that seemed possible as Sunderland led through two Phillips strikes, while Oxford held Middlesbrough, but four Boro goals in 18 minutes at the start of the second half consigned Sunderland to the play-offs with the largest-ever points total not to be promoted automatically.

Sunderland bundled past Sheffield United to set up a play-off final against Charlton, a game recently voted the best ever played at Wembley. Needless to say, Sunderland lost. Northeastern teams always have, every time they've been there since 1973. Glorious as the FA Cup final victory over Leeds was, it exacted a terrible price, as though all the luck were used up in one go. First, there was Newcastle hammered by Liverpool in the 1974 FA Cup final, and then beaten by Manchester City in the League Cup in 1976. Sunderland lost the League Cup final to Norwich in 1985, a play-off final against Swindon in 1990, and an FA Cup final against Liverpool in 1990. Middlesbrough, having suffered defeat to Nottingham Forest in the Zenith Data Systems Cup in 1990, lost in both FA Cup and League Cup finals in 1997, and were then beaten by Chelsea in the League Cup final the following year, as Newcastle suffered the first of two successive FA Cup final defeats. Throw in Darlington's defeat to Plymouth in the third division play-off final of 1996 and northeastern teams had lost on their previous 12 visits to Wembley. Sunderland were about to make it 13.

On a fraught and humid afternoon, Sunderland held the lead three times but drew 4-4, reined in by a hat trick from Clive Mendonca, a Sunderland fan with a heavy Wearside accent. The first 13 penalties of the shoot-out were scored. The 14th was taken by Sunderland's left-back, Michael Gray. He scuffed his kick, Sasa Ilic saved, and Charlton were promoted. As Niall Quinn gave an emotional pitch-side address, it did not escape notice that Dichio, who had come off the bench to replace Phillips, had not taken a penalty. Kevin Ball, not the most technically gifted player, had taken one, as had the right-back Chris Makin. Quinn had not been in the initial five, presumably reasoning that he was not the cleanest striker of a ball, but when it went to sudden death, he had recognised his moral responsibility to volunteer. Dichio, though, still hung back. Quinn was sixth also on the Republic of Ireland's list in their World Cup second-round game against Spain in 2002. On that occasion, Ireland had lost before he was needed; his autobiography is littered with references to the guilt he felt, perhaps still feels.

That would have been bad enough, but Dichio compounded the fault the following season in a 7-0 home win over Oxford. When Sunderland, already 2-0 up, were awarded a 38th-minute penalty, Dichio demanded it, and helped himself to a cheap goal. Easy enough to score a penalty when a game is already won and your side is cruising to a record-breaking promotion, but when the pressure was on, Dichio had vanished. Faced with a do or die situation, Dichio had gone for don't.

And so, of course, only playing because of an injury to

Patrick Agyemang and almost certainly oblivious to all that history, Dichio chose that game to end a 41-game drought and score his first league goal for Preston, arriving unmarked to nod in Graham Alexander's 18th-minute cross.

'It's definitely the most difficult game we've had so far,' Keane had warned beforehand. 'This is the first time under my management we've come up against a top-six side who are in the middle of a good run.' Still, even he, presumably, had not expected it to be as difficult as it turned out to be, even if those difficulties were largely self-inflicted. Sunderland had arguably been the better side until falling behind, but having done so they capitulated. 'It was disappointing,' said Keane. 'A bad game.'

Alexander converted a penalty awarded for a foul by Nosworthy on Simon Whaley and an own-goal from Dean Whitehead, turning the ball into his own net as he attempted to prevent Dichio reaching a David Nugent cross, gave Preston a 3-0 half-time lead. Nugent hit the bar soon after the break, before Whaley added a fourth with a deflected drive after Sunderland had reacted slowly to a lobbed through-ball. 'Conceding four goals shouldn't happen,' Connolly admitted. 'This is a tough league and just because we're a big club with a well-known manager, it doesn't mean we can just walk into the Premiership. What the manager says in the dressing-room stays there, but he was disappointed, and so were we.'

Although Stanislav Varga pulled one back almost immediately with a header from Liam Lawrence's corner, the game was already well beyond them. 'It was a good test for us,' Keane claimed, as he sought to draw positives from another game that had exposed the defensive frailties that lay behind the authoritative veneer of his side's passing. 'Preston were organised and worked their socks off. It has set a good benchmark for us. We hope to learn a lot from the game.'

Saturday, 14 October, Championship

Preston North End	4-1	Sunderland
Dichio 18		Varga 56
Alexander (pen) 31		
Whitehead (og) 35		
Whaley 55		

Preston: Nash, Alexander, St Ledger, Chilvers, Hill, Sedgwick, McKenna, Pugh (Davidson 79), Whaley (Neal 74), Nugent (Ormerod 70), Dichio
Subs Not Used: Lonergan, Wilson
Sunderland: Alnwick, Nosworthy, Varga, D Collins, Clarke, Lawrence, Whitehead, Leadbitter, Hysen (Wallace 52), Murphy (Yorke 62), Connolly
Subs Not Used: Ward, Brown, N Collins
Ref: M Jones (Cheshire)
Booked: Dichio (Preston); Nosworthy, Varga, Wallace (Sunderland)
Att: 19,603
League position: 17

There were no immediate signs of lessons having been learned the following Tuesday, though, as Sunderland went to Stoke and were unsettled by the physicality of Tony Pulis's side. From the dawn of time matches between Sunderland and Stoke have been ugly, niggly affairs. Alan Durban, the manager who once reacted to criticism of a pragmatic performance by saying that if you want entertainment you should go to the circus, moved to Sunderland from Stoke in 1981, and when the two meet it is as though they feel compelled to honour the memory of his time in charge. And Pulis, whose teams tend to be uncompromising and often unpleasant, is the nearest the modern age has to a Durban.

This was Sunderland back in Ipswich mode, kicking anything that moved, and this time they got a kicking in return. That said, there was nothing malicious about the clash that led to Rory Delap, making his home debut for Stoke, being ruled out for the season. As Darren Ward threw the ball out after 11 minutes, Delap challenged for it with Robbie Elliott. Delap was fractionally slower, took Elliott's follow-through full in the shin, and broke both tibia and fibula. 'I felt sick to the stomach,' the full-back said. 'You don't like to see that happen to any player, but when it's a friend it's even worse.'

Elliott was one of five changes to the team that had lost at Preston – 'the party's over' said Keane – with Ward being given his debut in place of Ben Alnwick, and Dwight Yorke starting. The Tobagan responded with his first goal since his return to English football, turning sharply in the box to lash in after Steve Simonsen, the Stoke goalkeeper, had spilled a Liam Miller corner. Within ten minutes of the start of the second half, though, the lead had become a deficit, and again defensive sloppiness was to blame. First Lee Hendrie was left untended to equalise as Mamady Sidibe helped on a Simonsen clearance, and then Vincent Pericard met Andy Griffin's cross with a powerful downward header to beat Ward. Danny Collins wasted a late chance and Chris Brown had a decent shout for a penalty turned down, but there was little sense of injustice about the result. 'We had a crazy ten minutes in the second half and that cost us,' said Ward. 'On another night we might have had a penalty and come away with a draw.' That other night, when Sunderland would scrape a barely deserved draw against Stoke, was still to come.

Tuesday, 16 October, Championship

Stoke City	2-1	Sunderland
Hendrie 50		Yorke 28
Péricard 54		

Stoke: Simonsen, Hoefkens, Higginbotham, Duberry, Griffin, Delap (Chadwick 12), Russell, Diao, Hendrie (Brammer 79), Sidibe (Fuller 68), Péricard
Subs Not Used: Bangoura, Wilkinson
Sunderland: Ward, Nosworthy, Varga, D Collins, R Elliott (Clarke 46), L Miller, Leadbitter, Whitehead (Brown 69), Wallace (Murphy 69), Connolly, Yorke
Subs Not Used: Alnwick, Lawrence
Ref: P Walton (Northamptonshire)

Booked: Diao (Stoke); R Elliott, Nosworthy (Sunderland)
Att: 14,482
League position: 19

Nobody quite dared say it, but after seven games that had produced just ten points, and with the club back in 19th place in the table, there was suddenly a danger that the season might descend into a relegation battle. Given the ricketiness of the back four, and the psychological damage from the previous relegation campaigns, that did not bode well. 'The game is full of bluffers,' Keane had written in his autobiography, 'banging on about "rolling your sleeves up", "having the right attitude" and "taking some pride in the shirt you're wearing". A manager who trades in those clichéd generalisations – and there are many of them – is missing the point. Brian Clough dealt in detail, facts, specific incidents, and invariably he got it right. Playing for him was demanding.' Now was the time for him to prove that he was not one of them.

Keane later spoke of how 'hectic' the first two months in the job and been, of the crazy rush to bring in players before the transfer deadline and how he and Tony Loughlan would 'hit the wall' at six or seven o'clock every night. 'Me and Tony, we were renting a house together, we were getting pulled left, right, and centre, sorting so much out, everything,' he said. 'We were coming back and falling asleep. It was a mad, mad few months. We knew it would be like that, of course, we wanted to change a lot of things around the club. It was like a crash-course in management. I suppose that was the only way it was going to be. I wasn't going to come into a big job like this without the club having its difficulties. Those first two or three months in the job I wouldn't wish on anybody. Absolute madness.'

On the surface, though, he remained serene, continuing the

pruning of his squad as the left-winger Andy Welsh was sent on loan to Leicester. There was also an acknowledgement of the problems at left-back, where Robbie Elliott, Danny Collins, and Clive Clarke had all been tried without a huge amount of success, as Keane took the 18-year-old Lewin Nyatanga – a centre-back who could also play on the left – on loan from Derby until January.

Looking back at the end of the season, Keane spoke of 'the many moments' when things had gone right for his side, edging the momentum in Sunderland's direction. Dean Whitehead's goal in the home game against Barnsley was undoubtedly one of them. Sunderland had won seven of their preious eight home fixtures against Barnsley, but the match had not been going well. Two away defeats had trimmed 9,000 from the gate – an indication of just how precarious fans' faith in the new beginning was – and, with ten minutes to go, the decision to stay away was looking increasingly prudent. The game had been scrappy and disjointed, a swirling wind combining with an obvious nervousness to make all the brave talk after the Sheffield Wednesday game seem a distant memory. But then Liam Lawrence, shirt hanging loose, blond hair awry, picked up the ball on the right, and advanced with stooping menace. Nyron Nosworthy, sprinting head-back, chest pumped out like Eric Liddell, surged by in a flurry of stripes outside him, leaving Robbie Williams for dead. Lawrence, weighting his pass perfectly, pushed the ball into his path so Nosworthy didn't even have to take a touch, merely slowing before driving in a low cross. Dean Whitehead got across his man at the near post, and, just as it seemed the ball may get caught between his feet, managed to shovel it out with his right, sending a shot scuttling across Nick Colgan, the

Barnsley keeper, and in at the far post. It was a goal that not merely won the game, but restored confidence. Grabbing a victory as the game seemed to be drifting away was, after all, indicative of the sort of mental resilience that had been so evidently lacking. Late goals would become a habit. There was even one more to come in this game, as Ross Wallace jinked by two men on the left and clipped over a deep cross that was met at the back post with a downward header from Chris Brown.

Manchester United's surge to the treble in 1999 was characterised by last-gasp goals and dramatic reversals of fortune – the result, it was said, of great fitness – mental and physical – and of belief. United came to believe they would score late, and, equally, opponents began to believe that they would concede. Perhaps it was the memory of that campaign that inspired Dwight Yorke's post-match comments, which at the time seemed ludicrously overconfident. Where most were grateful for a ground-out victory that might help to drag the team towards a respectable mid-table finish, he saw greater things ahead. 'I feel we have a good chance of promotion,' he said. 'Part of the reason the gaffer brought me here was for my experience. Sometimes you need an older head to calm things down. I see myself as a leading figure in our dressing-room. I was confident we would get a result.'

It was a theme Keane picked up as he praised the value of 'perseverance'. 'We have to be patient,' he said. 'The great teams win a lot of games in the last five or ten minutes. We're nowhere near good enough at the moment to think we can beat any team in the first twenty minutes. Barnsley were there to make it hard for us and there was going to be an edginess on the back of a couple of bad results. You tend to get people questioning things and the panic sets in. You just have to keep going. Keep bloody going.'

Saturday, 21 October, Championship

Sunderland   2-0   Barnsley
Whitehead 82
Brown 88

Sunderland: Ward, Nosworthy, Varga, Cunningham (Nyatanga 46), D Collins, Lawrence, Whitehead, Yorke, Murphy (Wallace 74), Connolly (Leadbitter 83), Brown
Subs Not Used: Alnwick, L Miller
Barnsley: Colgan, Hassell, Reid, Kay, Williams, Devaney, Howard (Healy 72), Togwell, McIndoe, Richards (Wright 71), Hayes (Nardiello 84)
Subs Not Used: Letheren, Heckingbottom
Ref: N Swarbrick (Lancashire)
Booked: Reid, Healy.
Att: 27,918
League position: 17

Relief rather than exultation, though, was the dominant emotion after the Barnsley game. The late goals had yet to be recognised as a pattern and the win was, frankly, a touch lucky. Keane spoke of the need to build on the victory and Liam Lawrence spoke of how back-to-back victories could be a springboard for success, but three successive away defeats had frayed confidence, even among the 4,000 fans who made the trip down the east coast for the game at Hull. 'We will be a force to be reckoned with at home; the question mark is away,' Yorke said. 'Our away form is a little bit dicey and we need to sort that situation out.'

Sunderland found themselves comfortably the better side, although they did show a worrying vulnerability to the long diagonal ball. For the most part, it seemed a question of when the goal would come, but, after a deflected shot had smacked the bar and Chris Brown had stabbed wide from three yards, and with the game into its third and final minute of injury-time, there was a sense of considerable relief when it finally arrived. As Ross Wallace drifted in from the right, Brown laid the ball on to him, and the Scot, opening his body cleverly, directed his finish inside Boaz Myhill's far post. The dam of frustration finally broken, he raced to the fans behind the goal, ripping off his shirt as he did so.

When Wallace finally emerged from the hugging and hair-ruffling, though, it was to be shown a red card, collecting a second booking for the over-enthusiastic nature of his celebrations. His first, just as needlessly, had come for dissent. Keane had spoken of the need to learn lessons, something Wallace, booked in similar circumstances at Derby, had evidently failed to do. He, though, seemed not to care, giving a double-fisted salute to the crowd as he left the field. 'Perhaps I'm going to have to staple my shirt on in the future,' he said. 'The lads have told me I'm like a little kid, but as soon as I see all the fans going mental, I just don't seem to be able to help myself. When you see all the fans jumping around you just want to get in amongst it, but I know I can't be doing that in the future.' For Wallace, it was six starts, two goals – both winners – and two red cards: cult heroes have been made of less. Keane, magnanimously, agreed 'not to crucify him'.

Saturday, 28 October, Championship

Hull City   **0-1**   **Sunderland**
                            Wallace 90

Hull: Myhill, Ricketts, Turner, Mills, Dawson, Fagan (Bridges 82), Ashbee, Delaney, Welsh (Barmby 72), Parkin, Forster (France 66)
Subs Not Used: Duke, Elliott
Sunderland: Ward, Whitehead, D Collins, Varga, Nyatanga, Lawrence (Connolly 67), Leadbitter, Yorke, Wallace, Murphy, Brown (N Collins 90)
Subs Not Used: Alnwick, Hysen, L Miller
Ref: R Beeby (Northamptonshire)
Booked: Fagan, Delaney, Mills (Hull); Leadbitter, Wallace, Varga (Sunderland)
Sent Off: Wallace 90 (Sunderland)
Att: 25,512
League position: 13

Up to 13th, and the optimists were stirring again, even if performances had given them little reason to do so. On song Sunderland held the ball as well as any Sunderland side in living memory, but they remained error prone at the back, and there were significant question-marks as to just how sharp their cutting edge was. Against Cardiff those worries were proved horribly apposite as a ghost of the season past chose Hallowe'en to return to haunt the Stadium of Light.

With a couple of minutes of the game to go, a lone magpie fluttered down from the sky above the Stadium of Light, circuited a couple of times, then landed by the touchline, pecking arrogantly along in front of the technical areas. Symbolically as well as actually, Michael Chopra's triumph was complete.

Chopra only scored one goal for Newcastle, but as far as he was concerned, it couldn't have been a better one. On Easter Monday the previous season, he'd done what every Geordie dreams of doing: he'd scored for Newcastle in a Tyne-Wear derby. Even better, it was a crucial goal, as he equalised on the hour to get Newcastle back into a game they'd looked like losing, inspiring a typical Sunderland capitulation to a 4-1 defeat. The only thing that could have made it sweeter would have been if Sunderland hadn't managed to render the game irrelevant by getting themselves relegated three days earlier.

In the build-up to his second visit, Chopra had made sure of a lively reception by saying he was looking forward to 'murdering the Mackems again'. His every touch was booed, but it didn't faze him. If anything, it inspired him, and he scored twice, his ninth and tenth goals of the season. Sunderland looked at a record that prolific with awe. Going into the game their top-scorer for the season was Dean Whitehead with three.

Keane spoke of top-of-the-table Cardiff as 'a gauge' to 'see how far we've come'. The answer was nowhere near far enough. The defending for Chopra's first goal was laughable. There was nothing particularly mysterious about Paul Parry's fourth-minute cross from the right, but the diagonal ball undid Sunderland yet again and Chopra was left eight yards out with only Darren Ward to beat. He had so much time he almost got over-casual about it, but eventually sliced the ball into the roof of the net. Chris Brown levelled from Tobias Hysen's cross six minutes later, but Cardiff were back in front before half-time. With Stan Varga and Danny Collins apparently impersonating an Antony Gormley installation, Chopra casually wandered between them to hook in what turned out to be the winner. Hysen had a spectacular volley superbly tipped wide by Neil Alexander and Dwight Yorke might have had a penalty when he seemed to be taken out by the goalkeeper, but Sunderland were well-beaten. 'We threw the game away,' said Daryl Murphy. 'You can't give easy chances like that to any team, let alone the team at the top of the league. I thought at 1-1 we could have gone on and won it, but we gave away another sloppy goal.'

He admitted 'there is probably only so much the manager can take', and certainly this was a grimmer-faced Keane than Sunderland had seen before. 'Poor,' he said. 'No pluses whatsoever.' When asked what had gone wrong he replied with just three words: 'Passing. Tackling. Movement.' He then, almost gnomically, suggested that 'real team-mates have a go at each other', a point he had evidently made to the players. 'We probably are a bit too nice,' Murphy admitted. 'We should bollock each other a bit more.'

The forward, though, was inclined to look on the bright side. 'We're still only six points off the play-offs,' he said. 'Two or three more wins on the bounce puts us right back up there.' Maybe so, but Sunderland were 14 points behind Cardiff, and the arrival of the magpie seemed a rather blatant reminder not merely of that, but also of past agonies.

Tuesday, 31 October, Championship

Sunderland	1-2	**Cardiff City**
Brown 10		Chopra 4, 37

Sunderland: Ward, N Collins (Kavanagh 69), Varga, D Collins, Nyatanga, Lawrence (Leadbitter 69), Whitehead, Yorke, Hysen, Murphy, Brown (S Elliott 82)
Subs Not Used: Alnwick, Caldwell
Cardiff: Alexander, McNaughton (Kamara 86), Purse, Loovens, Chambers, Ledley, Scimeca, McPhail, Parry, Chopra, Thompson (Campbell 46)
Subs Not Used: Johnson, Howard, Flood
Ref: C Boyeson (E Yorkshire)
Booked: Chambers, Chopra (Cardiff)
Att: 26,528
League position: 15

The magpie wasn't the only weird thing afoot: Mick McCarthy wanted to sign the lumbering Scottish defender Neill Collins for Wolves, presumably as part of his master plan to turn Molineux into a rest home for sluggish former Sunderland centre-backs. Jody Craddock and Gary Breen had seemed an ideal pairing, but perhaps Craddock wasn't quite flaky enough – and, in fairness, in his Sunderland days had had a certain elegance; what was needed, clearly, was somebody to put pressure on him, to keep him focused on his unreliability. Later in the season, when Wolves, after a run of nine games in which they had lost just once, suddenly imploded and lost 6-0 at home to Southampton, several pundits referred to it as 'freakish'. The only freakish thing was that they hadn't been letting in six every week. To Sunderland fans scanning their team-sheet and seeing Collins and Breen in tandem, with Craddock joining the fun with half an hour to go and two goals still to let in, the only freakish thing was that they'd lost just one of the previous nine.

The only other explanation was that McCarthy saw the signing of Collins as some kind of reparations for Saipan, an inventive means of achieving a rapprochement with Keane ahead of Sunderland's visit to Molineux the following month. 'He didn't go through an agent or the chairman or a friend of a player, he rang me direct,' Keane said. 'That was much appreciated.' Although surely not as much as the idea somebody was going to take Neill Collins off his hands; nobody in their right mind could tell anybody to stick that offer up their bollocks.

'It's good to move on in life because life is short,' Keane went on. Paul Parker had said at the start of the season that Keane had 'mellowed', that 'you'll see a change in him', but this was ridiculous. This was a man who had clattered Alf-Inge Haaland four years after the Norwegian had first offended him. What was going on? Was this the reason for Keane's beard-growth? He'd already started drinking green tea. Was he about to don psychedelic robes and start muttering about the dawning of the age of Aquarius? Had Quinn's socialistic utopia become a hippy commune?

'It was all very amicable,' Keane said. 'We did chat about what has gone on before and it's nice to put these things to bed. We were both happy to talk things over. Now it's done and dusted.' Collins went on loan until January, when he was signed on a permanent deal for £150,000, an ordinary, cumbersome defender with a place in history as the indirect architect of an unlikely peace. As Keane continued to trim his squad, Tommy Miller went on loan to Preston and, slightly surprisingly given how regularly he'd played, Liam Lawrence to Stoke. The assumption was that his laid-back languidness did not fit with the Keane master-plan, but subsequent events would suggest a more tawdry reason for his departure.

*

On the pitch things followed a predictably depressing course. Since the Milk Cup final of 1985, Sunderland have enjoyed a 'special relationship' with Norwich. Amid the violence and rancour of that darkest of seasons, events that March day at Wembley stood out as an example of what football could be about. Even before the horrors of Heysel and Bradford, 1984-85 had been bleak. Millwall fans had rioted at Luton, while both legs of Sunderland's Milk Cup semifinal victory over Chelsea had been marred by crowd trouble.

Sunderland won the first leg at Roker 2-0 through two Colin West goals – one a penalty, the other a rebound after his penalty had been pushed onto the post – as Chelsea were effectively reduced to nine men by injury, but the game was overshadowed by the violence that surrounded it. There were 96 arrests in total as Chelsea fans ripped out two hundred seats to use as missiles at Roker Park, attacked the Blue Bell pub in Sunderland and, in a strange echo of the vandalism of about 15 centuries earlier, smashed windows at Fulwell Library – and ripped out 200 seats to use as missiles at Roker Park.

With around 4,000 Sunderland fans inside Stamford Bridge for the second leg – and apparently a further 3,000 locked out – further disorder was inevitable. It came, although police stressed that almost all the 104 arrested were Chelsea fans. Having gone behind early on, Sunderland came back to win 3-2 – 5-2 on aggregate – but it was a night on which simply escaping unscathed was something of an achievement. The goalkeeper Chris Turner, hero of the quarterfinal victory over Tottenham, was kicked and the forward Clive Walker, a former Chelsea player, attacked in a pitch invasion that followed Walker's second goal, while Chelsea's defence appeared to be distracted by a policeman chasing a fan across the corner of the penalty area as Colin West headed the third. Most sickening was what followed in the streets afterwards, as hooligans blocked streets and attempted to drag fans off coaches to slit their faces.

So when, on the morning of the final, police heard stories of hundreds of Sunderland and Norwich fans converging in a car park just outside Wembley, their panic was understandable. Having mobilised emergency units, though, all they found was fans engaged in a huge, joyously unruly game of football. The amicable relationship continued, often with surreal results. When Dale Gordon scored a winner for Norwich at Roker Park in December 1990 after a neat passing move, the Fulwell End politely applauded. On 30 December 1993, Sunderland's away game at Tranmere was postponed because of a water-logged pitch (somewhat conveniently, given Tranmere's extensive injury list) but rather than turning back to the Northeast, hundreds of travelling fans decided to carry on and watch Norwich away at Everton. Television pictures of that game show the away end split between green-and-yellow and red-and-white.

After the 1985 final – the Friendly Final, as it became known – the Friendship Trophy was instituted, the winners determined by taking the aggregate score of the two league fixtures between the clubs any time they were in the same division. Sunderland, unfortunately, seem to have taken their duties of friendship rather too seriously. They haven't won at Carrow Road since their 3-1 victory eight days before that Milk Cup final. In the final itself, they not merely scored Norwich's goal for them, Gordon Chisholm chesting Mick Channon's shot past Chris Turner (who was partially unsighted by an offside John Deehan, but that's another story), but also missed a penalty. In fact, having instituted a competition in which there was only one other team, Sunderland have achieved the extraordinary feat of, in over two decades, managing to win it only once, back in the glory season of 1998-99 when a 2-2 draw at Carrow Road was followed by a 1-0 win at the Stadium of Light. That said, there is a theory Sunderland still retain the title, having not lost on aggregate to Norwich since, although the trophy remains at Carrow Road.

There was at least an improved performance from Sunderland, but, for the first time under Keane, they failed to score, and so the long run without success at Norwich continued. Yes, they were denied two fairly clear penalties in the space of a minute late on – Dion Dublin first hauling down Daryl Murphy and then handling – but the fault really was their own for not doing more with their possession, and not converting any of the half-dozen clear chances they did create. 'We have to do better in the last third,' Steve Caldwell said, after his first appearance under Keane. 'We have to use possession better and take our chances when they come. I also felt we could have fashioned a few more chances. We got some good quality balls in, but the play was a little one-dimensional. We could have had more variety in our game.'

Sunderland had 71 per cent of possession, and 13 chances to Norwich's two, but they didn't have a forward playing with the pace and poise of Robert Earnshaw. As Norwich broke six minutes after half-time, Sunderland's defence parted all too easily, and when Paul McVeigh curved a pass through for Earnshaw, he took one touch before firing a classy finish across Darren Ward and into the bottom corner. 'Credit to Robert Earnshaw,' said Keane. 'He's had one chance and he's taken it. There's a fine line between winning and losing. We were comfortable at half-time, but there's always a danger in football that you get hit with a sucker punch, and we did. Sometimes you need a bit of guile in the final third. We had decent possession, but we lacked the final ball. That's the hardest thing in football and it's what we're going to look at.'

Generally, he remained more upbeat than results suggested he ought to be. 'We can't feel sorry for ourselves,' he went on. 'We've got to bounce back. It just seems to be going against us at this moment in time, but we hope by the end of the season things will pan out.'

Saturday, 4 November, Championship

Norwich City **1-0** **Sunderland**
Earnshaw 51

Norwich: Gallacher, Colin (Eagle 84), Shackell, Dublin, Drury, Etuhu, Safri, Robinson, McVeigh (Hughes 74), Earnshaw, Huckerby
Subs Not Used: Ashdown, Thorne, Spillane
Sunderland: Ward, Whitehead, D Collins, Caldwell, Nyatanga, Lawrence, Kavanagh (Leadbitter 72), Yorke, Hysen (Murphy 68), Brown, Connolly (S Elliott 77)
Subs Not Used: Alnwick, Nosworthy
Ref: M Riley (West Yorkshire)
Booked: Gallacher, Huckerby (Norwich); Caldwell, Kavanagh (Sunderland)
Att: 24,652
League position: 17

A week later, though, it was pessimism continued with a deeply disappointing draw at home against Southampton. The media focus on Sunderland had waned, and so too, it seemed, was the momentum that had been generated by Keane's arrival. At least after Norwich there had been a sense that Sunderland had been unfortunate; here they knew they had been extremely lucky to get the point that they did. Darren Ward had received a call up to the Wales squad earlier in the week, and responded with a performance, that, Keane acknowledged, was the only thing that kept Sunderland from a comprehensive defeat. One save, midway through the second half, as he flew to his right to push a Pelé header up onto the underside of the bar was breathtaking. Keane described it as one of the best he'd ever seen, while George Burley, the Southampton manager, put it in the same bracket as Gordon Banks's save from a header by the other Pelé. 'One for the scrapbook,' Ward said modestly.

Ross Wallace, on his return from suspension, had given Sunderland the lead with a whipped free-kick – this time he remembered to keep his shirt on – but Southampton always had the better of the game. They finally got their reward in injury-time as a half-clearance fell to the full-back Gareth Bale. He didn't strike the shot particularly cleanly, but it cannoned off the heel of Steve Caldwell, leaving Ward wrong-footed and helpless as the ball ballooned past him. 'It was possibly a fair result,' the goalkeeper admitted, 'but it's difficult to stomach not holding on for a win. The lads are a bit down. When you concede an equaliser like that it feels like a defeat. You try to take the positives. It stopped the rot after a couple of defeats, and we were close to winning without playing particularly well.'

Keane was equally determined to be positive. 'Last week we played a lot better and ended up with nothing,' he said. 'Today we might have ended up with three points that we didn't really deserve, but that's football. Southampton had twenty-four shots on goal so the law of averages says one of them's going to go in.' As Sunderland slipped to 19th, though, just three places above the drop zone, there was even the odd mention of the dreaded R-word again.

Saturday, 11 November, Championship

Sunderland   **1-1**   **Southampton**
Wallace 62   Bale 90

Sunderland: Ward, Nosworthy, Caldwell, D Collins, Nyatanga, Whitehead, Kavanagh (S Elliott 80), Yorke, Wallace, Connolly (Leadbitter 75), Murphy (Brown 67)
Subs Not Used: Carson, L Miller

The *Cleadon* tug passes under the Wear Bridge, 1954 (*Sunderland Echo*).

Looking out from the Fulwell End, as crowds queue for FA Cup Final tickets, 1973 (*Sunderland Echo*).

OPPOSITE PAGE
Above Workers stream over the Wear Bridge, 1952 (*Sunderland Echo*).

Below A packed terrace at Roker Park (*Sunderland Echo*).

The World Cup comes to Sunderland. A queue forms for tickets (*Sunderland Echo*); Anatoly Banishevsky of the USSR challenges the Italian goalkeeper Enrico Albertosi in a World Cup game at Roker Park in 1966 (Getty).

The towering centre-forward: Quinn during his first coming to Wearside (Getty).

No bluffing, no bullshitting, no celebrating: Keane in typically pensive touchline mode (Getty); and preferring to view training from afar (*North News & Pictures*).

Two thirds of the Trinidad and Tobago connection: Carlos Edwards got most of the headlines, but Stern John and Dwight Yorke also had key roles to play (Getty).

Jonny Evans arrived on loan in January to form a formidable central defensive partnership with Nyron Nosworthy (Colorsport).

Dean Whitehead, Sunderland's undemonstrative but highly effective captain (Colorsport).

Daryl Murphy (right), who grew in stature as the season progressed, got the opener in the tumultuous 3-2 victory over Burnley; David Connolly (top) misses from the spot against Burnley, but had the bottle to convert a penalty late in the game; Carlos Edwards's late winner (centre) prompts delirium (all Getty).

The incisiveness of Carlos Edwards on the right made a huge difference after he signed in January (Getty); Edwards (centre and below) and Nyron Nosworthy (above) – and their pork-pie hats – celebrate winning the Championship at Luton (Getty and Colorsport).

Southampton: Davis, Makin, Lundekvam, Baird, Bale, Licka (Wright-Phillips 67), Wright, Pelé, Skacel (Surman 63), Jones (Rasiak 63), Dyer
Subs Not Used: Bialkowski, Sarmiento
Ref: K Friend (Leicestershire)
Booked: Nosworthy (Sunderland)
Att: 25,667
League position: 19

Having reached the end of Givens Street, I turned back on myself, walking up Benedict Road towards the park. The Harbour View, once all peeling white paint, has had a makeover, but Benedict Road is one of those streets that seem not to have changed in about a century. By this time people were beginning to stir. A white-haired man passed on the other side of the road, carrying a newspaper. A white van pulled up and a man in a blue boiler suit dashed out of his gate and jumped in the passenger seat. A woman coaxed an unenthusiastic terrier towards the park. As I passed her, the dog lurched towards me, and in stumbling to avoid it my gaze flicked right. Through a greasy net curtain, I saw a table set for breakfast. On a yellow checked tablecloth, there were four demure cups, upturned, four saucers on which were laid four teaspoons, four plates and four rounded knives. In the centre of the table, by the salt and pepper, was a thick round mat, set out presumably for the teapot. The scene, for reasons I don't entirely understand, affected me. Who sets the table for breakfast nowadays? It was, I suppose, a reminder of the past, of an old-fashioned northern civility. Maybe it's me; maybe other people do bother to sit down together for breakfast, rather than slurping at a bowl of cereal while tapping away at a laptop. Either way, it gave me a jolt, a sense of how distant I am now from that past.

There is a sense of continuity at the end of the street as well. The Blayney's that was drunk dry as thousands of fans queued overnight for tickets to the 1992 FA Cup semifinal has become a Booze Buster, but Armstrong's Aquatics still sells pets at the end of Bede Street, and, opposite, the Methodist church, where you used to be able to get tea or coffee and homemade cakes before games, is still there.

I turned into the park and wandered along past the ageing tennis courts and the pond, past the sculpture erected by the local Sunday Schools association. For some reason I'd always thought it was a memorial to those killed in the Victoria Hall disaster in 1883, when 183 children were killed, crushed in a stairwell as they raced to the stage to collect presents they'd been promised, but it turns out I was mixing it up with the real memorial in Mowbray Park.

At the bandstand, smaller than I remembered it, I headed down, and through the ravine – protected as representing a significant percentage of the 270 hectares of magnesium grassland that remains in Britain – and out on to the beach. The tide was almost in when I got there, leaving just a thin strip of sand running from the Cat and Dog Steps along to the Pier. In summer, this is probably the most popular section of beach, although it surely wouldn't be if the supposed etymology of the name were widely known. When cats and dogs in the town died, it was common practice to throw their bodies into the river. Rather than being washed out to sea, though, it was here, it is said, that the corpses tended to be washed up.

[7]

STIRRINGS

By the end of the season, Keane had become some kind of magus figure, bearded, intense, and seemingly capable of shaping events simply by talking about them. Perhaps earlier in the season the magic was dimmed by his exhaustion at the novelty of the situation, perhaps he was still learning how to harness his powers. It was in mid-November, in the week leading up to the Colchester game that the full magnitude of that faculty became apparent. My strikers must perform, he said, and so, quite abruptly, having given no prior indication they might be about to do so, they did.

Injuries had played their part, and the hangover from the previous season was still affecting confidence, but it was still a miserable statistic that, at that stage of the season, Chris Brown was still Sunderland's most prolific forward with three. Of the other forwards, Daryl Murphy and Stephen Elliott both had two, while David Connolly had played nine times without breaking his duck. 'The teams at the top tend to have goalscorers in top form,' Keane noted soberly. 'Sometimes that's all it comes down to. We're hoping that one or two of our strikers will kick into action and get some goals.'

Stephen Elliott, making his first start since August wide on the right in a five-man midfield, duly obliged, two strikes in eight minutes around half-time energising a performance sterile enough to have prompted grumblings of discontent within the opening half-hour. What invention there was came almost entirely from the Irish forward. He had slid a shot a fraction wide of the far post following a one-two with Liam Miller, but he did put Sunderland ahead on the stroke of half-time with a moment of rare imagination. Receiving a pass with his back to goal on the right-hand corner of the box, he shaped to turn right but, rolling the ball behind his standing leg, he span sharply to his left, fooling his marker, Chris Barker, and opening up space for a shot or cross. Aidan Davison expected the latter and took a hop across goal, only to see Elliott's strike from 18 yards dip and veer savagely in at his near post. It might have been a mishit, but his turn deserved some luck. 'That settled us down just before half-time,' Elliott said. 'We'd had plenty of possession, but didn't really have much penetration. Perhaps that was frustrating for the crowd, but when that first goal went in, the confidence returned to the stadium. The way we played improved in the second half and at times we looked a really good side.'

Nobody was getting carried away – this, after all, was only Colchester, whose away form remained inconsistent throughout the season – but a first win in four certainly helped to ease Wearside's anxiety. Elliott got his second eight minutes after half-time, touching in Dean Whitehead's pull-back, and he was denied a hat trick only when Davison produced an acrobatic tip-over to keep out his 25-yard clip. Chris Brown had a goal ruled out for offside, but, just as things were looking comfortable, Sunderland reacted slowly to some penalty-box pinball, allowing the substitute Chris Iwelumo to pull one back with 11 minutes remaining. Life is full of might-have-beens, but had Kem Izzet maintained his composure after a long ball caught Sunderland out a few minutes later, it is possible that the Keane revolution would never have gathered momentum. 'We deserved the win,' said Keane, 'but, as usual, we made it hard for ourselves. They got the goal and we invited pressure. In parts of the game we were really good, outstanding. We passed and moved well. If you get the third goal, the game's dead and buried, but when it's 2-0 and you concede, it seems to be natural instinct to drop back and try to hold on to it.'

Under little pressure and with just Ward to beat, Izzet spooned over. Sunderland survived and, in injury-time, Connolly took a ball from Graham Kavanagh down on his chest, turned and – at last – steered his first for the club into the bottom corner. 'Things haven't quite fallen for me since I came to the club,' Connolly said. 'There haven't been any tap-ins or anything, so it's nice to see the ball go in, and hopefully I can get a few more.'

Saturday, 18 November, Championship

Sunderland   3-1   **Colchester United**
S Elliott 45, 53   Iwelumo 79
Connolly 90

Sunderland: Ward, Whitehead, Varga, D Collins, Nyatanga, L Miller, Leadbitter (Kavanagh 83), Yorke, Wallace (Hysen 83), Brown (Connolly 69), S Elliott
Subs Not Used: Caldwell, Carson
Colchester: Davison, Halford, Baldwin, Brown, Barker, Duguid, Izzet, Jackson, McLeod (Jones 46), Cureton, Guy (Iwelumo 70)
Subs Not Used: White, Gerken, Richards
Ref: A Hall (W Midlands)
Booked: Brown (Sunderland)
Att: 25,197
League position: 16

A sense of stability returning was one thing, but Keane admitted he had been hoping for more. After bringing in Tottenham's Hungarian goalkeeper Marton Fulop on loan, with a view to a permanent move in January, he spoke of an irritation at the way the market worked and, more specifically, at the attitude of players. 'Sunderland are not the big pull everybody thinks they are perhaps,' he said. 'Half the battle's trying to get to speak to the players. Getting to first base is hard. Then the first question they ask is what kind of money they're going to be getting, and I find that amazing. So that's been frustrating, the boys putting the financial side before playing football for a top club like Sunderland. We're suffering as we try to bring quality players in due to the stigma of the relegations. A lot of people think Sunderland is Australia or somewhere. There's a stigma with the club, the area, the people. People believe here's not worth even visiting or travelling to, and they're so wrong.' The idea of Sunderland not being a 'big pull' was controversial, but by talking of Wearside as a wrongly neglected area, Keane was expressing a truth that had rankled for years.

In another week the issue would perhaps have been investigated more thoroughly; this particular week, though, it was rather lost. This was the week of Keane versus McCarthy: the return. To the disappointment of everybody hoping for blood on the touchline – and that presumably included Sky, who decided to show Sunderland's game at Wolves live on the Friday night – the Keane-McCarthy détente declared during negotiations over Neill Collins seemed firm. 'I will shake his hand, of course I will,' said McCarthy, 'and it will be a genuine gesture and not something for the TV cameras. I will also ask Roy into my office for a drink afterwards – I know he doesn't drink alcohol but I'll pour him a lemonade or a cola or a coffee or whatever he wants.' Keane too was in conciliatory mood, insisting it would not be the first time he had met McCarthy face-to-face since Saipan and that the matter had been 'put to bed' by their discussions over Collins. 'As far as I'm concerned it's about the players,' he said. 'It's Sunderland versus Wolves and everyone should be talking about that.'

Their handshake before the game was uncertain, Keane seemingly taken by surprise as McCarthy, tailed by a couple of dozen photographers, approached him. At the end, after the final whistle, it was embarrassed, at least on the part of Keane. Teeth clenching his upper lip, he shook his head as though slightly bewildered as he walked up to McCarthy, and from their body language as they exchanged a brief hug it was clear he was admitting that he had no idea how Sunderland had got away with a point. Keane later revealed that this was the second of three occasions over the course of the season when he lost his temper. His fury, though, was directed not at McCarthy, but at a lacklustre performance from his own side. Darren Ward made a number of fine saves, Leon Clarke missed a sitter, and so, when the ball broke from a scramble to land at Stephen Elliott's feet ten minutes from time, Wolves led by only a single goal, a beauty dispatched into the top corner by Jemal Johnson just before half-time. Elliott turned and, when he got his shot out from under his feet, it flicked off the calf of Mark Little past a wrong-footed Matt Murray, and Sunderland had an unlikely point. 'He's a goalscorer,' Keane said. 'There's no doubt about that. He's got his goals in the last two games, but some of his link-up play and work-rate has been outstanding. He's getting fitter and stronger. We hope he's one who can get near the top of the goalscoring charts because when you've got a striker in form in makes a hell of a difference.'

Keane admitted his side had been 'fortunate' and hailed Ward as an undoubted man of the match. Few were arguing. 'He's our form player,' said Dean Whitehead. 'He kept us in a couple of games recently that we could easily have lost badly.

Some of his saves have been top class and he's been a great influence because he fills people with confidence. He comes for crosses, kicks well and he's making great saves. If a few of us could match his form, we'd climb this league.'

Ward himself was just grateful to be playing after two frustrating seasons at Norwich, in which he had managed just one start and two substitute appearances as he deputised for Rob Green. 'When I was sitting at home in the summer wondering where my next club was coming from, I could never have imagined what was ahead,' Ward said. At 32, he was happy to arrive on Wearside as cover for Ben Alnwick, but after replacing him for the 2-1 defeat at Stoke in October, he never looked back, and was eventually rewarded with a contract extension that ties him to the club until the summer of 2009.

Friday, 24 November, Championship

Wolverhampton Wamderers	1-1	Sunderland
Johnson 43		S Elliott 8

Wolverhampton: Murray, Little, Breen, Craddock, Clapham, Gobern, Olofinjana, Henry, Jones, Bothroyd (Clarke 63), Johnson (C Davies 84)
Subs Not Used: Ikeme, Collins, Potter
Sunderland: Ward, Whitehead, D Collins, Varga, Nyatanga, L Miller (Kavanagh 64), Leadbitter, Yorke (Hysen 46), Wallace (Nosworthy 76), S Elliott, Connolly
Subs Not Used: Carson, Caldwell
Ref: M Pike (Cumbria)
Booked: Jones (Wolves); Yorke, Varga (Sunderland)
Att: 27,203
League position: 16

As was the way at that stage of the season, the iffy performance at Wolves was followed by a very good one away at QPR the following Tuesday, although again the combination of profligacy and defensive vulnerability threatened to undermine Sunderland. Excellent as Johnson's strike had been for Wolves, given he had been allowed time to turn, advance and line up his shot, it had not been beyond prevention.

QPR had won three of their previous four games, but for long periods against Sunderland they were so outclassed that John Gregory, the QPR manager, cried off the post-match press conference with a headache. Daryl Murphy ended a 13-match goal-drought to give Sunderland the lead, flicking in a half-blocked drive from Grant Leadbitter, and then Leadbitter, thriving in an advanced role through the middle as Sunderland played a 4-5-1, ran on to Ross Wallace's through ball, and rounded Simon Royce for an elegant second. Ray Jones pulled one back after taking down Nick Ward's chipped through-ball on his knee, and, with 17 minutes to go Sunderland were faced with a Colchester situation, as they had to battle to win a game they should have won comfortably. If Ross Wallace hadn't been involved in his own private miss of the season competition – he won it by slicing wide of an open goal from six yards – and David Connolly's late drive had flashed an inch to the right rather than cannoning back to Royce off the post, the scoreline would have reflected the performance. As it was, Sunderland were left hanging on. 'It could have been 5-, 6- or 7-1 tonight, the number of chances we created,' Keane said. 'I'm sure it was a great game to watch for the neutral, but not from our point of view, and probably not for the supporters. But we got there in the end and that's the important thing.'

Monday, 28 November, Championship

QPR   1-2   Sunderland
Jones 73   Murphy 17
                Leadbitter 45

QPR: Royce, Mancienne, Rehman, Stewart, Bignot, Ward, Rowlands, Smith, Cook (R Jones 46), Gallen, Blackstock (Furlong 82)
Subs Not Used: Cole, Bailey, Nygaard
Sunderland: Ward, Nosworthy, Caldwell, Varga, Collins, L Miller (Connolly 57), Kavanagh, Leadbitter (Whitehead 63), Wallace, S Elliott, Murphy

Subs Not Used: Fulop, Hysen, R Elliott
Ref: U Rennie (S Yorkshire)
Booked: R Jones (QPR); Wallace (Sunderland)
Att: 13,108
League position: 14

Four games unbeaten, and suddenly eyes were looking up the table rather than down again. 'This run will build confidence, but we've been on this kind of run before and not kicked on from it,' Graham Kavanagh said. 'The two home games coming up are vital. If we can get six points it will set us up nicely going into Christmas. If we can keep the run going we can send out a real statement that we're capable of promotion.' What is remarkable, with hindsight, is to think that even at the end of November, that still needed spelling out.

Keane too felt that things were moving in the right direction. 'I'm glad to be getting up towards the top half of the table,' he said the day before the home game against Norwich. 'I've seen progress. It's going to take time, but the signs are there. The fans might not see what goes on off the pitch, but hopefully that will start to reflect on results. We're getting a group of players who have a togetherness and are really knuckling down. It's a lot better. We [the coaches] know the ins and outs now. There were far too many players here when I got the job.' Given Arnau Riera and William Mocquet had just been farmed out on loan – to Southend and Rochdale respectively – having played less than one half of first-team football between them, that could have been taken as a criticism of Quinn's transfer policy, but the point was never pressed. 'In the first month or two it was so hectic,' Keane went on, 'but things are starting to settle down. We've got more ideas about the players and they've got more ideas about us. You want players to be a proper team and to run through brick walls for each other.'

Sunderland knew only too well how destructive a lack of dressing-room unity could be. In the fifties they had been the 'Bank of England' club, but the stars they signed never gelled. Len Shackleton was so put out by the arrival of Trevor Ford that, late in games in which Sunderland were comfortably ahead, he would deliberately feed him passes loaded with so much spin they were almost impossible to control. As the Welsh centre-forward's touch let him down again and again, Shackleton would turn to the Fulwell End and shrug, as if to ask, 'You prefer this clown to me?' A decade later the signing of Jim Baxter served only to divide the dressing-room into cliques as Charlie Hurley was edged aside to accommodate the prodigiously-gifted but unruly Scot.

There were signs of the togetherness of Keane's side against Norwich as Sunderland reverted to patchiness – even Danny Collins was moved to complain of a 'scrappy game' – but fought out a 1-0 win, keeping their first clean sheet in seven games. Peter Grant, the Norwich manager, claimed the game had been a mirror image of the match at Carrow Road a month earlier, but Norwich never enjoyed the long spells of pressure Sunderland had had then. Sunderland themselves were far less effective, and, particularly towards the end of the first half, there was a distinct restlessness among fans.

The winner came from nowhere, Daryl Murphy spinning on the edge of the box and shaping a left-foot shot into the bottom left corner. 'It was very frustrating up until the goal,' Murphy said. 'It was just a battle and the pitch really cut up. The fans were frustrated and so were we, but they tried to stay with us and we got the breakthrough in the end.'

'It was a top finish from Murphy,' Keane said. 'Before the

game I told him not to rest on his laurels after the QPR game and he certainly didn't do that. It was a fantastic finish, a great goal. Murph has the potential to be a top, top player, but we need consistent performances from him.'

Saturday, 2 December, Championship

Sunderland   1-0   Norwich
Murphy 76

Sunderland: Ward, Whitehead, Caldwell, Collins, Nyatanga, S Elliott, L Miller, Kavanagh, Leadbitter (Yorke 74), Wallace (Hysen 85), Murphy
Subs Not Used: Fulop, R Elliott, Connolly
Norwich: Camp, Colin, Shackell, Dublin, Drury, Hughes, Etuhu, Robinson (Eagle 77), Huckerby, Earnshaw, Safri (Thorne 80)
Subs Not Used: Lewis, McVeigh, Ryan Jarvis
Ref: P Joslin (Nottinghamshire)
Booked: L Miller (Sunderland); Shackell, Drury (Norwich)
Att: 27,934
League position: 14

Murphy's performance wasn't the only thing to delight Keane. 'It was a very, very scrappy game but I don't care,' he said. 'It's the happiest I've been after a game since I came to the club. My players showed a lot of character out there.' That might have surprised those who sat through it, but then Keane has always argued that there is more to football than brilliance. Bryan Robson became his hero precisely because he was 'not brilliant, but awesome'.

In his early teens Keane was regularly overlooked for regional or national representative honours and failed to catch the eye in a number of trials. In his autobiography, though, he notes as an absolute the lesson he learned while playing for Rockmount Under-11s. 'I listened to our coaches, Timmy Murphy and Gene O'Sullivan, particularly when they referred to attitude,' he said. 'Their credo was simple yet true: take the field with the wrong attitude and no matter how much ability you possess, you'll lose.' With suspensions and injuries taking their toll,

Dean Whitehead pushed himself through the game with a strained hamstring, while Keane had particular praise for Liam Miller. 'He was in Ireland at a funeral on Friday,' he said. 'He missed training and I gave him the opportunity to have the weekend off but he said that he wanted to come back and play and that says a lot about the lad.'

Until that moment, Keane had been sparing in his praise of individuals, at least in public. Perhaps it was coincidence, but if it were, it was one of a huge number over the course of the season. Keane seemed to have an uncanny gift for either predicting or pre-empting the future. Here he had drawn attention to the commitment of one of his players; five days later, it seemed he had been issuing a warning to those who were not quite so focused as *The Sun* broke news of a sex video scandal involving Liam Lawrence, Ben Alnwick, Chris Brown, and Martin Woods. The seven-minute video showed the four, along with two others, presumed not to be footballers, who remained clothed throughout, 'roasting' 'a busty female fan'. The 'mystery brunette' later turned out to have been only 16, and claimed to have had no knowledge she was being filmed. Brown, aping the style of John Motson, maintained a running commentary throughout, referring to the non-players as 'the watching faithful', while Woods never removed his jumper. 'We will be handling the matter internally,' said Sunderland's communications and marketing director, Lesley Callaghan, earning herself an award from an American television programme for best unintentional innuendo of the week. One of the players later rang *The Sun* anonymously, saying 'What we did was wrong, but everyone was consenting.'

Woods had left the club the previous August, and none of the other three had been near the team for weeks. Lawrence was already on loan at Stoke; he was sold in January. The window also saw Alnwick finalise his move to Tottenham in a swap with Fulop and Norwich sign Brown for £325,000. For Keane, evidently, commitment had to be absolute. For fans, though, the story was great news. This was the sort of scandal that was only reported if it involved players from big clubs; the fact that it had got national coverage suggested just how seriously the rest of the world was taking Sunderland. Wrongly neglected no more.

The renewed sense of confidence was seen against Luton as a crowd of over 30,000 turned up at the Stadium of Light for the first time since the victory over Sheffield Wednesday at the end of September, but things didn't begin well. When Stanislav Varga blocked Dean Morgan's cross after five minutes, the ball cannoned back to the forward, who controlled it and hit a shot across Marton Fulop – making his debut in place of the flu-stricken Darren Ward – and into the bottom corner. 'It wasn't very nice,' the Hungarian said, 'but I put it to the back of my mind and we all knew there would be plenty of time to get back into the game.'

It took Daryl Murphy just four minutes to pull Sunderland level as he muscled by Leon Barnett on the left, cut into the box and slammed an emphatic finish into the roof of the net for his third goal in as many games. Sunderland's winner came eight minutes into the second half. David Connolly had looked lively throughout, and it took an excellent save from Dean Kiely to deny him his second for the club just before half-time as he latched on to an under hit back-pass. That second goal did come, though, and it was very similar to his first, as he turned just inside the box, and hammered a low shot just inside the left-hand post. 'We're gaining momentum,' he said, before outlining his belief that a top-two spot was a realistic target.

'We showed good character,' said Keane, apparently deter-mined to hammer home the message of the previous week. 'We were slow out of the blocks, but again we were digging deep, we're grinding out results. I've always said it's going to take time, but we're heading in the right direction, and we're going to give ourselves a chance. We're going to be playing catch-up, probably until the last day of the season.' How right he was.

Saturday, 9 December, Championship

Sunderland	2-1	Luton Town
Murphy 9		Morgan 5
Connolly 53		

Sunderland: Fulop, Whitehead, Caldwell, Varga, Collins, S Elliott, L Miller, Kavanagh, Wallace, Connolly (Leadbitter 78), Murphy
Subs Not Used: Carson, Nyatanga, R Elliott, Yorke
Luton: Kiely, Foley, Heikkinen, Barnett, Emanuel, Edwards, Bell, Robinson, Brkovic, Vine (Feeney 76), Morgan (Boyd 76)
Subs Not Used: Beresford, Perrett, Langley
Ref: A Penn (W Midlands)
Booked: Brkovic (Luton)
Att: 30,445
League position: 12

There are times when a draw, by the manner in which it is attained, can be more pleasing than a victory. The feeling had been growing that Keane was instilling in Sunderland the qual-ities that made Manchester United great, and it seemed to be confirmed with a most untypical comeback to steal a point away to Burnley.

This was the kind of thing that Sunderland sides simply did not do. The last ten minutes, that is; the first 79 were all too familiar. Daryl Murphy conceded possession inside the Burnley half nine minutes in, and Steve Jones's ball released Wade Elliott on the counter. With Sunderland overmanned, he slipped the ball left to Kyle Lafferty as Stan Varga attempted to close him down and the teenager, advancing, stroked a calm finish past Darren Ward. Lafferty, having cleared a Steven Caldwell effort off the line, made it 2-0 seven minutes after half-time with another fine finish after being sent through by a weak back-header from Dwight Yorke.

Yorke, playing in the deep central midfield role he had occupied for Trinidad and Tobago in the World Cup, looked out of sorts throughout, and it was only when he and Ross Wallace were withdrawn for Liam Miller and Graham Kavanagh just after the hour, that Sunderland really began to impose themselves. Still, things seemed to be sliding away from them when, with ten minutes remaining, Leadbitter picked up the ball 30 yards from goal, drifted through a couple of half-challenges, then pinged a drive into the bottom corner. 'I was a little bit lucky still to be on the pitch because I wasn't myself,' the 20-year-old said. 'When I saw Kav and Liam waiting to come on, I thought it would be me coming off, but thankfully the gaffer kept me on.'

And the goal? 'I just turned and saw there was a little space to shoot at.' Easy as that. It was his third of the season, and all three had been spectacular.

The momentum had taken a decisive shift Sunderland's way. This was like watching United in their pomp, pummelling an opponent into submission in an eternal final few minutes. Caldwell made a superb tackle to deny Jones as Sunderland were caught up field, but the equaliser did arrive, deep in injury-time. As Ward's long clearance was nodded on, Connolly took a touch to set himself, then looped an arcing drive across Danny Coyne and into the top corner. 'We had loads of fans there,' Connolly said. 'The whole stand was packed, and it would have been a shame for them to come all the way here and watch us roll over. I was thinking before the game that I'd not had the opportunity to go over to the fans after I'd scored. So I decided that if I scored I would do it.'

As the *Sunderland Echo* commented, Keane's side suddenly seemed bullet-proof. 'In terms of getting a result when we don't play well,' Keane said, 'it was pleasing. We keep giving ourselves mountains to climb, but to be fair to the players, we keep climbing them. People will remember Grant and Dave for the goals, but I'll also remember two saving tackles from Steve Caldwell.'

Saturday, 16 December, Championship

Burnley	2-2	Sunderland
Lafferty 9, 52		Leadbitter 80
		Connolly 90

Burnley: Coyne, Thomas, McGreal, Duff, McCann, Elliott (Spicer 66), Hyde, Mahon, Jones, Lafferty, Noel-Williams (Branch 90)
Subs Not Used: Sinclair, Garreth O'Connor, Foster
Sunderland: Ward, Whitehead, Caldwell, Varga, D Collins, S Elliott, Leadbitter, Yorke (L Miller 62), Wallace (Kavanagh 62), Murphy (Hysen 74), Connolly
Subs Not Used: Nyatanga, Fulop.
Ref: M Dean (Wirral)
Booked: Hyde (Burnley); Yorke, Caldwell (Sunderland)
Att: 14,798
League position: 11

A wrongly neglected area, Keane had said, and he was right. Perhaps there is an element of provincial chippiness about this, but, as Bryan Talbot's brilliant comic novel *Alice in Sunderland* sets out in the course of arguing that Alice's Wearside roots are overlooked as part of an Oxford conspiracy, just about the only people who haven't neglected the area are the Normans, who razed Sunderland twice before building a new castle on the Tyne to ensure the subjugation of the North, and the Germans, who bombed it so heavily during the Second World War that 267 civilians were killed, and over 4,000 houses destroyed or significantly damaged.

The decline over the past 100 years has been obscene. In the late seventh century, Sunderland – or at least the monastery of St Peter at Monkwearmouth – was one of the foremost centres of learning in Europe. St Peter's was the first building in Britain to have stained glass windows. For much of the late second millennium Sunderland was one of the world's greatest industrial cities. Yet, by the late twentieth century, it was notable only for having achieved the unique double of being both the largest city in Europe without a cinema and the largest city in Europe without a mainline rail station. It had become a poor adjunct of Newcastle, not even connected to the Tyne-Wear Metro until 2002, 22 years after it had opened.

Bede, one of the greatest of all British intellectuals, was born near St Peter's. He entered the monastery as a seven year old, became deacon at 19 and priest at 30. It was his scholastic achievements, though, for which he is remarkable. He was 59 when he finished the *Historia Ecclesiastica Gentis Anglorum* (*Ecclesiastical History of the English Peoples*), an astonishing work that references not merely the church fathers, but also classical writers such as Horace and Lucretius. Using unprecedented techniques for assessing the value of evidence – and so gaining a reputation as the 'father of history' – he set down in writing for the first time the notion of Englishness, and also began the practice of dating events since the birth of Christ. Most modern accounts suggest he spent the majority of his adult life at St Paul's at Jarrow, St Peter's sister monastery. Certainly he seems to have followed the abbot Ceolfrith there at the age of 12, after the death of Benedict Biscop, who had founded the monasteries and brought the glassmakers over from Italy. After that, though, evidence is scarce and what is odd is the idea that he stayed on Tyneside, when the great library was at St Peter's. Nonetheless, the tourist attraction of Bedeworld is in Jarrow, not Monkwearmouth.

The neglect is universal. Who invented the light bulb? Thomas Edison? Nope: it was Joseph Swan, born in Bishopwearmouth, and royally stitched up by Edison. First secretary of the Football Association, father of the FA Cup, and international football? Charles William Alcock, born in Sunderland. Then there's America. George Washington's family came originally from Wearside, and the Stars and Stripes takes its basic design from his coat of arms.

So having given only football, the modern calendar, historiography, electric light, the USA and England to the world, it's understandable people should think Sunderland not worth bothering about.

[8]

CHRISTMAS WOBBLE

Selhurst Park has never been good to Sunderland. It's never really been good to anybody. It's a horrible place, and it offers a disturbing vision of the future. This is what life will be like when the world has become a giant sprawl of suburbia. Its traffic jams are eternal. Eerily calm men in suits hang around outside churches with unlikely names. Even in midwinter, the whole place is redolent of fresh creosote and dismal barbeques. Nothing quite seems to function. The platform at Selhurst station is so low in comparison to the trains that stop there that the very young and the very old have to be lifted down. The stewards are the biggest jobsworths in the country, probably the world, and seem inordinately proud of the accolade, strutting with self-importance, puffed up like a blackbird after a particularly satisfying bath. Even the pitch has a sponginess that seems to suck the life out of games.

Sunderland fans probably hate it more than most, though. Just as they have become experts in promotion, so they are connoisseurs of relegation, and they haven't known one worse than Selhurst Park 1997. Some relegations linger fondly in the memory as poignant outpourings of pride. Mention Maine Road 1991 to those who were there, and even now they will have to choke back the tears. Officially there were seventeen thousand Sunderland fans among the 39,000 attendance on the final day of the season; in reality there were many more. A goalless draw against the champions Arsenal a week earlier had put Sunderland level on points with Luton Town, with the same goal-difference. Luton, though, had scored four goals more, meaning that if Sunderland were to stay up, they needed a better result away at Manchester City than Luton achieved at home to Derby, who were already relegated.

For about a minute, it even looked possible, as Marco Gabbiadini's equaliser was rapidly followed by a diving header from Gary Bennett. That should have been omen enough – the last time he'd scored one like that had been in the heartbreaking 4-3 play-off semifinal second-leg victory over Gillingham in 1987, when Sunderland became the only team ever relegated on the away goals rule. Even as Sunderland fans celebrated, City levelled, and by the time Niall Quinn – football again offering the illusion of meaning through its interconnectedness – added his second of the game to make it 3-2 late on, the news that Luton were leading 2-0 had rendered it academic.

That was a day that lives on in the collective memory of Sunderland as a festival of fandom. That had been a remarkable, ridiculous season. Sunderland had finished a distant sixth the previous year, had beaten Newcastle in the play-off semifinal (0-0 at Roker, with Paul Hardyman sent off for kicking John Burridge in the head after missing a last-minute penalty; a glorious 2-0 at St James' – Gates 13, Gabbiadini 85, as it is tattooed into the consciousness of any Wearsider sentient at the time), before losing to Swindon in the play-off final thanks to an own goal from – well, who else? – Gary Bennett. Swindon, though, were then found guilty of making illegal payments to players, and Sunderland, with a palpably inadequate squad, were promoted in their place. There was an acceptance of the likelihood of relegation from the offset, but rather than the despondency of 2005, it provoked a fey sense of carnival. If Sunderland were going to tilt at windmills, they were determined to enjoy it. The statistics speak of a lack of goals, only 38 scored in 38 games, but that was a season char-acterised by ebullient away support and epic topsy-turvy matches: the defeat at Maine Road was Sunderland's fourth 3-2 reverse of the season, and there were also two 3-3 and two 2-2 draws. There was an over-riding sense of fun, and the final day spoke of defiance as fans gloried in what they saw as hero-ic failure. Perhaps, in retrospect, that was Sunderland in what Keane would later dismiss in the Irish as 'happy camper' mode. Convince yourself it's all a lark and you probably shouldn't be there in the first place, and you are insulated against the pain of disappointment. Keane, in his autobiogra-phy, speaks of how footballers must never allow themselves to recognise the 'childishness' of what they do for a living; great-ness, for him, comes from the fear of just that pain. Maine Road 1991 was one of the great days, but it was also a day that explained why Sunderland were doomed to yo-yo. Perhaps, in the economic circumstances it was realism, but it also demon-strated an acceptance of failure. Perhaps that is even prefer-able, for failure is far more common than success, but Keane would not have tolerated it.

Still, however you looked at it, Maine Road 1991 was better than Selhurst Park 1997, where there was no fun, little pride, and not much in the way of defiance. That was simply a day of failure. The emotion had come the previous week, in the final game at Roker Park before the move to the Stadium of Light. As Chris Waddle scored his only goal for the club he had sup-ported as a boy, a free-kick arrowed into the top corner,

Sunderland, carried on a wave of nostalgia, produced their best performance of the season in beating Everton 3-0. The hard part seemed to have been done. That lifted them to 40 points, the traditional target for teams looking to avoid the drop and, crucially, two points clear of Coventry in the third relegation place. To stay up, Coventry had to beat Tottenham away on the final day, and hope Sunderland did not beat Wimbledon.

Abjectly, Sunderland lost 1-0, but that wasn't the worst of it. Coventry's game, as it had 20 years previously when they had conspired with Bristol City, kicked off late. The abiding memory of Maine Road had been the seething mass of candy-stripes after Bennett's goal; at Selhurst Park it was of the wait after the game had finished, sitting, minute after agonising minute, for confirmation from White Hart Lane. The Sunderland centre-forward Craig Russell slumped disconsolately on the pitch, watching fans in the stand listening nervously to their radios, waiting, praying for a Tottenham equaliser. It never came. Coventry won 2-1 and Sunderland, once again, were relegated.

December 2006 at Selhurst Park was only marginally better. With the fixture brought forward to the Friday for television, a win would have lifted Sunderland level on points with Colchester in sixth, but their seven-game unbeaten run came to a glum end. Fog had threatened a cancellation, but with it lifting partly so only isolated sections of the pitch remained invisible, the game went ahead. As Croydon enacted its vampiric effect, Sunderland wished it hadn't: they had more of the ball and the territorial advantage, but they seemed one-paced and bereft of imagination. Liam Miller dragged an effort wide from no more than a dozen yards, eight minutes in, and, although Dean Whitehead and Stan Varga both went close with second-half headers, they never had a better chance.

Palace's threat was even more limited, but they got the only goal of the game four minutes before half-time. Shefki Kuqi held off Whitehead to nod Danny Butterfield's cross back for Mark Hudson, and the centre-back, unmarked at the edge of the box, beat Ward with a crisp falling volley.

Other managers might have pointed out how their side had dominated the statistics, but Keane was unflinching. 'We didn't deserve anything,' he said. 'You have to earn the right to win a game of football and it just passed us by, which makes it all the more frustrating. We started slowly. We were expecting someone else to do it, but our players have got to step up to the plate. The game was there for the taking; there's no doubt about that. We were looking to go on to the next step in terms of getting near the play-offs, but clearly we're not ready for that. Some of our players aren't ready for the next challenge. You've got to take risks in football, especially in the attacking third. We got into decent positions, but we ended up going back towards our own goal and that's no good. You want players who can go and try something, and if they're trying to do that they can't be criticised. But if they keep going back to the keeper they will be criticised – because anyone can do that, and we don't want that at Sunderland.'

Friday, 22 December, Championship

Crystal Palace   1-0   **Sunderland**
Hudson 41

Crystal Palace: Speroni, Ward, Hudson, Butterfield, Borrowdale, McAnuff, Soares, Fletcher, Kennedy (Lawrence 89), Morrison (Freedman 83), Kuqi (Scowcroft 71)
Subs Not Used: Flinders, Reich
Sunderland: Ward, Caldwell, Varga, Nosworthy, D Collins, Whitehead, Leadbitter (Wallace 60), Kavanagh, L Miller (Yorke 75), Murphy (Brown 75), Connolly
Subs Not Used: Fulop, Nyatanga
Ref: L Probert (Gloucestershire)
Booked: Fletcher (Palace); Varga (Sunderland)
Att: 17,439
League position: 11

The Boxing Day defeat to Leeds has become almost as much a part of Christmas tradition on Wearside as the charity dip in the North Sea that precedes it. Sunderland had lost seven of their previous eight home league games against Leeds, the last two of those coming on 26 December. Arguably, it was the defeat in 2002 that had relegated Sunderland that season. Leading 1-0 through Michael Proctor's goal, they then conceded to James Milner, making him, at the time, the Premiership's youngest goal scorer, before Robbie Fowler converted a penalty three minutes after arriving as a substitute. Sunderland went on to take just one more point all season.

At last there came a win, but, while it was comfortable enough, that had more to do with Leeds's manifold inadequacies as any great improvement on Sunderland's part. It certainly was nothing like the 3-0 victory at Elland Road in Keane's second game. For around an hour it was the same story as at Palace: a lot of huff and puff, not a lot of quality and the teasing question of how a side that ordinary could possibly draw a crowd in excess of 40,000. Everything changed, though, with the introduction of Ross Wallace, who had been left on the bench for a second successive game. That was widely perceived as an expression of frustration at his inconsistency, but Keane revealed that illness would probably have prevented him playing a full game anyway. After a bright start to his time at Sunderland, his form had drifted, but his pace and his willingness to get behind Leeds gave Sunderland an extra dimension. 'I have been a bit disappointed in my performances,' he acknowledged. 'I know I have to improve. I don't think I have played as well as I can, and I have to show the manager that I should get a place in the team.'

As Wallace's imagination on the left forced Leeds deeper, space opened up for Dwight Yorke, who had been ineffective until then, and his quality finally began to emerge. David Connolly took most of the credit for his opportunism in scoring the opener, but the build-up was all about Yorke and his ability to stitch passages of play together. Receiving the ball from Dean Whitehead, he exchanged passes with Connolly, delayed a fraction, and then played a perfectly calibrated ball into the box for the on-rushing forward. Connolly seemed to be too near the goal line for anything but a cross, but, as Daniel Nardiello had from a similar position for Barnsley a month earlier, he turned back inside Matt Heath, and slid a shot in at Tony Warner's near post. 'He's actually disappointed because he thinks he should have got two or three,' Keane said. 'But I'd rather give him credit for the one he did get.'

Yorke played his part in the second, too, combining with Liam Miller to feed Daryl Murphy. As he cut infield the ball ran slightly ahead of him, falling conveniently into the path of Grant Leadbitter, who sent another of his speciality 20-yard drives fizzing just inside the post. Two great goals, and with Leeds so demoralised as to be almost supine, the game was won. The sense that they had suffered a total meltdown of discipline was confirmed as their assistant manager, Gus Poyet, was sent off for throwing a spare ball on to the pitch in an attempt to stop a Sunderland attack, apparently believing his action was justified because a home fan had done similarly a few minutes earlier. When a coach can't see that he and a supporter have utterly different moral responsibilities, a club really is in trouble. While the home fans delighted in Leeds's humiliation, it also served to highlight the effectiveness of Keane's minimalist approach to touchline emotion. It is surely easier for a man who looks in control to be in control.

Tuesday, 26 December, Championship

Sunderland   2-0   Leeds United
Connolly 65
Leadbitter 81

Sunderland: Ward, Whitehead, Varga, Caldwell, Nyatanga (D Collins 58), S Elliott
(Wallace 58), Leadbitter, Yorke, L Miller, Murphy (Hysen 90), Connolly
Subs Not Used: Fulop, Nosworthy
Leeds: Warner, Richardson, Heath, Ehiogu (Kilgallon 72), Foxe, Lewis, Douglas, Derry
(Healy 72), Westlake, Kandol, Beckford (Moore 72)
Subs Not Used: Sullivan, Howson
Ref: G Salisbury (Lancashire)
Booked: Douglas (Leeds)
Att: 40,116
League position: 11

After one FA Cup final victim, the other. Beating Preston in
1937 was no shock, but it did end what seemed, at the time, an
unfeasibly long run without a Cup success for the six-times
league champions. Preston, perhaps, could be grateful it was-
n't eight-times. Sunderland had applied to join the league in its
inaugural season in 1888-89, but had been denied entry on the
grounds that they were too far away (which seems rather to
undermine the suggestion that 1888 saw the birth of a 'national' league), and Preston won the first two so-called titles (the
Midlands/North-West Combination, as it should surely now
be recognised). Sunderland were finally admitted the following
year, and went on to win three championships in their first five
seasons with their 'Team of all the Talents', so called because,
after seeing his team beaten 7-2 by Sunderland in 1890, the
Aston Villa director William McGregor was heard to comment
that 'they have a talented man in every position'. There was
even a poem written about them:

The team of all the talent,
The cream of all the land,
The best of forwards, halves and defence,
Picked by a master's hand.
The League is at their mercy,
Should one team make a slip,
And surely now can nothing
Stand twixt cup and lip.

Not now they'd been admitted to the league, anyway. Sunderland may not have won either of those first two titles, but it is hard to believe they would not have been challenging, particularly given they beat Preston 3-1 shortly after they'd won the double in 1889.

When Frank O'Donnell put Preston ahead just before half-time in that 1937 final, it seemed Sunderland, inexplicably flat, were going to suffer again the heartache of 1913, when they had been denied the double by Aston Villa. That great team, still unfulfilled, had been broken up by the War, and it had taken two decades to form one of even vaguely comparable quality; this one, at least, league champions in 1936, would win one more trophy before war again tore everything apart. The wing-halves, Charlie Thomson and Sandy McNab, were born anew at half-time, and, six minutes into the second period, Sunderland had their equaliser, Bobby Gurney, the goalscorer supreme, glancing in Raich Carter's header from a corner. It was Carter himself, the cerebral inside-forward who had married on the Monday before the final, who got the second, before Eddie Burbanks, who would go on to score Sunderland's last goal before the war and their first goal after it, sealed the victory with a third from a tight angle. In Sunderland, it is said, streets that had been empty for the duration of the game as everybody gathered around radios, spontaneously filled in celebration.

Sunderland returned home by train to a reception of pride and relief. From Darlington north the tracks were lined with well-wishers, while there were so many fans at Newcastle station that it took the team 25 minutes to reach their connection to Monkwearmouth. Tugs and vessels on the Wear tooted in acknowledgement as they crossed the bridge in four coaches, before squeezing down Fawcett Street which was, it is said, lined 30 deep on either side. 'Sunderland had gone crazy,' said Carter. 'My arms ached from holding aloft the Cup. This was my home town and these were my own folk. I was the local boy who had led the team to victory and brought home the Cup for which they had been waiting for fifty years. What more could any man ask?' The procession, looping back, moved on through the throng on Bridge Street, Roker Avenue and Brandling Street to Roker Park, where there were 20,000 to welcome them. And then it was on to the main business at the Trade Union Club on Frederick Street, where a bottle of beer had been kept since the defeat in the 1913 final. The curse seemingly lifted, Carter and the rest of the team drunk away its memory.

The final game of 2006 brought no such joy. It rather highlighted the problems that had blighted Sunderland since Keane's arrival – a defensive sloppiness and an inability to turn possession into chances. With Dean Whitehead again drafted in at right-back, and Nyron Nosworthy starting in an unfamiliar position on the left, it came as little surprise that Keane was in talks with Manchester United to sign two defenders – Jonny Evans and Phil Bardsley – on loan until the end of the season. Nobody but Darren Ward reacted as Danny Pugh hooked the ball over an advancing defence and, as Brett Ormerod, denied a clear strike by Ward, hooked the ball across goal, David

Nugent arrived ahead of Nosworthy to nod over the line. 'You can't expect to come from behind every week and keep climbing the league,' admitted David Connolly. 'It's a big loss and it's left us with more ground to make up. We threw everything at them in the second half, but it just wouldn't go in for us. We didn't have any clear-cut chances.'

Saturday, 30 December, Championship

Sunderland   **0-1**   **Preston North End**
Nugent 36

Sunderland: Ward, Whitehead, Caldwell (Nyatanga 16), Varga, Nosworthy, L Miller, Yorke (S Elliott 46), Leadbitter, Wallace (Brown 67), Murphy, Connolly
Subs Not Used: Fulop, Hysen
Preston: Nash, Alexander, St Ledger, Chilvers, Hill, Sedgwick, Miller, Davidson, Pugh, Ormerod (Anyinsah 81), Nugent (L Neal 90)
Subs Not Used: Lonergan, Wilson, McGrail
Ref: C Foy (Merseyside)
Booked: None
Att: 30,460
League position: 12

Keane accepted much of the blame himself, admitting it had been 'a mistake' to allow ten players to leave on loan. 'I need to bring players back,' he said. 'We've been down to the bare bones and a club like Sunderland shouldn't be in that situation. I take responsibility for that because I allowed those players to go out on loan.' He hardly helped the situation, though, by immediately allowing Robbie Elliott to leave, the former Newcastle player joining Leeds after Sunderland decided not to prolong his month-to-month contract.

So the year ended with Sunderland in twelfth with 37 points from 26 games, ten points behind Preston in second. Two defeats in three games had dampened much of the optimism generated in the seven-match unbeaten run that had preceded it, and most fans looked to the play-offs at best.

To the left, the beach stretches north, rounding Roker Cliff Park, the headland dominated by the old lighthouse that used to stand at the end of the South Pier, then on to Seaburn, and the site of Sunderland's great doomed attempt to drag itself upwards in the Eighties. Outside what is now the Marriott Hotel there is a roundabout. It used to be the biggest fountain in Europe.

As the mines and the shipyards closed and unemployment mounted, Sunderland, inspired by the MEP Alan Donnelly, constructed a fountain that had a greater throughput of water per minute than any other on the continent. The problem is that fountains are judged not by size, but by beauty. We may not have had a cinema or a mainline railway station, but we did have a very big hosepipe with a very ugly sprinkler-head attached.

That would have been bad enough, even without the fact that the fountain was stuck in the middle of a busy road junction about 20 yards from the North Sea.

Traffic aside, it is a beautiful spot, but much of the appeal lies in its ruggedness, in the way that when the wind is up, the waves lash against the sea-wall and grasp at the land with great claws of spume. This being the North Sea, the wind is up a lot, and wind tends to blow things around, even the water produced by the biggest fountain in Europe. When the fountain is in the middle of a roundabout, that can dangerously reduce visibility for drivers – especially when the gag of tipping a box of washing powder into the churning water never diminishes in hilarity. Eventually, the roundabout was grassed over, and, like an abbreviated chimney, it stands now as a bizarre reminder of the idiocy of the Eighties.

I turned right, past two crows fighting over a polystyrene tray of last night's half-eaten chips, and towards a far more successful redevelopment where the old North Dock used to be. The marina, crammed with small yachts and ringed by a genuinely tasteful range of housing, feels somehow incongruous. The red-tiled roofs recall Whitby or one of the other villages a little further down the coast, but that morning as the water lapped gently round the dozens of boats, only the grey skies spoiled the illusion that this could be some favoured corner of the Mediterranean.

The bank climbs away from the marina, up to Look Out Hill, which would offer a fine panorama of the estuary were it not for the aspen and the hawthorn that have overwhelmed the area. This is deeply irritating. The riverbank should be spectacular, but the shrubs are overgrown and strewn with litter, and anything not organic is daubed with graffiti; having invested in doing the area up, why has more not been done to keep it looking good? On the highest point stands a sculpture of a telescope, pointing straight into the shrubs, and alongside it, carved of stone, a stool, a Gladstone bag, a picnic hamper and diary, part of the Sculpture Trail that dots the north bank. Two centuries ago, a gun battery stood near here, defending the port against naval attack, initially from the privateer John Paul Jones, who carried out raids down the east coast in support of the Americans during the War of Independence. A similar battery stood across the river, and it was there, local legend has it, that a soldier on watch duty, startled by the mewing of a black cat after falling into a drunken sleep one moonlit night, insisted he'd been approached by the devil incarnate. From then on, it became known as the Black Cat Battery, and the black cat took a central place in the folklore of Wearside and, particularly, its football.

In 1905, a little over 100 years later, a cartoon of the club's chairman, Frederick William Taylor, a local businessman, depicted him by a football on which sat a black cat. In 1908-09 a black cat featured in the official team photograph and, confusingly, a later postcard entitled 'The Original Black Cat and Kittens' shows several players surrounding a cat and its litter. From the players featured, the photograph appears to have been taken sometime between 1911 and 1913. Several fans travelling to Newcastle for an FA Cup tie in March 1909 took with them images of black cats done up with red ribbons, while the *Sunderland Echo* reported that crowds who saw off the team as they left Monkwearmouth station bound for the 1913 Cup final 'prominently sported button-holes of red and white flowers and ties of club colours, each decorated with a tie-pin composed of a black cat'. Match programmes of the 1930s frequently featured cats on their covers, while a 12-year-old fan called Billy Morris smuggled a black kitten – a red and white ribbon around its neck – into Wembley for the 1937 FA Cup final. The supporters' club adopted the logo in the 1960s, and the club finally took up the nickname following a vote in 1997. Dreadful modern marketing said some, but the tradition is secure.

[9]

NEW YEAR, NEW HOPE

Leicester was the beginning. Nobody – with the possible exception of David Connolly, who mentioned the phrase 'top-two finish' every time he came within sight of a microphone, and perhaps Keane himself – saw it coming, and even after it had begun, it was a long time before anybody recognised the fact. The statistics are there, though, irrefutable: after the indifferent Christmas, the long surge to the summit began at the Walkers Stadium on New Year's Day.

Sunderland's victory, although it was only sealed with two goals in the final 11 minutes, represented probably their best performance of the season to that point. Still, even the *Sunderland Echo*, usually such a tub-thumping outlet for optimism, was saying no more than, if performances like that could be maintained, the club 'could still mount a genuine bid for promotion'. The biggest doubts concerned their potency in front of goal. Having dominated so comprehensively, the critics asked, just why had it taken them until the 79th minute to open the scoring?

Even when they did finally take the lead, the fates, it seemed, had done their best to deny them. Dean Whitehead, overlapping from full-back, sent in a fine cross to the near post, where a stretching Daryl Murphy stabbed a volley against the bar.

The rebound eluded Grant Leadbitter, but fell for Tobias Hysen to head in his first goal since he had equalised against Leicester at the Stadium of Light earlier in the season. 'I should have got three or four goals in the game,' the Swede said, 'but that's what happens when you haven't been involved for a while. I snatched at a couple when I should have done better. We were always on top, but we didn't take the chances and their keeper did well a couple of times.'

Hysen also had his part to play in the second four minutes later; his header from Paul Henderson's clearance sending Murphy through one-on-one against the keeper. Henderson saved, and as Murphy closed in on the rebound, he responded sharply to hack the ball away. It fell, though, for Connolly, who swept the ball into an empty net. 'There is great belief in the squad,' Hysen went on. 'We always feel we can get goals late in games if we need them.'

Monday, 1 January, Championship

Leicester City   0-2   Sunderland
Hysen 79
Connolly 83

Leicester: Henderson, Stearman, McCarthy, Kisnorbo, Kenton, Hughes, Wesolowski (Cadamarteri 62), Williams, Porter, Fryatt, O'Grady (Hume 62)
Subs Not Used: Logan, Tiatto, Maybury.
Sunderland: Ward, Whitehead, Varga, Nyatanga, Wallace, S Elliott, Yorke (Leadbitter 60), L Miller, Hysen (Hartley 84), Brown (Murphy 59), Connolly
Subs Not Used: Fulop, Welsh
Ref: S Mathieson (Cheshire)
Booked: Kenton (Leicester); Whitehead (Sunderland)
Att: 21,975
League position: 10

The Leicester game set the tone for the new year on the pitch, and it wasn't long before a positive note was struck off it as well, as Carlos Edwards arrived in a £1.4million deal from

Luton, whose manager Mike Newell announced how impressed he'd been by Sunderland's professionalism and openness in completing the deal – rare praise from a man who had frequently accused his fellow managers of sharp practice. 'I'm sure they'd been watching him before that, but I got a phone call a week or so after we played them from Roy Keane,' he said. 'The way they went about their business and the way they did everything was what you would expect of a top club.' The right-side of midfield had been a problem position from the start of the season, and Edwards was to add the sort of creative thrust from wide areas that had been so lacking in Sunderland's struggles to turn possession into chances. Keane spoke of his delight at signing a player who had been targeted by a number of clubs after his impressive performances for Trinidad and Tobago at the World Cup, while Edwards revealed that it had been his international team-mate Dwight Yorke who had persuaded him to join. 'Dwight had a huge part to play,' he said. 'He told me he has been at other clubs like Manchester United and Aston Villa, but he has never seen facilities like he has at Sunderland.'

To rather less fanfare, although his eventual impact would be just as great, Jonny Evans arrived on loan from Manchester United a day later. Keane spoke of his 'delight' at acquiring a player of such quality. 'He's going to be a top, top player,' he said. 'Unfortunately, it's probably going to be for United, not for Sunderland. He's got talent and that's important, but the most important thing if you want to be a top player is mental strength and he's got that. He's not a cocky lad.'

Most Sunderland fans knew little of the Northern Ireland defender, but they soon would. By the end of the season there were even those who would swear he was a match for Shaun Elliott, the very idea of which at one time would have seemed blasphemous. Evans practically committed blasphemy himself in his first interview, when, after dropping in the usual platitudes about how great Niall Quinn and Kevin Phillips had been, he compared Sunderland to Royal Antwerp, where he had spent the early part of the season on loan. 'They're a big club,' he said. 'They're in the second division, but they really belong in the top division.' More encouraging was the revelation that he had bumped into Keane in a cinema in the summer, and chatted to him about his future, something that added to the feeling of everything slotting together as though to some greater plan. The sense of design may have been bogus, but it was reassuring.

There was still one setback to come, but it was the sort of setback that can be a blessing: defeat in the Cup to Preston. Could Sunderland have maintained their charge with the distraction of a Cup run? Well, possibly, but they didn't have to. Three years earlier, McCarthy's side had lost in the semifinal of both the FA Cup and the play-offs, and the anti-climactic end to that season was fresh enough in the mind to leave fans well aware of the dangers of fighting on two fronts.

Still, a third defeat in a season to Preston, title-thieves, was frustrating. Sunderland had had the better of the opening half-hour, but fell behind on 31 minutes as Brett Ormerod latched on to Callum Davidson's through-ball, rounded Darren Ward, and guided his shot past Evans on the line. 'It's like déjà vu from last week,' Keane said. 'It was a sloppy goal. We gave away possession and then we tried to play offside. When a player has time on the ball like that it's always dangerous. One mistake and we got punished. There was a warning sign before the goal, and I wasn't sure why we were still trying to play offside. I don't encourage that.'

Six minutes later Liam Miller scythed down David Nugent,

was shown a second yellow card, and the game was as good as over. 'I've no complaints about the sending-off,' said Keane. 'Liam set himself up with the first yellow card and then the referee made the right decision, but that left us with a mountain to climb.'

Saturday, 6 January, FA Cup third round

Preston North End   1-0   Sunderland
Ormerod 31

Preston: Nash, Alexander, Chilvers, Wilson, Hill (Whaley 56), Sedgwick (L Neal 72), McKenna, Davidson, Pugh, Ormerod (Anyinsah 79), Nugent
Subs Not Used: Lonergan, McGrail
Sunderland: Ward, Whitehead, Varga, Evans, Wallace, S Elliott, Leadbitter (D Collins 77), L Miller, Hysen (Yorke 39), Connolly, Murphy (Edwards 61)
Subs Not Used: Clarke, Fulop
Ref: I Williamson (Berkshire)
Sent Off: L Miller 37 (Sunderland)
Booked: Pugh, Nugent (Preston); L Miller, Varga (Sunderland)
Att: 10,318

Within two days, though, there was more good news, as Sunderland signed the 18-year-old Irish forward Anthony Stokes from Arsenal for £2million. After becoming, while on loan at Falkirk, the first player to score back-to-back hat tricks in the Scottish Premier League on his way to 16 goals in 18 appearances, he had looked set to join Celtic, before the Keane factor had the desired effect. 'I spoke to Roy Keane about everything,' he said. 'He told me his hopes for the club and that helped make up my mind. I'm very excited about the move. The fact that there are such strong Irish connections at Sunderland helped me to make the decision because that's going to make it easier to settle in.' Even better, the omen-hunters noted, he shares a birthday with Kevin Phillips.

As Stokes arrived, and the signing of Carlos Edwards freed Stephen Elliott to play as a centre-forward, so Keane felt in a position to allow other forwards to depart. Chris Brown, the last of the sex-video quartet still at the club, left for Norwich, while Jon Stead, his loan spell at Derby complete, was sold to Sheffield United.

Stokes spoke optimistically on his arrival of Sunderland being just three points of the play-offs, but, perhaps emboldened by the performance in the away win over Leicester, Keane was talking tough ahead of the visit of Ipswich. 'Any more defeats are going to be difficult to make up,' he said, drawing attention to the fact that Sunderland had lost more often than any other team in the top half of the table. 'We've had one or two disappointments when we've given bad goals away, and one of them was at Ipswich. We can't afford any more slip-ups like that, giving two or three sloppy goals away. If you do that, you're going to get nowhere as a team.' His belief that a top-two place was a possibility, though, remained undimmed.

That would take several weeks, but Sunderland at least climbed into the top ten for the first time with a 1-0 victory over Ipswich. Windy conditions meant the performance was never going to hit any great heights, but there was sufficient to suggest the impact Keane's new signings could have. Stokes left the field to a standing ovation when he was substituted two minutes from time, and it was his combination down the right with another new signing, Carlos Edwards, that led to the only goal as Stokes outpaced Dan Harding before crossing for Connolly to side-foot in his fifth in eight games. 'Dave Connolly showed his experience,' Stokes said. 'He pulled away at the back post and the defenders didn't track him. Obviously there are four strikers here and there will be different partnerships, but Dave is a great striker to work with.'

Saturday, 13 January, Championship

Sunderland   1-0   Ipswich Town
Connolly 13

Sunderland: Ward, Whitehead, Evans, Nosworthy, Wallace (D Collins 66), Edwards,
  Leadbitter, Yorke, Hysen (Murphy 64), Stokes (S Elliott 88), Connolly
Subs Not Used: Fulop, Clarke
Ipswich: Price, Wright, Naylor, De Vos, Harding, Roberts (Clarke 81), Williams,
  Legwinski, Garvan (Currie 71), Richards (Haynes 61), Lee
Subs Not Used: Supple, Bruce
Ref: L Mason (Lancashire)
Booked: Yorke (Sunderland); Roberts (Ipswich)
Att: 27,604
League position: 9

Victory had been good, but had it really been that good? The
behaviour of crowds continues to defy explanation. Why then?
What was the spark that sent a manic optimism fizzing
through Wearside again? What had people seen in a wind-
blasted 1-0 win over Ipswich that suddenly persuaded people
that this was for real? After all, on the face of it, things were
little brighter than they had been before. The debts still stood
at £40million, they were out of the FA Cup, and they remained
ten points behind the league leaders Birmingham. And yet
somehow, somewhere, the collective pulse had been set throb-
bing, and over 6,000 Sunderland fans bought tickets for the
away game at Sheffield Wednesday. Even Keane sounded
impressed, possibly moved, by such a show of faith. 'There's
not many clubs could do that,' he said, which is probably for
the best. Why would people flock to watch the team ninth in
the second flight play the team 11th in the second flight? Was
it really just the boost of seven wins in 11 Championship
games? 'Quite a feel-good factor around the club,' was Keane's
dry explanation. When it was announced that an extra 150
tickets would be put on sale at two o'clock on the Tuesday

afternoon, people began queuing at ten in the morning. This was mass hysteria on the scale of the Salem witch-trials. Weirdly, it turned out to be justified.

Perhaps it could be explained by the fact that comebacks are such a feature of the history of the club. Recent history provided the examples of 2003-04, 1997-98 and 1975-76, when appalling starts had given way to much-improved form, but the greatest of them all came in 1912-13. Sunderland had not won the league since 1902 and after seven years in the job the pressure was beginning to mount on Bob Kyle, Sunderland's first Irish manager (and the only non-Scot to hold the role until the arrival of Alan Brown in 1957). The season could hardly have begun worse. A 1-1 draw against Newcastle was followed by defeats to Blackburn, Derby and Blackburn again, at which the directors sacked the goalkeeper, Walter 'Buns' Scott.

Sunderland lost 3-0 at Oldham, and drew 2-2 at home to Tottenham. Kyle then brought in a new goalkeeper, signing the former miner Joe Butler from Glossop North End. He made his debut in a 2-0 defeat at Chelsea, but the arrival of the full-back Charlie Gladwin from Blackpool turned the season around. Having taken two points from their opening seven games, Sunderland suddenly won five games in a row and, with Charlie Buchan and Jackie Mordue in their pomp on the right flank, went on to lose just two of their final 23 games, clinching the title with a 3-1 win at Bolton in their penultimate game.

Keane, at least, had started the recovery a little earlier. 'I'm reasonably happy with how things are developing,' he said. 'You don't really get time to reflect, there's that much happening.' So much, in fact, that in an unguarded moment he spoke of 'upheaval'. 'We're taking baby steps, and we made another few steps last week in terms of getting a good result, and three lads making their home debuts. I've never been one for looking too far down the road. Maybe you have to change that a little as a manager. The changes we have made have all felt to be right, whether it's players coming or going, changes in the staff.'

Keane had repeated again and again since his arrival that 'change is good', but, in hindsight, the scale of the changes had been extraordinary. In a little over six months of Quinn's leadership, there had been 28 permanent deals involving players either coming or going, not to mention 15 loans. 'Maybe three, four months ago I wouldn't have thought there'd be that many but it's just happened, natural progression,' Keane said. 'Hopefully all those changes have been spot-on.'

He was rather less sanguine after the game, after a sloppy performance that nonetheless brought a 4-2 win. It would seem uncharacteristic, but perhaps Keane for once felt the pressure of expectation, as he lost his temper for the third and – he subsequently claimed – final time that season. Even in that, he won the favour of the fans. Scales were being lifted from eyes: after the years and years of making the best of things, of being grateful for every win no matter what the circumstances, here at last was a manager who looked beyond the result to the performance, and who was driven to seek perfection in everything.

Sunderland's problem that afternoon was that they seemed to find it rather too easy. A cleverly worked one-two with Jonny Evans, following a short corner, laid in Dwight Yorke to loft the first over Mark Crossley after 21 minutes, and Tobias Hysen made it two on the stroke of half-time, smashing in a cross from Dean Whitehead after he had been released by David Connolly. When Connolly then converted an angled ball from Hysen just before the hour, the game seemed won.

Certainly Sunderland seemed to think so, and they eased off, allowing Wednesday to mount an improbable comeback. A Chris Brunt free-kick flashed through the wall and past a wrong-footed Darren Ward, and then Wade Small lashed in the rebound after Nyron Nosworthy had blocked a shot from Marcus Tudgay. Minds lurched back to March 1991, and the squandering of a three-goal lead away to a Dean Saunders-inspired Derby. This Sunderland, though, had the steel to regroup, and Carlos Edwards made sure of the victory in the final minute, finishing off after Crossley had palmed out a cross-cum-shot from Daryl Murphy. 'We got away with it,' Keane growled. 'We encouraged them and it annoyed me. We were sloppy. We made it a difficult situation by giving the ball away. If we'd kept passing and doing what we had been doing, we'd have won the game easily.'

Saturday, 20 January, Championship

Sheffield Wednesday	2-4	Sunderland
Brunt 82		Yorke 21
Small 87		Hysen 45
		Connolly 58
		Edwards 89

Sheff Wed: Crossley, Bullen, Coughlan (McAllister 37), O'Brien (Clarke 30), Folly, Whelan, Lunt, Brunt, Small, Tudgay, MacLean (Burton 62)
Subs Not Used: Adamson, Graham
Sunderland: Ward, Whitehead, Evans, Nosworthy, D Collins, Edwards, Hysen (Wallace 90), Yorke, L Miller (Leadbitter 63), S Elliott, Connolly (Murphy 75)
Subs Not Used: Fulop, Varga
Ref: A D'Urso (Essex)
Booked: Yorke, D Collins (Sunderland)
Att: 29,103
League position: 7

The carnival had ended in victory, and that was enough to maintain the bandwagon's momentum, but the relentless self-analysis was universal. 'We've got to look at things we can improve,' Hysen said. 'Had we kept a clean sheet, he would have been happy, but to give away two goals like that could have been very bad for us. Had they got a third goal, then it would have been a disaster in a game we controlled for eighty minutes. He was very upset about it and told us so. He is making sure we don't kid ourselves. We have to kill games off and he expects one hundred per cent work-rate. If he gets that, the results will take care of themselves. He won't settle for anything else – he is honest and says what he wants.'

Given Keane's reaction to the victory was at once both utterly characteristic and memorably unexpected, it was appropriate that it was at Hillsborough that Sunderland fans finally came up with a song with which to serenade him. As with so many of the lines that best capture a moment, it was not planned but sprang spontaneously from the away end as 'Hey Jude' was played over the PA to welcome Sheffield Wednesday back on to the field after half-time. Suddenly 'Hey Keano' had become the anthem of the season.

Understandably, a lot of the focus fell on Sunderland's travelling support. 'It was unbelievable,' said Darren Ward. 'In the first half, when we were two goals up, I had a full view of them from the other end, and it was amazing to see. The place was bouncing. The passion of the fans has struck me from the word go. In my first game at Stoke, there was a hefty following for a night match. It's brilliant for a player to be playing here.'

Still, though, Niall Quinn wanted more. The committed few may have become the committed many, dashing off on pilgrimages with the eagerness of medieval penitents, but he knew that, astonishing as it is to take 6,000 to Hillsborough, he needed more fans at home games if his economic model was to work. Being Quinn, he dressed up his marketing plea in quasi-evangelical terms he probably believed himself. 'The momentum is starting to gather pace and we need our fans to get behind the team in numbers,' he said. 'Now is the time for those who may have wavered in the past to stand up and be counted and back what we're trying to achieve here. We need to send out a statement of intent to teams coming to the Stadium of Light – the crowd made such a difference at Sheffield Wednesday and I'd like to see that replicated in home turf. The club needs the fans and now is the time to make some sacrifices and back your team.'

His words, at least then, fell largely on stony ground, and there were under 27,000 there for the visit of Crystal Palace, despite the arrival of two more new signings – the centre-forward Stern John from Coventry and the right-back Danny Simpson on loan from Manchester United. In mitigation, it was a Tuesday night, and it was against Crystal Palace. There must have been a good game between Sunderland and Palace sometime, but not in living memory. This was another stinker, Sunderland's first goalless draw in over a year being as effective a rebuttal of Quinn's case as was possible, and presumably boring the Countess of Wessex, a guest and patron of the club, sufficiently that she won't venture anywhere near a football ground in the near future. Anthony Stokes saw a goal-bound shot deflect to safety off the back of Leon Cort, but that was about it, apart from two decent shouts for penalties. Still, given Sunderland hadn't been awarded one for almost 15 months – and that in the last minute when they were already 3-0 down to Aston Villa and referees were going through a phase of giving penalties against Liam Ridgewell for just about anything – they were uttered more in hope than expectation.

Tuesday, 30 January, Championship

Sunderland   0-0   Crystal Palace

Sunderland: Ward, Whitehead, Nosworthy, Evans, D Collins, Edwards (Leadbitter 66), L Miller (Murphy 77), Yorke, Hysen (Wallace 73), Connolly, Stokes
Subs Not Used: Fulop, Simpson
Crystal Palace: Kiraly, Hudson, Butterfield, Cort, Lawrence, Green (Freedman 76), Kennedy, Fletcher, McAnuff, Ifill (Soares 74), Kuqi
Subs Not Used: Speroni, Ward, Morrison
Att: 26,958
Ref: T M Kettle (Rutland)
League position: 9

'Palace came with a game plan,' said Dean Whitehead. 'They'd had us watched, packed midfield and put nine or ten players behind the ball all the time. It was difficult to up the tempo because the pitch was terrible. We got our point and a clean sheet and it's better than nothing, but teams know what we're about. They know we're a good side when we pass it so we could be in for a frustrating few games.'

A certain amount of frustration at Sunderland's inability to make the most of their possession was understandable, but then again, it was a long time since Sunderland had gone into games in the position of being favourites and had opponents close the game down against them. 'The way Palace played, with one up front, is a mark of respect for my players, a compliment to us,' said Keane. 'You don't get anything easy in football, and I told the players that afterwards. I was probably more pleased with this performance than when we scored four at Sheffield Wednesday and won. I'm happy with the lads in terms of their effort and commitment, and I'm happy with the clean sheet and the point, but we didn't do well enough in the final third to win it.'

To outsiders it is probably laughable that Sunderland and Newcastle fans speak of themselves as supporting big clubs. After all, Sunderland last won the league in 1936, Newcastle in 1927. Newcastle's last trophy was the Fairs Cup in 1969 and Sunderland's the FA Cup in 1973, a victory that was notable, standing 'as the greatest fairy-story Wembley has ever known' (™ – everybody who's ever mentioned it in print), only because Sunderland were by then so far from the pinnacle of English football.

'It seemed as though … the experts said … it couldn't happen, except it looks as if it's going to,' a barely coherent Brian Moore roared over the closing seconds. 'They came from the Northeast with hope, and they're going to go back with the Cup … A great result for Sunderland and, with all due deference to Leeds, a great result for football.' Well, yes, all fine stirring stuff, but it is a touch patronising. And, in a sense, deservedly so. It was a great result for football purely because Sunderland were by then, in the eyes of the world south of Easington and north of Ashington, a little club – albeit it one with an unfeasibly large support.

Some statistics, then, to give a degree of legitimacy to what may otherwise seem a delusion. Sunderland have won the league six times, three of them in a four-year spell in the early 1890s when, given football barely existed outside of Britain, they could realistically claim to be the best side in the world. In 1895 they even won what was dubbed the 'championship of the world' by beating the Scottish champions Hearts 5-3 at an exhibition in Edinburgh. Up to the Second World War, only Aston Villa could match Sunderland's record of league success. Even now, Sunderland stand sixth in the all-time list.

In a table calculated from all results in the top flight of English football (using two points for a win, as that was the system under which most of those games were played), Sunderland in summer 2007 stood ninth, three places clear of Chelsea. In a table calculated using all results in all divisions Sunderland stand seventh, although the relevance of that statistic is rather undermined by the fact that two of the teams above them are Wolves and Preston. Still, they both had a two-season start, and Aston Villa are only 16 points clear, so they could be caught in 2007-08 (although with two points for a win, it would be some achievement).

Does any of that mean anything? In the modern age, probably not, other than that statistics can be twisted to mean almost anything. Still, the point is that Sunderland have a long history and, near its beginning, it was a successful one. There is a long-held expectation of achievement, which has, perhaps, become counter-productive. That is often – rightly – taken to mean that fans demand too much, too soon, but there is also a sense in which the desperation for success means it is celebrated too wildly on the odd occasion when it does arise, rather than being used as a platform for building.

That is perhaps something that has afflicted English rugby since the World Cup victory in 2003 and English cricket since the Ashes success of 2005, and it is something that comes up repeatedly when you talk to members of Sunderland's 1973 squad – a feeling that the opportunity was never seized, that, rather than investing and building, Sunderland allowed a very, very hot iron to cool. By the time promotion was achieved three years later, the moment had passed, the team was in transition, and the result was instant relegation.

10

MOMENTUM MAINTAINED

If there were fears the Crystal Palace game would prove another stutter, they were not reflected in the crowd, as 33,000 turned up for the Saturday visit of Coventry, a game that revived memories of another of Gary Bennett's greatest moments. Which Sunderland fan, after all, can think of Coventry without thinking of the infamous League Cup tie in January 1990 and the incident midway through the second half when the Coventry forward David Speedie clattered his studs into the side of Bennett's knee, a hideous challenge in any circumstances, but particularly bad given he'd just had surgery on it?

Bennett was already a huge favourite of the Sunderland fans, but it was his response that made him a legend. He was a rubber-limbed limousine of a defender who cruised through games with an aura of imperturbable calm, and even here, as he got to his feet, picked up Speedie by the throat and hurled him into the Clock Stand Paddock, there was a great sense of languid deliberation about his actions. As Speedie, falling backwards into the terracing, scrambled away from a beating, Bennett, without waiting to see the red card, began a trudge to the dressing-room that rivalled Antonio Rattin's in 1966 for prolonged outrage. He had the full width of the pitch to cross, and as he went, he unpicked the ties that held his sleeves in place, and threw them disgustedly to the ground. It was a gesture that somehow combined fury with a tremendous dignity, and as he went he kept finding new pieces of string to rip off and fling down. This was revelatory. Sunderland fans had long admired his nonchalant suppleness, but nobody had ever realised he was born not of man but of macramé. All the excitement, though, was rather ruined when Coventry won the replay 5-0.

Keane had stressed after the draw against Palace the importance of scoring an early goal, and after Sunderland had managed one, they were rewarded with a relatively comfortable 2-0 victory. It probably helped that Coventry's two goalscorers against Sunderland on the opening day had both moved on. Gary McSheffrey had been sold to Birmingham long before Stern John made the move to Wearside. John was given his debut, meaning Sunderland lined up with three Trinidad and Tobago internationals and, remarkably, only one Irishman. Keane's transfer policy had evidently broadened its scope: he was now interested in anybody from an island noted for its laid-back approach to life.

The Celtic influence was further diminished with the sale of Steve Caldwell to Burnley for £400,000, but, for all the changes to personnel, Keane was adamant that his overhaul of the club was still in its early stages. 'People think I've made lots of changes,' he said, 'but really I haven't even started. There's so much I want to do to get the club in tip-top shape and to have a real cutting edge to it. Whether it is the first team, the reserves, or the kids, you want people to sit up and take notice of Sunderland and how they are playing.'

Caldwell's departure left Keane needing a new captain, and, to nobody's great surprise, he turned to Dean Whitehead, who, in his undemonstrative way, had established himself as a reliable performer in the midfield and a minor crowd favourite since joining the club from Oxford for £150,000 in 2004. Having been linked with both Liverpool and, more realistically, Reading in the close season, he had not been fazed by dropping a division, and had been admirably willing to shift back from his preferred midfield role to cover at right-back. 'It's not too bad,' he said, 'but I'm just filling in until the other lads are back. I see it as an emergency role, and I hope the gaffer does.'

Keane, given his obsession with attitude, was understandably impressed. 'Dean has been outstanding since I came to the club,' he said. 'No one has to remind me what his preferred position is, but because of the numbers situation, we've been short at full-back. Nyron Nosworthy was set to come in and play regularly, but he picked up a knock so we had to slot Dean in at right-back. He's got the ability to do that. There's no doubt in my mind that Dean is a top-class midfielder and could hold his own in the Premiership. It just shows you what a good attitude he's got and what a good professional he is. All I can say is that you need players like that at a club if you're going to be successful.'

John was denied a scoring debut against his former club, but there was a boost for him afterwards when Keane, asked how he thought the new boy had looked, replied that he thought stripes suited him. He also got to celebrate goals from both his compatriots. 'I would have loved to have scored on my debut,' he said, 'but it was a good win for us and we are closer to the pack. A lot of teams are going to be scared to play against Sunderland because we're playing the game the way it's supposed to be played.'

It began with more defensive sloppiness, though, Leon McKenzie running on to a simple ball over the top and being denied only by a fine block from Darren Ward. Yorke, who was becoming increasingly influential after an indifferent start to his Sunderland career, put Sunderland ahead after 19 minutes, heading home from close range after Stan Varga had hooked Ross Wallace's free-kick back across goal. 'Yorkie's been different class,' Keane said. 'His performances have been good and he's knocked in a few goals in the last few games. In the middle of the park, he's a vital addition to any team, just to help them keep their heads, keep the ball and try to dictate the pace of the game.'

The three points weren't wrapped up, though, until a deflected drive from Edwards flashed into the top corner with six minutes remaining. 'We can play better,' said Keane, his body-language screaming out 'not getting carried away'. 'But we've played better in the past and got nothing, so that's football.'

Saturday, 3 February, Championship

Sunderland   **2-0**   **Coventry City**
Yorke 19
Edwards 84

Sunderland: Ward, Whitehead, Nosworthy, Varga, D Collins, Edwards, Leadbitter (Simpson 72), Yorke, Wallace (Hysen 61), John, Murphy (Stokes 60)
Subs Not Used: Clarke, Fulop
Coventry: Steele, Whing, Hall (Virgo 46), Hawkins, McNamee, Doyle, Thornton (Tabb 35), Hughes, McKenzie, Kyle, Mifsud (Adebola 81)
Subs Not Used: Lee-Barrett, Birchall
Ref: S Mathieson (Cheshire)
Booked: Leadbitter (Sunderland); Whing (Coventry)
Att: 33,591
League position: 7

By that stage belief was rampant. At Plymouth, Sunderland were so sharp that the opposing manager Ian Holloway was left drooling at how consistently they were 'on the money' in terms of their pressing, and later he cited their example as the reason his team enjoyed a surge of form in the weeks that followed. The first goal didn't come until the 69th minute, but even as Carlos Edwards cleared off the line from Rory Fallon, there was always the sense that the win would come. Fittingly it was Anthony Stokes, who had made his debut for the Republic of Ireland against San Marino earlier in the week, who got the opener, a strike that spoke volumes for the confidence in the side. Dean Whitehead, running on to Edwards's floated chip was forced wide to the left of the box, but rather than attempting to check back on to his right foot, or to win a corner, he calmly turned, and rolled the ball back into the path of Stokes, who took a touch before firing a low shot in at Luke McCormick's near post. 'This has been the best week of my career,' Stokes said. 'Playing for my country was my life's ambition and to get my first goal for Sunderland is really pleasing.'

Two minutes later, John flicked on a Jonny Evans clearance, David Connolly ran on and rounded McCormick for a smoothly-taken second. 'First and foremost we had to be solid,' said Keane. 'It's a very good result and a good performance, especially in the last half-hour. Stokesy gives us plenty of options. He's the kind of player we can bring off the bench and that could be the difference come the end of the season.'

Saturday, February 10, Championship

Plymouth Argyle	0-2	Sunderland
		Stokes 69
		Connolly 71

Plymouth: McCormick, Connolly, Doumbe, Timar, Capaldi, Norris, Buzsaky (Summerfield 72), Nalis, Halmosi (Sinclair 61), Fallon, Ebanks-Blake (Gallen 72)
Subs Not Used: Sawyer, Gosling
Sunderland: Fulop, Simpson (L Miller 89), Evans, Nosworthy, D Collins, Edwards, Whitehead, Yorke, Hysen (Stokes 66), John (Leadbitter 74), Connolly

Subs Not Used: Carson, Cunningham
Ref: K Stroud (Hampshire)
Booked: Doumbe (Plymouth)
Att: 15,247
League position: 7

Six games in 2007 had brought 16 points – more than Sunderland had achieved in the whole of the previous season. 'I always say that when I took the job I asked the players to give ourselves a chance, and that's what we're doing,' Keane said. 'I still think we've got the most difficult run-in of all the teams above us. We still have to play four of those above us.'

As matters improved on the pitch, so Keane's redevelopment of the club carried on off it. Bobby Saxton, appointed assistant manager by Quinn and moved sideways to become director of scouting on Keane's arrival, was relieved of his position, as was the chief scout, Bob Shaw. 'It's one of those things in football,' Keane said. 'In my first few months at the club everything was a hundred miles an hour and Sacko was a great help, but now things have settled down, I'm looking to bring in one or two of my own people.' Earlier on in the season, that might have seemed capricious; by this stage it was just seen as another example of Keane's pleasing ruthlessness. There was no suggestion of a link between the two events, but when, a week later, the chief executive Peter Walker resigned after nine years with the club, it was hard not to interpret it as evidence of the Keane-Drumaville desire to overhaul the club from top to bottom.

What was needed was to transfer that hard edge to the pitch. Behind all the obvious progress that had been made, the only shadow was the sense that Sunderland still did not quite make the most of themselves. They were conceding fewer soft goals than they had earlier in the season, but they perhaps weren't quite getting the results at the other end. Southend at home was the kind of game Sunderland expected to cruise, even if Steve Tilson's side had won 3-1 at Birmingham and hammered QPR 5-0 in two of their previous three games. For once they did, taking the lead after four minutes and going on to produce a performance of rippling authority. It wasn't just that they won 4-0 that was so encouraging; it was the utter control they demonstrated. Darryl Flahavan in the Southend goal made a number of useful saves, and Stern John, Liam Miller and Dean Whitehead all hit the woodwork. It might not quite have been the equivalent of the 7-0 win over Oxford in 1998-99 – or even over Southend in 1987-88 – but it wasn't far off. 'The last three or four home games have not been too good to watch, but we showed we can pass and move and it was a deserved victory,' said Whitehead. 'We could have ended with five or six.'

It was the Trinidad and Tobago connection that started things, Stern John flicking on for Carlos Edwards, who got behind Peter Clarke and crossed low to David Connolly to tap in. Connolly laid in Tobias Hysen to make it 2-0, and, with 77 minutes left to play, Southend settled for a desperate exercise in damage limitation. It was moderately successful in that the third goal did not arrive for another 64 minutes, but when it did, it was a significant one. After seeing Flahavan tip over a header in the first-half, John had lain still for several moments, before slowly clambering to his feet. His disbelief was clear, almost as though even in his third game, having been denied so often, he had begun to wonder whether a first goal would ever arrive. When it did, it could hardly have been easier, as he knocked the ball into an empty net from eight yards after Whitehead's cross-shot had bounced back off the post. His second arrived almost straightaway. A cleverly worked move down the right led to Edwards feeding Miller, and when he pulled his cross behind the posse at the near post, John was there to sweep in at the back. 'Stern deserved his goals because of his overall work-rate and general play,' Keane said. 'He's a big strong lad and showed some great bits of skill. A lot of people were probably surprised when I bought him, but now they've seen what he can do.'

Saturday, 17 February, Championship

Sunderland   4-0   Southend United
Connolly 4
Hysen 13
John 77, 78

Sunderland: Fulop, Simpson, Nosworthy, Evans, D Collins, Edwards, Whitehead (Leadbitter 82), L Miller, Hysen (Stokes 72), Connolly (Wallace 71), John
Subs Not Used: Ward, Yorke
Southend: Flahavan, Hunt, Clarke, Sodje, Hammell, Gower (Foran 68), McCormack (Moussa 68), Maher, Campbell-Ryce, Bradbury (Harrold 69), Eastwood
Subs Not Used: Francis, Collis
Ref: N Swarbrick (Lancashire)
Booked: Whitehead (Sunderland); Clarke, Maher, McCormack (Southend)
Att: 33,576
League position: 6

Sunderland were up to sixth, and, finally, in the play-off positions. Typically, though, that was portrayed not as an achievement in itself but as another staging post en route to a greater goal. Keane's refusal to engage with the general optimism was becoming almost self-parodic. 'You've always got to have a bit of hope and belief,' he said. 'That's why I took the job, in the hope we could turn things around. We haven't turned anything around yet. We've just got away from the bottom of the table. If the players didn't have the ability to challenge for promotion, they wouldn't be here. We've been playing catch-up. We've managed to squeeze into the play-offs but we're not going to rest on our laurels.'

Carlos Edwards was more reflective of the general optimism,

appropriately so, given he was to a large degree responsible for it. To call him the new Julio Arca would be unfair, but he certainly filled the creative gap left by the Argentinian. He was quick, he was inventive and he could cross. Moreover, he had two feet, and in that regard his style was reminiscent less of Arca than of Allan Johnston, although there was a greater robustness to his play than there had been to the Scot's. Certainly there had been nobody since Johnston who had the crowd holding its collective breath as he swooped in from the wing to line up a shot with his supposedly weaker foot. 'It's in everyone's mind that we get straight back to the Premiership,' he said. 'That's the only thing the manager has instilled in us. He's not looking to next year – this year he wants to be promoted and that's our mentality. The gaffer won't accept us playing for sixth or seventh or settle for a play-off spot. We're looking to be promoted without having to play extra games.'

The path drops through the bushes to the river. From the far bank, where the south dock still bustles, rise a couple of cranes. Still, walking through the bamboo and the aspen, it is hard to believe that just half a century ago, these banks were home to Britain's most productive shipyards, and had been for over 100 years. In 1834, the Lloyd's Register recorded that Sunderland was 'the most important shipbuilding centre in the country, nearly equalling, as regards number and tonnage of ships built, all the other ports together'. Between September 1939 and the end of 1944, 249 vessels totalling over 1.5 million tons were built on the Wear, 27 per cent of the UK's output over the period. To put that in context, the output of the entire United States in

1938 was only 201,251 tons. And now, it is all gone.

Tragic as that is, there's no point pretending the yards could have gone on dominating the world for ever. For one thing, the river is too narrow and too shallow for the bulk of modern ships; for another, globalisation has produced a workforce elsewhere willing and able to produce the same product to a similar standard but at a cheaper price, but the end still seemed particularly cruel. Inevitably, it came by Thatcher's hand, as, in 1988, shipbuilding on the Wear was sacrificed to secure a European subsidy for Scottish shipyards. After a protracted death, mining finally came to an end six years later. At its peak in the eighties, unemployment in Sunderland reached 22 per cent and well into the nineties the city was in the top 10 per cent of Britain's most depressed communities.

My theory is that in such circumstances, the identification of the city with the football club becomes of increased importance. It is, essentially, all the people have left. Even now, as Sunderland begins uncertainly to rise again thanks to Nissan and the computer industry – in 2007 Sunderland gained a top-seven ranking from the Intelligent Community Forum for an unrivalled fifth time – the football club has a vital role in maintaining a continuity of identity. The transformation of the city – psychologically at least – I find astonishing. One in ten members of the workforce is now self-employed, suggesting a reawakening of the entrepreneurial spirit that brought those early settlers from the Tyne. All that is positive and necessary, particularly as the remaining heavy industries continue to decline, but it is hard to see how there can be the same civic pride about enhanced broadband speeds, or the production of another Micra, as there was about something as vast and magnificent as a ship. Only the football club can provide that now.

That sense of continuity, of the past echoing through the

new, becomes clearer the nearer you come to the bridges. I passed by the National Glass Centre, a nod to the glass industry that until very recently had remained strong in the town since Benedict Biscop, abbot of St Peter's, had first brought over craftsmen from Rome in the seventh century. St Peter's is still there, a squat, robust building, clearly designed with defence in mind, and in front of it, where once the ballast from ships formed ever shifting mountains, is the main campus of Sunderland University. This, without question, has been a triumph, recently being voted one of the five best in the country.

On the paving stones between the lecture halls and the river stands a sculpture of a pile books, an open one at the front designed deliberately to recall the Wearmouth-Jarrow Bible. Three were originally produced in the twin monasteries under Ceolfrith – beginning in 682, when he was granted extra land on which to raise the 2,000 head of cattle required to produce the necessary quantity of vellum to produce the bibles – but the only one to survive is now in Florence, miraculously preserved after Ceolfrith died en route to Rome to present a copy to the pope.

A little further on I come to more sculptures, an outsize nut and bolt, and then probably the crowning glory of the Sculpture Trail, *Shadows in Another Light*. It is, ostensibly, a metal tree on a plinth, one arm arcing out from the trunk towards the river. The obvious association is the tree of knowledge, extending its reach further and further, but then you notice the odd patterning of the paving stones. Viewed from above and behind, from the bridge perhaps, or in the mirror by the base of the trunk, it becomes apparent that the shape formed is that of a hammerhead crane, industry's shadow reaching out from knowledge, the past reaching back from the present.

11

THE BIG THREE

Having, as Keane had demanded, got themselves in a position to challenge, Sunderland came to the crunch as they faced, in the space of 11 days, three games against teams above them. Keane denied, at least in public, they were 'make or break', but he was the only one. Falter and the season would be reduced to an undignified scramble for the play-offs; soar, and not only would Sunderland benefit in terms of the league table, but the sense of Keane as progenitor and conductor of an unstoppable force would be established as an all but irrefutable fact.

First up came Birmingham at St Andrews, and a reunion for Keane with Steve Bruce, who had been designated to look after him when he arrived at Old Trafford in 1993. 'When I first went to Manchester United,' Keane said, 'shall we say I was not the perfect professional? As a young lad I was out and about a bit, but he was always there and his advice was much appreciated. When I look back over my career, I don't get the buzz from looking over medals or money, but appreciating the players I played with, and Brucie was one of them. He's a great bloke.'

Bruce returned the compliment, calling Keane 'a leader among men', and the closeness of their relationship perhaps explained Keane's magnanimity after the final whistle. 'Maybe a draw was a fair result,' he said. It wasn't. Birmingham rallied after half-time, but in the first half Sunderland were magnificent, producing a performance of such poise and class that it could have been a Premiership side taking apart a team of non-league chuggers. The only problem was that it produced only one goal. 'It was one of those nights when we needed the second goal,' Keane said. 'I do believe we had the chances to kill the game off, and when you don't it can come back to hurt you.'

The goal they did get was superb; a 25-yard drive from Carlos Edwards, but it represented a troubling pattern. Sunderland were getting their share of brilliant goals, but they seemed to struggle for the mundane. Possession did not simply produce goals, as it seemed to for other sides. David Connolly had an early effort saved by Colin Doyle, and then saw his volley from the resulting corner bounce over the bar, Anthony Stokes struck a chance too close to Doyle when well-placed, and Dwight Yorke, with a shooting opportunity, tried instead to lay in an offside Stern John.

Half-time, though, checked the momentum and, after Martin Fulop's outstretched boot had kept out a Sebastian Larsson effort early in the second half, Birmingham had a couple more chances to equalise before, in the final minute, DJ Campbell, who had orchestrated Sunderland's FA Cup exit at Brentford the previous season, forced in a Rowan Vine cross to equalise. 'We had a lead that we should have held and could have extended,' Fulop said. 'We're looking at it as two points dropped.'

Tuesday, 20 February, Championship

Birmingham City	1-1	Sunderland
Campbell 90		Edwards 27

Birmingham: Doyle, N'Gotty (Campbell 83), Jaidi, Martin Taylor, Sadler, Larsson, Muamba (Danns 75), Clemence, McSheffrey, Bendtner (Vine 75), Jerome
Subs Not Used: Maik Taylor, Nafti
Sunderland: Fulop, Simpson (L Miller 57), Evans, Nosworthy, D Collins, Edwards, Whitehead, Yorke, Stokes (Leadbitter 85), John (Hysen 64), Connolly
Subs Not Used: Ward, Wallace
Ref: M Halsey (Lancashire)
Booked: N'Gotty, McSheffrey (Birmingham); Evans (Sunderland)
Att: 20,941
League position: 5

Keane was more upbeat. 'The more the game goes on,' he said, 'the greater the chance they're going to score. To get a draw at Birmingham is not the end of the world. It was an open game, an entertaining game. If we'd managed to get that second goal, I'm sure we'd have gone on to win it. We've got to take the positives and look forward to another big game on Saturday.' Although the scale was different, the effect was not dissimilar to Quinn's famous Wembley oration, when, within the space of three or four minutes, he turned the pain of the 1998 play-off defeat into the spur that would lead Sunderland to savage the division the following season. It's not the disappointment; it's how you respond to it.

The next game, though, at home to Derby, took a worryingly similar course, as Sunderland dominated the first half, failed to take full advantage, and let things slip in the second. This time, though, there was to be a happy ending.

In that the game kicked off at 3pm on a Saturday, there was a happy beginning as well. Sky had initially wanted to show the game on the Monday evening, but then, because of Derby's progress in the FA Cup and the possibility they might require a replay to settle their fifth-round tie against Plymouth, they shifted it back to the Saturday, but with a scheduled start of 5.15pm. Niall Quinn refused, believing that the traditional

3pm start suited the majority of fans better. 'We turned down a significant amount of money,' he said, 'to benefit our team and our fans.' It would be churlish to suggest he just wanted to get down the pub quicker, but not as churlish as David Sullivan, the owner of Birmingham City, who, having been criticised for agreeing to an 11.30am kick-off against Stoke for the purposes of television, bafflingly claimed that Sunderland had not turned down a Sky game at all. It later emerged Birmingham had been misled by an email from 'a senior individual at the Football League', prompting a profusion of apologies.

That was a shame, not so much because Sullivan's initial chippiness had given the impression that Birmingham were undergoing some sort of psychic meltdown, but because it distracted from the fact that Quinn, by luck or by judgement, had somehow managed to channel the energy of 1933, another game against Derby, and the most famous accommodation of fans in Sunderland's history. That season was a bleak one, not only for the club but for the whole region as the depression bit hard. Food was more important than football, and, with sacrifices having to be made, a home game against Bolton in October 1932 drew a crowd of just 9,000. Only the Cup offered salvation.

For Sunderland, the FA Cup had taken on the quality of an epic quest. By 1933 they had reached four semifinals, but remained the only club of equivalent stature never to have won it. After beating Hull City in the third round, Sunderland faced Aston Villa, the team who had beaten them in the final in 1913 and against whom they had never won a Cup tie. As Bobby Gurney hit a hat trick in a 3-0 win, belief began to swell. Blackpool succumbed to another Gurney strike in the fifth round, setting up a classic away to Derby in the quarterfinals.

Sunderland were 2-0 down inside quarter of an hour, but fought back to lead 3-2. Derby equalised, but Gurney's second of the game put Sunderland 4-3 up, only for Dally Duncan to hit a last-minute equaliser. Breathless, energy-sapping stuff, and everybody wanted to be part of the replay.

It was scheduled for the following Wednesday – no police-imposed ten-day notice periods back then – but, in the days before floodlights, that meant an afternoon kick-off, when most of the population – or at least those who still had jobs – would be at work. So they closed the mines and the shipyards. In the middle of the depression, when money was appallingly tight and every order counted, every major employer gave their workers half-days so they could go to an FA Cup quarterfinal replay. Admittedly they were expected to make up the time the following Saturday, but Sunderland were away at Bolton, so it hardly mattered. The effect was to make the game into a festival, and 75,118 turned up, still the largest attendance for a game at Sunderland. Raich Carter spoke of having to fight his way through a 'dense mob' even to get to the ground, and inside the situation was even worse. 'Inside,' he wrote, 'was pandemonium. The spectators spawned out from the stands over the cinder track and across the touchline onto the pitch itself. We did not know how and where we were going to play. I do not think the match should have started. Players could not be expected to do themselves justice in such conditions although there probably would have been a riot if the game had been called off.'

A big occasion? Fans gripped by excitement and expectation? There could be only one outcome, and it arrived sure enough, as Derby's Peter Ramage scored the only goal of the game. Hope and anti-climax, heroic comebacks, and dismal underachievement: it was the way Johnny Cochrane's

Sunderland had always been, and, until Carter's influence really began to be felt three years later, the way it would continue to be.

Keane's Sunderland were under slightly less pressure, but there was still a crowd of over 36,000 at the Stadium of Light, perhaps guilted by Quinn's gesture into being there. Whatever the reason, Quinn's decision to reject the television money was emphatically justified. The pressure, in fact, seemed rather to be felt by Derby, who could have gone nine points clear of Sunderland had they not lost at home to Stoke the previous Wednesday. Given their previous game had been a 2-0 Cup defeat to Plymouth and they had drawn against Hull the match before that, they seemed to have been afflicted by the same neurosis that caused every team who topped the Championship last season to be undermined by the position. Helpfully, Keane pointed that out. 'Mentally, teams at the top will, and certain players will, lose the plot,' he said, a trick straight out of the Sir Alex Ferguson book of destabilising the opposition. His own dressing-room, by contrast, was full of 'tough players'. Certainly there were few there who had ever been troubled by being top of the table.

It seemed to work as well, as Sunderland controlled the first half, eventually taking the lead through a 27-minute David Connolly penalty. Sunderland had not been awarded one in their 63 previous games (not quite the '65 years' Keane later claimed, but not far off) and Marc Edworthy must have felt mightily aggrieved that, when a number of blatant offences had been allowed to pass in that period, he should be pulled up for a slight tug on Connolly's shirt. Yet again, though, Sunderland were left wondering how such dominance had produced such little reward. The danger was that Derby, as Birmingham and QPR had, would regroup and rally in the second half.

Thanks to the arrival of Giles Barnes as a half-time substitute, they did. The 18-year-old had already put a free header over, when, just before the hour, he embarrassed Danny Collins with a pirouette on the edge of the box, and cracked a low shot past Darren Ward. Given Steve Howard had also had a header cleared off the line by Tobias Hysen and Ward had made an athletic back-pedalling tip-over to keep out a Howard shot that deflected awkwardly off Collins, it began to seem that a draw would not merely be a fair result, but even a slightly lucky one.

The introduction of Grant Leadbitter for Hysen, though, tipped the game back Sunderland's way. Daryl Murphy clipped a drive against the post, before, finally, in injury time, Liam Miller got between Michael Johnson and Matt Oakley to touch Leadbitter's cross beyond Stephen Bywater. 'We conceded a very late equaliser at Birmingham and felt we should have won that game,' Connolly said. 'We didn't want to feel the same disappointment again – and it would have been disappointing to draw against Derby. You could see our attitude with the winner. Liam Miller was still getting into the box after ninety-odd minutes and that's what you get when you gamble. It's what you get when you're being brave and go for it.'

Saturday, 24 February, Championship

Sunderland   **2-1**   **Derby County**
Connolly 27 (pen)   Barnes 57
L Miller 90

Sunderland: Ward, Simpson, Nosworthy, Evans, D Collins, Edwards, L Miller, Yorke, Hysen (Leadbitter 69), John (Murphy 58), Connolly
Subs Not Used: Fulop, T Miller, Varga
Derby: Bywater, Edworthy, Moore, Mears, McEveley, Teale (Barnes 46), Oakley, Pearson (M Johnson 83), Jones, Howard, Fagan (Peschisolido 71)
Subs Not Used: Grant, Macken

Ref: M Atkinson (W Yorkshire)
Booked: Connolly, D Collins (Sunderland); McEveley, Edworthy (Derby)
Att: 36,049
League position: 4

As Miller ran and slid on his stomach in front of the corner of North and East Stands, the Stadium of Light reacted as though the league had been won at that moment. Fans saw the play-offs as a given, the only question being whether they could haul themselves up into the top two. Miller himself, having been part of the Leeds side defeated by Watford in the play-off final the previous season, spoke of wanting to avoid the play-offs at all costs.

Keane, meanwhile, was swift to dismiss the idea his side was the best in the division. 'Right now we're the fourth or fifth best team in the league because that's where we are in the table,' he said. 'If we'd have drawn today we would have been back down in ninth.' Because winners must never be happy. With Sunderland just three points behind the leaders West Brom, though, nobody really believed he was thinking like that, even if Derby, also three points ahead, had a game in hand.

The only negative was the suggestion that Anthony Stokes had been left out of the squad for disciplinary reasons, an issue which had led to questions by journalists at press conferences. 'Absolutely not,' Keane insisted. 'There were other players left out too and they would all be disappointed. Stokes was left out like Ross Wallace was left out, like Kenny Cunningham was left out. I can only pick eleven players and have five on the bench and I just felt he's had three games on the bounce so I thought we'd get him ready for next week.' Then again, in his autobiography he makes clear his support for the Ferguson method of pursuing discipline in private, while defending players in public, so it was hard to be sure.

*

The mood was good, Sunderland's form was good, and still Niall Quinn wasn't happy. He wanted more. Sunderland's crowd against Derby may have been double that Blackburn attracted against Portsmouth in the Premiership the following day, but it was still 12,000 short of capacity (and, for that matter, under half of what they'd attracted against the same opposition 74 years earlier). So the chairman wrote to 7,000 season-ticket holders who still hadn't returned, setting out his vision, and encouraging them to leap on the bandwagon, and planned a series of six meetings at social clubs where he would meet fans, explain his plans and take their questions. 'We're saying, "Come back, it's a little bit different now." I know they were hurt, I know they were fed up and I know the apathy that was in the air, but we're trying to change that. We're trying to keep our side of the bargain. When I meet people who haven't come back I say to them that before last summer they said if there was a new regime they'd come back. Then they said if there was a good manager they'd come back, then they said if we signed players they'd come back, then they said if we won games they'd come back. We're kind of doing a lot on our side. I've sent these letters out to invite them to ask me about anything that is still bothering them. I'm trying to make them understand that the club is a different place now. Any bad experiences they have had I hope will be erased and we can make them proud of their club again. We kind of get the feeling that it's going that way, but I need the people. We need forty thousand crowds, and the only other thing I can do is go round people's houses and drag them there myself.'

This was not, he insisted, a 'marketing ploy', rather it was an effort at 'reconnection'; an unfortunate term in that it sounded so much like, well, the kind of word a marketing executive would use. After eight years of frozen prices – indicative of frozen development – he acknowledged there would have to be a small increase for the following season, but, as he said, for those who renewed early, he was still offering the possibility of Premiership football at Championship prices. This, of course, for all his protestations, was marketing; what redeemed it was that at its heart lay a viable dream.

What made the dream viable, without question, was Keane, and he was somebody with no great fondness or aptitude for marketing. He just said what he thought. Four wins and a draw in five games in February earned Keane the manager of the month award – he would win it again in March – a prize he seemed to regard as almost perverse. 'I can't get my head round why they give out these bloody awards month to month,' he said. 'I'm not bothered about it. I'll stick it in the garage. It's about where you finish at the end of the season. That's the time to reflect, and if you feel a team deserves some-thing you give them the award, not individuals and certainly not the manager. I don't get sucked into all that nonsense.'

Ungracious, perhaps, but no Sunderland fan cared. A refusal to accept undue praise is, after all, part of the heritage of the city, part of the ethos of not showing off. Jack Crawford is probably Sunderland's most celebrated military hero, but he hated his fame, however deserved it may have been.

On 11 October 1797, at the height of the Napoleonic Wars, a British party under Admiral Duncan, on the lookout for ships bound for France to assist a putative invasion of Ireland, engaged the Dutch navy just off the coast at Camperdown. Blocking a possible retreat, Duncan forced the Dutch to fight, and at first the battle was even. As a Dutch cannonball struck the top of the mainmast on the Admiral's ship, though, bring-ing down his flag, the British seemed to be facing defeat.

Duncan's men were confused and dispirited, seeing the apparently lowered colours as a gesture of surrender. Realising the problem, Crawford, then just 23, seized the flag, some nails and a marlinspike, and climbed what remained of the mast to re-raise the Admiral's colours. As he reached the platform halfway up, a musket-ball struck the mast by his head, unleashing a volley of splinters, one of which embedded itself in his cheek. Regardless, he carried on his climb, and successfully reattached the flag. Morale raised, Duncan's men inflicted on the Dutch a crushing defeat, and Crawford was hailed as a hero.

Seeing his act as nothing more than his duty, though, he was uncomfortable with the acclamation, and turned down an extraordinary offer of £100 a week to re-enact the battle at the Vauxhall Pleasure Gardens. Crawford refused even to take part in the official parade of honour through the streets of London. His place was taken by an actor, who had so much money thrown into his carriage that he never had to work again. Keane probably had little idea of the tradition he was invoking, but it didn't matter. This was exactly the toughness fans loved to hear from him, the practical disregard for fripperies that exposed the inner steel.

Keane, the manager, though, was about more than mere toughness, as became apparent at the Hawthorns. Yes, he could buy the right players, yes he could motivate, but, the odd quibbler asked, what was he like as a tactician? Against West Brom the world found out: he was very astute indeed. Tony Mowbray's side was, by popular consent, the best to watch in the division. Their method, though, was simple, arguably one-dimensional: Kevin Phillips and Diomansy Kamara made angled runs behind the opposing defence, and Jason Koumas tried to find them. Stop them doing that, and you'd stopped West Brom.

Sunderland simply defended very deep, with Dwight Yorke

and Dean Whitehead forming an extra barrier in front of them. West Brom were frustrated, sufficiently so to leave a baffled Mowbray grasping for excuses. 'We have to be gracious in defeat,' Mowbray said, a sure sign he was about not to be. 'But I like to think we were a better team than them on the day and over our next ten games I would suggest we'll get more goals and more points than Sunderland.' It was one of those claims so bizarre, so divorced from reality, that the press-conference room reacted with an audible gasp. A series of frantic glances followed between journalists looking for reassurances that it wasn't just them who had seen the game – and filed their first edition pieces – in a wholly different light. For the record, West Brom went on to take 13 points from their remaining ten matches, scoring 19 goals; Sunderland over the same period scored 24 and took 25 points.

Sunderland were, initially, committed to preventing their opponents from playing, but, having examined them and found that they weren't perhaps quite as frightening as had been made out, they began themselves to probe, taking the lead with their first meaningful thrust. Danny Simpson, cutting in from the right, laid the ball forward to Stern John, who touched it off for Dwight Yorke to side-foot his finish into the bottom corner. 'I told him to sit,' said Keane, 'so I don't know what he was doing bombing on.'

Among the Sunderland fans at the other end of the pitch a giant Trinidad and Tobago flag was unfurled, and it was waving again four minutes after half-time as Stern John was left unmarked to head in Dean Whitehead's corner from close range. 'When you look at the stand and you see a Trinidad and Tobago flag it makes you get goose bumps,' John said.

Only superb saves from Dean Kiely, who had joined them from Luton in January, prevented Anthony Stokes and Tobias

Hysen from increasing Sunderland's advantage and, even after Darren Carter had pulled one back with a controlled volley to set up a late siege, the only real chance of the final minutes fell to Connolly, who was denied by a quite astonishing reflex save from Kiely. The dismissal of Paul Robinson for a supposed professional foul on Liam Miller with three minutes remaining confirmed Sunderland's victory. It was later overturned on appeal. 'We're gonna win the league,' chanted the away fans. The previous season it had been belted out with ironic gusto, self-deprecation being the last refuge of the damned. Here, it was just as heartfelt, but entirely serious.

Saturday, 3 March, Championship

West Bromwich Albion   1-2   **Sunderland**
Carter 72   Yorke 23
                                        John 49

West Brom: Kiely, McShane, Clement, C Davies, Robinson, Koumas, Chaplow, Greening (Carter 55), Koren (Gera 55), Kamara, Phillips (MacDonald 55)
Subs Not Used: Daniels, Albrechtsen
Sunderland: Ward, Simpson, Evans, Nosworthy, D Collins, Edwards (Hysen 41), Whitehead, Yorke (L Miller 73), Stokes, Connolly, John (Murphy 62)
Subs Not Used: Fulop, Leadbitter
Ref: D Gallagher (Oxfordshire)
Sent Off: Robinson 87 (WBA)
Booked: Clement (WBA); Whitehead (Sunderland)
Att: 23,252
League position: 4

There was a downside, and it was a significant one. Carlos Edwards, easily Sunderland's most creative presence since his arrival, was left with a dislocated shoulder after a challenge from Richard Chaplow that had the famous vein in Keane's forehead pumping as he berated Dermot Gallagher, the referee, from the touchline. 'He said he was going to retire last year,' Keane said darkly, before, after an electric pause, continuing. 'Maybe he should have.'

That was just the start of a master class in deadpan grumpiness. While others marvelled at how comprehensively Sunderland had tamed the division's other form team, Keane was evidently thinking up ways to improve. 'We made it hard work,' he said. 'We should have maybe finished it off earlier. We could have maybe kept ball a bit better, made more of our breaks. If you don't take opportunities then they get a goal out of nothing and suddenly you're under the cosh. We had to dig deep, but you've got to dig deep to do anything in life.'

Surely he could draw satisfaction from taking seven points from three successive games against Sunderland's direct promotion rivals? 'Should have been nine,' Keane replied gruffly. Impressed, then, by how Nyron Nosworthy had dominated aerially? 'That's what I expect.' Credit to Darren Ward for his command of his box? 'That's why he's got the gloves on.' Excellence, now, was expected as standard.

Most football rivalries are simply that – hatreds between two teams who, for whatever reason, have found reason to dislike each other. Occasionally, there is a deeper logic to it, usually rooted in religion, class, or history. The Tyne-Wear rivalry, I would suggest, is unique in Britain, not in terms of depth of feeling – again, I find such arguments facile – but in terms of the fact that it involves two separate cities whose centres are just 13 miles apart. These are entities that have clashed over just about everything for centuries; football happens to be the stage on which it is most obviously played out in the modern age.

There is little evidence for this, but it is not hard to imagine that those who had seen their village twice destroyed by the Normans in the late eleventh century felt a sense of grievance against the settlement that surrounded the castle built on the Tyne to ensure their subjugation. Newcastle, similarly, presumably resented those who had left the guilds on the Tyne to set up anew four centuries later, and from the moment the Tyne guilds persuaded Charles I to award them a monopoly on exporting coal from the eastern coalfields, the animosity had a specific focus. Sunderland, understandably, rallied to the parliamentary cause during the civil war, and became a landing point for Scottish mercenaries fighting on the Roundhead side. Newcastle, meanwhile, housed a Royalist garrison.

The respective armies met at Boldon Hill in 1644, with the Roundheads triumphant. Newcastle was besieged and taken and, briefly, Sunderland enjoyed trade benefits. Come the Restoration, though, and a number of retaliatory royal charters restricted trade on the Wear. This, of course, raises the question of whether Sunderland was always less prone to emotional extremes than Newcastle and so temperamentally more attuned to the Puritanism of the Parliamentarians, or whether the Civil War shaped the local character. Not surprisingly, come the second Jacobite Rebellion of 1745, Sunderland again backed the rebels and Newcastle George III – the other explanation of the etymology of 'Geordie' ('Geordie' being a local familiar form of George), if you reject the theory of the lamps.

Towards the end of the nineteenth century, industrial riots became increasingly common, and in the early twentieth, football often provided the trigger. A riot at a derby at St James' on Good Friday 1901, when 25 policemen tried to control a 70,000 crowd, led to an abandonment and numerous injuries, there was a stampede at a Cup tie in March 1909 and in further disturbances at a league game at Roker two months later a police horse was stabbed.

More recently, the debate has centred around the legacy of the Tyne–Wear Development Agency, which was seen in Sunderland as favouring Newcastle. The development of the airport to the north of Newcastle was unpopular but probably justifiable; the 22-year delay in bringing to Sunderland the Metro, for which it had been paying from the start, was frankly outrageous.

Even now, as the two cities slowly grow into one another, and it becomes increasingly common to live in one and work in the other, the rivalry endures, often in ludicrous forms. In *The Far Corner* Harry Pearson speaks of having seen two men almost come to blows on a train as they argued over which city had the better shopping facilities, while I confess I feel an irrational pride in the fact that the Empire in Sunderland has a better ghost story than the Theatre Royal in Newcastle. They have only a Grey Lady, supposedly the spirit of a woman who committed suicide by jumping from the gods in the nineteenth century. The Empire matched that with the ghost of Vesta Tilley, an early vaudeville star who laid the foundation stone in 1906, edged ahead with the ghost of Molly Moselle, a stage manager who went out to buy a birthday card during a run of Ivor Novello's *The Dancing Years* in 1949 and was never seen again, and then took a surely insurmountable lead with the ghost of Sid James, who had a heart attack on stage in 1976, and died before he reached hospital. His lascivious laugh can, it is said, still be heard in the dressing room he occupied that night, and so terrified Les Dawson during one performance that he refused ever to return. Vesta and Molly, you imagine, aren't too delighted either.

The problem with the football rivalry is that for a long time it justified mediocrity. Each club defined itself primarily by reference to the other, and only afterwards by reference to the rest of the world. Who cared if Sunderland finished 16th in the second flight, just so long as Newcastle finished 17th? That changed to an extent as Newcastle rose under Keegan in the nineties, but the sentiment still endures. It was dropping Alan Shearer for a defeat to Sunderland – the glorious derby in the rain in August 1999, when Kevin Ball hit his own bar from 40 yards in the dying minutes with a lunging tackle that went wrong – that led to Ruud Gullit's demise as Newcastle manager, and it surely is no coincidence that Glenn Roeder resigned on the day Sunderland won the Championship. Given the limitations of the squad at his disposal, and the injury problems with which he had to deal, there was no disgrace in leading Newcastle to a mid-table finish, but the impact of Roy Keane and his ability to draw headlines increased the pressure on Newcastle and Roeder until it became intolerable.

[12]

BUSES AND TAXIS

If the surge in demand for away tickets for the Sheffield Wednesday game had been inexplicable, at least there was logic to the collective madness that saw 8,000 buy tickets for the away game at Barnsley. There were still ten games remaining, but the rest of the country – with the possible exception of three pockets in the Midlands – saw Sunderland's rise as inevitable. Keane, predictably, did not. Having made several references to how Barnsley would be battling hard to get themselves away from the danger of relegation, he launched into a warning against complacency. 'We can't be thinking the hard work is done, far from it,' he said. 'Barnsley will be just as hard as the last three games.'

Perhaps that was why he chose to make a point when three players – Anthony Stokes, Marton Fulop, and Tobias Hysen – arrived late for the bus taking them to Barnsley the day before the game. The bus set off without them and, after the players had followed it in their cars for several miles, they were told to turn round and go home. 'They couldn't make it for the 4.15pm coach yesterday afternoon, although we'd finished training just past noon,' Keane explained. 'If you can't get home and get your bag organised, get in your nice car and be on time, there is something drastically wrong. I've played with players for twelve, thirteen years and they were never late once. I've been at the club six months and there's been a number of players who have been late – late for training, late for team meetings. That's not good enough. In the past I have the feeling that players at the club have thought Sunderland is a soft touch. No more. If you work in a normal job in a factory you punch in. That's what I used to do years ago. So I left them behind.'

Keane hadn't always had such a close relationship with punctuality. Yes, he was so determined to make it to his first Manchester United training session on time that he hired a taxi to drive in front of him and show him the way, but there had been an incident on an end-of-season tour to the US with the Republic of Ireland in 1992 on which Keane kept the rest of the squad waiting. It was, admittedly, on the final morning of the tour – 'a meaningless exercise, part-competitive, part piss-up,' as Keane dismissed it in his autobiography – as they were about to set off for the airport, and so had no impact on the preparation for any game, but, still, the incidents drew comparison. When Mick McCarthy, the Ireland captain, told Keane he had been 'out of order', Keane had told him to 'go and fuck yourself', bringing into the public domain for the first time the tension between the two that would erupt in Saipan. When Jack Charlton, the manager, upbraided him, Keane told him he should have left without him. Stokes, Fulop, and Hysen had been warned.

Keane's calmness in press conferences had drawn much comment, but, when the US incident was recalled, his temper, briefly, flared. 'You're saying there's one rule for me and a differing one for the players?' he snapped. 'Get your facts straight. This wasn't the first time they were late. One or two, maybe, is OK. But three? No way. So don't patronise me. I'm for the team always, and nothing will stop that.'

Yet the strange thing was that Keane *had* been consistent. The bus incident in the US was, in a sense, the prologue to the Keane-McCarthy feud; the bus incident on the way to Barnsley was the epilogue. This was Keane the uncompromising, wanting standards imposed. What seems to have angered him about the Republic of Ireland's trip to the US was the general sloppiness, in which McCarthy, as he said elsewhere, had been complicit and which, he implied, McCarthy had allowed to spawn at Sunderland. In the US, he had been allowed to get away with keeping people waiting as he went for a drink with Steve Staunton. The bus should have gone without him, which would have spared him the confrontation with McCarthy. If he and Staunton had had to make the trip to the airport themselves, the point would have been made. When Keane left Fulop, Stokes, and Hysen behind, the point *was* made: for Sunderland, the McCarthy era was over, and they were playing by new rules. 'It might hurt you leaving players out, but if they disrespect their team-mates then so be it,' Keane said. 'It's a serious game, we should be in the Premiership and that's what I'm trying to do. All this stuff, be it preparation or training, we're trying to give them a chance to do that. I'm trying to change the mentality of a lot of things at Sunderland, be it a yo-yo club, where you feel you could be late for training or not train hard all the time; be it getting two or three weeks out of a week-long injury, taking days off left, right and centre. I had these vibes when I got the job. We needed to remember what this club is about. It's no good talking about where it should be. Judge people by actions, not intentions.'

Of course, it could have backfired dreadfully. Fulop they could do without, but in the absence of Carlos Edwards, Sunderland were short of attacking width, and either Stokes or

Hysen could have provided it. Whether that was the reason for a slightly flat display is impossible to say, but Sunderland did, eventually, get the win, and, as though to prove that Keane had got it right, the first goal came from the player he deployed in that troublesome right-wing position – Grant Leadbitter. There seemed little obvious danger as Leadbitter received the ball from Daryl Murphy at the top of the box, but having been given time to line up his shot, he fired it low across Nick Colgan and into the bottom corner. 'The gaffer's asked me to get in scoring positions and pick up some goals,' he said. 'I think I can do that quite well.'

Barnsley responded with a series of long balls, and it was with a long ball – or at least a huge headed clearance from Jonny Evans – that Sunderland got their second, in injury time. David Connolly held it up well and, as players arrived to draw away defenders, he worked space on the edge of the box and hooked a low shot into the bottom corner. It was his 11th of the season, and just reward for a game in which he had led the line tirelessly.

Inevitably, though, it was the bus and the crowd that occupied the headlines. 'Playing in front of those fans was an incredible experience,' said Leadbitter. 'It was the best away support I have ever seen. When I came out before the game I had a look round at our crowd and it gave me an even bigger lift.'

Saturday, 10 March, Championship

Barnsley	0-2	Sunderland
		Leadbitter 66
		Connolly 90

Barnsley: Colgan, Austin, P Reid, Nyatanga, Heckingbottom, Devaney (K Reid 63), Togwell, McCann, Howard, Ferenczi, Rajczi (Nardiello 70)
Subs Not Used: Lucas, Kay, Eckersley
Sunderland: Ward, Simpson, Evans, Nosworthy, D Collins, Wallace, L Miller (T Miller

73), Whitehead, Leadbitter, John (Murphy 57), Connolly
Subs Not Used: Wright, Cunningham, Carson
Ref: R Beeby (Northamptonshire)
Booked: Austin (Barnsley); L Miller (Sunderland)
Att: 18,207
League position: 3

The Barnsley Three must have spent an uncomfortable weekend, training with the reserves on the Saturday, but after they arrived so early for training on the Monday that they, in Keane's phrase, 'brought the milk in', all was forgiven. That Sunderland had won at Oakwell presumably helped. 'The three lads are all good lads, it was just an unfortunate thing,' Keane said. 'I've spoken to the players this morning; they've held their hands up. They made a genuine mistake and I'm not going to crucify them.'

Darren Ward spoke of an increased 'nervousness' around the squad, but also of how they recognised Keane's action as a means of dispelling complacency. The table, anyway, should have been motivation enough. Keane's children had spent the weekend calculating permutations, while the coaching staff had begun working out how many points history suggested would be necessary to secure automatic promotion. Only Keane seemed immune. 'Some of the staff have been mentioning that, when they've got a bit of spare time – or nothing else to do – they've been on the Internet checking up past leagues and what we might need,' he said. 'These things change; I wouldn't have a clue about what the average is to go up.' His indifference to statistics was probably wise. After all, Sunderland had won the division in 1996 with 86 points, but had missed out on promotion two years later with 90. And anyway, it's best not to take anything for granted ahead of a game against Stoke.

Stoke are a nightmare, but they are also a conundrum. Given

they are invariably so hard to play against, it makes little sense that they never win anything, never even really threaten to be promoted. After nine wins from their previous 11 games, perhaps Sunderland had to stutter somewhere, but there was an inevitability about it happening against Stoke. This was, by some distance, Sunderland's poorest performance of the year, and, having been all but impregnable at the back, they suddenly looked hesitant.

Darren Ward will take the blame for the first, as Darel Russell's drive slithered under his body, but Sunderland had been strangely diffident throughout the move that led to the goal, so as Russell lined up his shot from 25 yards out, nobody moved to close him down. Dean Whitehead cancelled that out with a smart finish from 20 yards after David Connolly had chested back Grant Leadbitter's cross, but sloppiness at the back handed Stoke the lead again. As first-half injury-time drew to a close, Sunderland seemed to be waiting for the whistle as they allowed a half-cleared ball to drop to Carl Hoefkens. With Danny Collins jumping vaguely in his general direction, Hoefkens took the ball down on his chest and fired a crisp shot into the bottom corner.

'It was great to get the equaliser soon after the first goal, so they didn't get a feel for being in the lead, but it was a sloppy goal we gave away just before half-time,' Keane said. 'There were a few harsh words said.'

Sunderland improved after the break, but not much. Mamady Sidibe hit a post with a deft backheel, but for once it was Sunderland who punished a side for not taking their chances. A left-wing corner was cleared only to halfway, and a secondary clearance fell to Leadbitter on the left. He crossed again, Nyron Nosworthy flicked on, and, at the back post, Daryl Murphy pivoted to hit a first-time shot low past Steve

Simonsen. To the side of the bench, Keane ran a few paces forward, his right fist clenched above his head – by some distance his most emotional celebration of the season. Even better news was to follow, as it emerged that Derby had only drawn at home against QPR, while Birmingham had lost at Norwich, and Wolves, who had been mounting a charge that was worrying in that nobody at Sunderland wanted to finish below a Mick McCarthy side, went down at Coventry. Quite apart from the psychological benefits of preserving the unbeaten record, it turned out that, rather than being two points dropped, this was one point gained.

'It was a good point,' Keane agreed, 'because the goal came so late in the game. Credit to the players because they showed great desire to get a result when we didn't play too well, especially in giving two bad goals away. The players are disappointed, but you're not going to win every game you play. Even the best teams in the world don't do that.'

Saturday, 13 March, Championship

Sunderland	2-2	Stoke
Whitehead 23		Russell 21
Murphy 89		Hoefkens 45

Sunderland: Ward, Simpson, Nosworthy, Evans, (Wallace 46), D Collins, Leadbitter, Whitehead, Yorke (L Miller 68), Hysen, John (Murphy 55), Connolly
Subs Not Used: Funlop, T Miller
Stoke: Simonsen, Hoefkens, Zakuani (Dickinson 82), Higginbotham, Griffin, Fortune, Lawrence, Diao, Russell, Sidibe (Eustace 86), Parkin (Fuller 61)
Subs Not Used: Hoult, Martin
Ref: M Jones (Chester)
Booked: Simpson, D Collins, Miller (Sunderland); Hoefkens, Lawrence (Stoke)
Att: 31,358
League position: 3

To those on Wearside who had embraced the illusion that Sunderland were due recognition as the natural heirs of the Real Madrid of the late fifties or the AC Milan of the early nineties, that came as something of a jolt. More realistic observers seemed to agree that this side wasn't quite a match for Sunderland's 1998-99 record-breakers (it tends to be over-looked that that team had been weakened by the loss of Lee Clark, Allan Johnston, and Michael Bridges by the time it finished seventh in the Premiership the following year), but was far superior to either the 1995-96 or the 2004-05 vintages. It might not overwhelm teams as the 1998-99 side had done, but it did share with the 1995-96 team a resolve that allowed it to grind out results. Nobody could claim that the victory over Hull that followed the draw against Stoke was thrilling, but it was impressively comprehensive. Tick the box, check the table and move on. Certainly Jonny Evans was already counting down the games, counting off the points after scoring his first goal for the club. 'The last few games will be mentally testing,' said Evans. 'We've got the ability to finish in the top two; we've seen that against some of the top teams recently, and now we've got to hold our nerve. These last seven games will be a mental test for us, especially after the run we've had, but we're confident.'

Stokes could consider himself fully rehabilitated as he returned to the starting line-up, and was full of contrition. 'It was great to be back and involved with the squad,' he said. 'I've worked hard since missing the bus – I've been getting in to training early. That's all I could do. It was up to the gaffer after that and I have to thank him for putting me back in. He told us in no uncertain terms that it's not acceptable. It was our fault because we did a stupid thing. The gaffer's a fair fella and has not held a grudge. It was a wake-up call for me.'

Keane's campaign for punctuality turned to the fans, as his side decided to punish those slow to take their seats by going ahead within three minutes. Dean Whitehead bent in a free-kick from the right, and Evans, doing a decent impression of Gary Bennett's telescopic neck, arched backwards to guide a header into the bottom corner. The floodgates, though, steadfastly refused to open. Sunderland had 68 per cent of possession, Evans was denied a second headed goal from a corner by a sharp save from Boaz Myhill and David Connolly missed a sitter, but the second didn't arrive until injury-time. Myhill sliced an attempted clearance, and John, presented with the ball 40 yards from goal, had the presence of mind to advance, round Myhill and score. Sunderland climbed to second, albeit only until Birmingham drew with West Brom the following day, and so entered the automatic promotion positions on the same weekend McCarthy's side had two years earlier.

Saturday, 17 March, Championship

Sunderland   **2-0**   **Hull City**
Evans 2
John 90

Sunderland: Ward, Simpson, Nosworthy, Evans, D Collins, Whitehead, L Miller (Wallace 63), Yorke, Murphy, Stokes (Leadbitter 64), Connolly (John 83)
Subs Not Used: Funlop, T Miller
Hull: Myhill, Ricketts, Turner, Delaney, Dawson, Livermore (Barmby 54), Ashbee, Parlour, Elliott (Vaz Te 53), Forster (Marney 74), Windass
Subs Not Used: Coles, Duke
Ref: A Bates (Staffordshire)
Booked: Delaney (Hull)
Att: 38,448
League position: 2

Cardiff. The clouds glowered a gun-metal blue, the wind howled and the rain lashed horizontal, and in the teeth of the tempest Sunderland were saved by their Prospero. Having failed to use the weather to their advantage when it was at their backs in the first half, Sunderland toiled at the beginning of the second as the conditions intensified, before, about 20 minutes in, the rain eased, the wind abruptly dropped and the skies brightened. Keane the master motivator and tactician is one thing, but in Cardiff it seemed he could bang his staff on the ground and control the weather. The game was won for Sunderland by Ross Wallace, brought on as a substitute after Keane had a premonition. 'He's a quality player,' Keane said. 'He's got a left foot and there aren't many of them around these days. He's been in and out of the side for the last month or two, but he's been outstanding in training the last couple of weeks. I can't see into the future, but I just had the sense he'd get the winner today.' With his burgeoning grey-flecked beard, intense stare and disconcerting air of studied calm, this was Keane as Eastern Orthodox mystic, and it was a terrifying transformation.

Saturday, 31 March, Championship

Cardiff City	0-1	Sunderland
		Wallace 72

Cardiff: Alexander, Gunter, Johnson, McNaughton, Ledley, Parry (Feeney 74), McPhail, Scimeca (Walton 46), Whittingham, Thompson, Chopra (Byrne 86)
Subs Not Used: Forde, Blake
Sunderland: Ward, Simpson, Evans, Nosworthy, D Collins, Leadbitter (Stokes 73), Whitehead, L Miller, Hysen (Wallace 57), Murphy (John 72), Connolly
Subs Not Used: Fulop, T Miller
Ref: A D'Urso (Essex)
Booked: Whittingham, McPhail, Walton (Cardiff); Evans (Sunderland)
Att: 19,353
League position: 2

'It was a scrappy game,' Danny Collins said, not for the first time: the Wales international, perhaps understandably, seemed to have become Sunderland's official spokesman on desperately bad matches. 'The weather hasn't helped, but it was a good result for us in the end. At the start of the second half it wouldn't have been good for the crowd to watch and it certainly wasn't good to play in, but it settled down after about twenty minutes and then we got it down and created a couple of good chances.'

Scrappy wasn't the half of it. This was a truly shocking game, and the conditions couldn't take all the blame. Without Carlos Edwards, Sunderland looked short of imagination, and when Tobias Hysen and Grant Leadbitter did get the ball in wide areas, their delivery was poor, although Hysen was unfortunate that his volley from a Leadbitter cross bounced over the bar. In that second half, though, Sunderland proved their mettle beyond any doubt. The Cardiff forward Steve Thompson is not, by any stretch of the imagination, a great player, but he is big, and he is awkward, and he is good at using his bigness and his awkwardness to telling effect. With Cardiff pumping balls towards him on the wind, many defenders would have wilted; Nyron Nosworthy and Jonny Evans grew stronger. Nosworthy loomed colossal, an implacable tower of a man, while Evans not merely won ball after ball, but had the presence of mind regularly to take it down and play it short – the hardest thing to do under the circumstances, but exactly what was needed. Keane had said on his arrival that Evans could become 'a top, top player' and if there had been any doubt, it disappeared at Cardiff. This was a performance of both physicality and intelligence, a display of extraordinary maturity for a player of just 19.

'I think the sky's the limit for Jonny,' said Kenny Cunningham. 'He's got everything. He ticks all the boxes and could play a big part in Manchester United's future. Sunderland have just got to be grateful they've had him this season.' They were, and they were grateful, in particular, for the effect he seemed to have had on Nosworthy. When he'd arrived, Sunderland had been as leaky as a rickety church roof.

Few thought Neill Collins was up to it, while fans were beginning to grow impatient even with Stan Varga, who had taken on semi-cult status by combining being enormous with having a delicately wafty demi-mullet. Varga's greatest strength is also his great weakness. He is built like an oak, but is only marginally faster, and probably slightly less nimble. He defends as one of Tolkein's Ents would. In a crisis you could rely on him to respond with courage and decency, and sling a passing hobbit – or perhaps Ross Wallace – on to his broad shoulders and carry him to safety, but only if that crisis wasn't moving at more than about three miles an hour.

Evans himself was pleasingly modest about his impact, speaking of 'the great bond between the players'. 'I think success has stemmed a lot from the fact that everyone trusts each other on the pitch and wants to back each other up. I've been proud to be part of this back four, with Darren Ward behind us, because we've worked hard on our communication with each other. People have been kind enough to talk about my partnership with Nyron, but I've got a partnership with Danny Collins on the other side and Danny Simpson has worked on his own understandings with Nyron.'

Still, it was Evans who stood out at Cardiff. From him was emitted a confidence, and after Wallace had arrived to add pace and guile, Sunderland had begun to threaten even before the weather eased. Nonetheless, that Sunderland won was in the end down to something as prosaic as a faulty defensive wall. Wallace's free-kick from the right corner of the box scudded through the gap that appeared in the middle of it, and Neil Alexander, partially unsighted, was slow to get down, the ball squirming through his grasp to nestle just inside the post. 'We have a knack of getting goals just when we need them,' said Wallace. 'I've practised free-kicks a lot in training and always fancy myself to get a decent effort on target. The goalkeeper gave me a lot of room at the near post, and thankfully it squeezed in.'

It was for what followed the game, though, that it will be forever remembered because it summed up what Niall Quinn was about. Having spoken frequently and eloquently of community and the club's place in the city, he proved in Cardiff that he was prepared to put his fine words into practice.

The 'Niall Quinn's Disco Pants' ditty was created by Manchester City fans on a pre-season tour to Penola in Italy in 1993. Quinn had been drinking, celebrating the Irish boxer Michael Carruth's gold medal at the Olympics in Barcelona, and ended up in a fight with City's new signing, Steve McMahon. First he broke his nose with a crunching right-hander and then, when McMahon picked himself up and came back for more, he shoved him through a plate-glass window. Quinn was left with his shirt ripped and spattered with blood, so he took it off. A little later, a group of City fans spotted Quinn in a club, dancing frenetically while wearing just a pair of cut-off jeans. And so was born the song that, Quinn admits, will probably be his epitaph:

> *Niall Quinn's disco pants are the best*
> *They go right from his arse to his chest*
> *They're better than Adam and the Ants*
> *Niall Quinn's disco pants.*

Sunderland fans adopted it with gusto, with a group of them gathered by the fanzine *ALS* releasing it as a single in April 1999. It got to number 56 in the charts, but when fans, seeing Quinn on board their EasyJet flight back to the Northeast from Bristol, launched into an alcohol-fuelled rendition, airline staff were unimpressed. An attempt to eject the singers for 'disruptive behaviour' dragged on, and, after the plane missed its take-off slot, the flight was cancelled. 'The airline offered those passengers not involved a free transfer on to the next available flight and hotel accommodation,' an airline spokesman said.

Fans insisted the airline had over-reacted. Airline security took away one fan who had stolen a sign, but that aside, there seems to have been little problem. The chanting, witnesses said, had gone on for no more than a minute. After frenetic discussions between airline staff, and frequent visits by stewards to the cockpit, a number of police cars came screaming up to the plane, and a stewardess came round and, apparently at random, selected fans to be kicked off the flight. One fan, Simon Dickinson, enquiring as to why he was being ejected, was told that the stewardess 'didn't need a reason'. Another fan was expelled seemingly for listening to his iPod. Worst of all though, was the ejection of a fan with learning difficulties, again for reasons that were never explained. Other fans, unwilling to leave friends behind, then began to disembark of their own accord, before Quinn left his seat in an attempt to intervene on behalf of the fans, admonishing airline staff with a line that, for all its undertones of dictatorial demagoguery, will live for ever in Wearside legend. 'These are my people,' he said. 'You cannot treat them like this.' Dickinson later claimed that a policeman admitted his embarrassment at the whole incident, saying that from EasyJet's calls they had been expecting a riot, only to find passengers sitting patiently in their seats waiting for take-off.

'The mood was humorous and everyone was in good spirits after our fine victory,' Quinn maintained. 'Nevertheless we were faced with a situation where our fans were stranded and needed assistance.' So he did the decent, if unthinkable, thing, and, after hiring buses proved impossible at such short notice, shelled out about £8,000 on taxis to take around 100 Sunderland fans back home. 'The club was happy to provide transport back to the Northeast for the group, which included children, elderly, and disabled fans, as their safety and wellbeing was paramount,' he explained. 'We also deny the airline's claim that overnight accommodation was offered and this was witnessed by several independent parties. Thankfully everyone returned home safely and we will now draw a line under this. To any fans who still feel aggrieved, remember the three points came home as well.'

Aggrieved? Not a bit of it. It just added yet more lustre to Quinn's halo. These were willing subjects. 'It shows again that he's the most decent bloke in football,' said another of the fans involved. 'I can't think of a single chairman or a single club that would do something like that for its fans. Everyone thanks him from the bottom of their hearts.' And, just to prove it, Quinn's song gained a new verse that included, just for good measure, a gratuitous dig at his Newcastle counterpart, Freddy Shepherd:

> *Niall Quinn's taxi cabs are the best,*
> *So shove it up your arse, EasyJet,*
> *Fat Fred wouldn't do it for the Mags,*
> *Niall Quinn's taxi cabs.*

The story is told of how at the first training session the following week, Keane announced he was hiring a private detective. Employees looked around nervously, at which Keane continued. 'There's got to be some dirt on that man,' he said. 'Nobody's that good.'

Across on the other side of the river, jostling against the bridge, where the old *Echo* office used to be, stands a new block of luxury apartments, the Echo 24. It is an undeniably thrusting, modern building, but it seemed to me that morning somewhat out of place, rather too big for its surroundings. It is at least, I suppose, a sign of affluence. Niall Quinn has a flat there, overlooking the river, and several of the other apartments have been taken by Irish businessmen, keen to take advantage of the city's unsteady emergence from the gloom of the nineties.

Certainly the block is a rather more valuable addition to the city than *Ambit*, a vaguely ship-shaped sculpture made of 22 steel cylinders that, in 1999, was briefly installed in the river just in front of where Echo 24 now stands. The Tyne had the Baltic, the Sage, and the Millennium Bridge; Sunderland got some floating pipes. They glowed at night, but in the city that had invented the light bulb 150 years earlier, that didn't really impress any more. And anyway, as was widely joked at the time, those who wanted a river that glowed at night only had to pop down the A19 to Middlesbrough. The real fear was that it was perhaps some enormous joke against the city, symbolising, as the name unfortunately suggested, stunted ambition.

Beyond the Echo 24, stretching towards the sea behind the old docklands is the old east end of the city, once Sunderland's slum area. It was there, among the open sewers and the narrow alleys, where pigs were bred in the streets, that in 1831, Britain experienced its first incidence of cholera, introduced by ships coming from the Baltic. The first victim was Isabella Hazard, a 12-year-old girl whose case featured in the *Lancet*. The second was Jack Crawford. Having spurned celebrity, the hero of Camperdown ended up working as a keelman, drinking heavily and dying in dreadful poverty. Those who reject fortune's advances can pay an awful price.

The East End, too, has been regenerated, and there is even – glory be – opposite the Echo 24, a cinema, opened in 2004. Sunderland has lost its fountain, is no longer the largest city in Europe without a cinema and, although a direct rail link to London has been long delayed, should soon cease to be the largest city in Europe without a mainline rail station. Three records gone and none will mourn them.

[13]

THE FINAL ASCENT

The win at Cardiff took Sunderland's league record since the turn of the year to 11 wins and three draws from 14 games, but even that only had Sunderland among the pack. The scramble for promotion out of the Championship had come to resemble a keirin bicycle race. Sunderland had now caught the group tailing the back wheel of the motorcycle, but the sprint to the line was still to come.

It began against Wolves, with Mick McCarthy's return to the Stadium of Light for the first time since his dismissal. Those despatched to report on touchline shenanigans between the combatants of Saipan left disappointed, as the two maintained the uneasy cordiality they had shown at Molineux. Keane even welcomed McCarthy in his programme notes. 'Obviously it didn't work out in the end,' he wrote, 'but it shouldn't be forgotten that he got Sunderland promoted with lots of goals and I think Sunderland fans will give him a very good welcome, which is what he will deserve.' He was indeed applauded, and there was even a brief chorus of 'there's only one Mick McCarthy'. It was, though, only brief. Nobody, after all, wanted to upset the new messiah by paying too much attention to his predecessor – not that anyone had ever thought of McCarthy as a messiah.

As Sunderland took the lead after 15 minutes, it was a hero from much longer ago that was called to mind, as football again indulged its habit of dealing in snapshots of the past. Daryl Murphy may have been a touch fortunate at the way the ball span up as he received a pass from Ross Wallace inside the box, but he took the opportunity superbly, flicking it over his head, taking Neill Collins out of the picture, before slapping a volley beneath Matt Murray. It wasn't quite Gary Bennett looping the ball implausibly over Gary Pallister before side-footing a volleyed winner against Manchester United in 1990, but it wasn't far off. Murphy was at the heart of the second as well, his cross from the right finding Wallace at the back post to head his fifth of the season. Andrew Keogh pulled one back with a diving header almost immediately, but Sunderland were comfortable enough. Insisting that 'you shouldn't judge a book by its cover' when his touchline *sang-froid* was remarked upon, Keane was in typically curmudgeonly form in the press conference. What, he was asked, had he enjoyed most about the performance? Winning, he replied.

Saturday, 7 April, Championship

Sunderland	2-1	Wolverhampton Wanderers
Murphy 15		Keogh 65
Wallace 63		

Sunderland: Ward, Simpson (Leadbitter 71), Nosworthy, Evans, D Collins, Edwards, Whitehead, L Miller, Wallace (Connolly 82), Murphy, John (S Elliott 72)
Subs Not Used: Fulop, Varga
Wolves: Murray (Budtz 72), Little, Breen, N Collins, Clapham, Kightly (Bothroyd 62), Olofinjana, Potter, McIndoe, Ward (C Davies 82), Keogh
Subs Not Used: Craddock, McNamara
Ref: N Swarbrick (Lancashire)
Booked: Nosworthy, Whitehead, L Miller (Sunderland); Keogh (Wolves)
Att: 40,748
League position: 2

A good day got even better as news came through that

Birmingham had lost to Burnley, meaning Sunderland were up once again to second, a point behind Derby, although the obvious caveat was that Birmingham still had a game in hand.

Ross Wallace had spoken about Sunderland's ability to come up with a goal just when they needed one; at Southampton they came up with two. This was Sunderland's season in microcosm: beginning with hope, as it became apparent that, with Birmingham having lost to Barnsley and Derby drawn with Coventry earlier in the afternoon they could go top of the table; passing through gloom and perhaps a touch of despair, before rising to a glorious crescendo. David Connolly had hit the post in a poor first-half, but, as both sides raised themselves after the break, it was Southampton who took the lead midway through the second half. Danny Guthrie's volleyed cross from Djamel Belmadi's long diagonal ball took a touch off Danny Collins, wrong-footing Jonny Evans and Nyron Nosworthy, allowing Marek Saganowski to beat Darren Ward with a half-hit, awkwardly-bouncing volley. It could have been worse had Ward not made a fine block with his legs to deny Jhon Viafara, and with 13 minutes remaining, Sunderland looked on course for their first league defeat of the year.

There had been vague hints of a rally, but there had been little real pressure on the Southampton goal when Carlos Edwards picked the ball up wide on the right. He drifted inside past Belmadi, went across Gareth Bale and kept going until, 22 yards from goal, he unleashed a left-foot drive that screamed into the top right-hand corner. 'They gave me the space to have a strike,' Edwards said, 'and I took the invitation.' Keane, by the bench, chewed his gum a little harder, and clapped his hands together six times, but was otherwise unmoved amid the pandemonium. He, obviously, had seen it coming; either that, or he remembered his previous visit to St Mary's when he was led away by police for taunting the home fans after Manchester United's victory had confirmed Southampton's relegation.

The momentum, suddenly, was with Sunderland. This again was them chasing a game, pounding away at an increasingly nervous and exhausted opposition until the winner came. With three minutes remaining, David Connolly did magnificently to hold the ball up, and, winkling a little space, nudged the ball through to Grant Leadbitter. The substitute took one touch, and then carved a shot away from the dive of Bartosz Bialkowski and inside the right-hand post. He ran to the corner where the away fans churned in a whirlpool of delight, sliding the final dozen of so yards on his knees. His judgement was as precise as his shot, as he came to a halt just touching the flag. 'The moment I hit the ball I was off,' Leadbitter said. 'I knew it was in. If we'd got the draw after being 1-0 down we'd have been reasonably happy, but with our players we always feel there are more goals in us.' That was the essence of the Keane revolution. It wasn't necessarily the players that were key, though: it was the belief.

Monday, 9 April, Championship

Southampton	1-2	Sunderland
Saganowski 67		Edwards 77
		Leadbitter 87

Southampton: Bialkowski, Ostlund, Baird, Pelé, Bale, Dyer (Guthrie 46), Wright, Viafara, Belmadi, Best (Wright-Phillips 53), Saganowski (Rasiak 86)
Subs not used: Davis, Suman
Sunderland: Ward, Simpson, Nosworthy, Evans, D Collins, Edwards, Yorke (Leadbitter 69), L Miller (Whitehead 46), Hysen, Connolly, S Elliott (Stokes 46)
Subs not used: Fulop, Murphy
Ref: P Taylor (Hertfordshire)
Bookings: Yorke (Sunderland)
Att: 25,766
League position: 1

The 'gremlins' Quinn had spoken of earlier in the season, the nervousness brought on by continual failure, were gone, and in their place was a guardian angel. 'Going top was a massive achievement,' said Nosworthy. 'It was a big step for us because we have been playing catch-up for so long. It's full steam ahead now. When we went behind, I always felt we could come back. That's the difference to last season; there's an in-built confidence about us. When we went behind, there was no panic.'

Quinn, meanwhile, continued to act as a travel agent to the fans. This time, when he discovered that several supporters had been left stranded in Southampton after their coach was vandalised, he had the team bus turn round to pick them up.

The belief had become an intoxication. In the aftermath of the victory at Southampton, it seemed that the only person who did not believe promotion was a certainty was Roy Keane. 'We don't know if this is a defining result,' he said. 'We'll only know that at the end of the season. It's in our own hands now. The games are running out, and if we keep winning the table will take care of itself. The priority is to be top at the end of the season, not with three or four weeks to go. My job is to make sure no one gets in the comfort zone but, to be fair, there have been no signs of that. I couldn't be happier working with these players. Every one of them has dug deep.' Promotion, Edwards revealed, was a banned word in the dressing room.

The hard work Sunderland made of beating QPR at home the following Saturday, though, restored a sense of anxiety. The problems were hardly unfamiliar – a failure to take chances while in control, a soft goal conceded – but that, if anything, just made them more troubling. Fortunately, the ability to find a late goal just when it was needed had not deserted them either.

It all began smoothly – rather too smoothly, perhaps – as

Sunderland took a seventh-minute lead with a goal of high quality. Nosworthy, bringing the ball out from the back, exchanged passes with Simpson and then pushed it forwards to Connolly. His reverse ball was perfectly weighted, meaning Whitehead didn't have to break stride as he slipped his finish under Lee Camp. Fans settled back for a win as simple as the one over Southend, but QPR levelled 16 minutes later. A Whitehead pass put Simpson under pressure, and when he lost possession, Dexter Blackstock burst into the box and was brought down by Ward. Martin Rowlands sent the goalkeeper the wrong way from the spot.

An edginess crept into Sunderland's play, but the winner did arrive eventually. Again it was Leadbitter who delivered it, sweeping yet another long-range effort into the bottom corner as Edwards, after shaping to float in a free-kick from the corner of the box, cleverly dragged it square for his onrushing team-mate. 'I thought today was a good performance,' Keane said. 'We created plenty of chances. Once again the players showed great character, but this was always going to be a difficult game for us. We gave away a sloppy goal – I suppose any goal you concede you can look at as sloppy – but the players came good again. We got the second one and managed to, I wouldn't say hold on, but it would have been nice to get a third goal. We are winning games and the players seem to be enjoying it. There's a good bond between them and I think that's beginning to show. They seem to enjoy each other's company. I'm sure they enjoy mine, but they enjoy each other's and that's ultimately what's important.'

Saturday, 14 April, Championship

Sunderland	**2-1**	**QPR**
Whitehead 7		Rowlands 23 (pen)
Leadbitter 76		

Sunderland: Ward, Simpson, Nosworthy, Evans, D Collins, Edwards, Whitehead, Yorke
  (Leadbitter 61), Wallace (John 46), Connolly, Murphy (Stokes 77)
Subs Not Used: Fulop, S Elliott
QPR: Camp, Bignot, Cullip (Kanyuka 43), Stewart, Timoska, Bolder, Rowlands, Lomas
  (Idiakez 83), Moore (Furlong 69), Blackstock, Smith
Subs Not Used: Cole, Nygaard
Ref: M Jones (Cheshire)
Booked: Simpson (Sunderland); Cullip, Bolder, Furlong (QPR)
Att: 39,206
League position: 1

Tellingly, even after what most saw as a performance that fell some way short of Sunderland's best, the opposing manager, John Gregory, was effusive. 'Sunderland – who are by far the best team we've played this season – West Brom and Southampton are probably the only teams in the Championship who get the ball off the goalkeeper and play it out from the back,' he said. 'Sunderland pass it as well as West Brom but with the intention of actually getting somewhere. They've just got that bit of devil in them which obviously comes from the manager.'

Gregory had begun the press conference by asking in bafflement, 'What's Roy done with Nyron Nosworthy? He was the best player on the pitch.' It was a fair question. There are those now who would have you believe that Nosworthy was an unqualified disaster the previous season, but that is not entirely true. 'Nuggsy', as he is known, was named as Sunderland's most under-rated player in the end-of-season *ALS* poll, and his popularity among fans was underlined by the fact that he also took the award for 'coolest player', an image which he tried to live up to by donning a terracotta-coloured Lester Young-style hat for the on-pitch celebrations at Luton. Still, he certainly tended towards the cumbersome and, although he was not the only one so short on confidence that he seemed at times in 2005-06 to find even the simplest of passes beyond him, it looked worse because of his size.

Even if he was never quite as bad as it has been made out, it is Nosworthy who represents Keane's greatest achievement. He had, in many ways, been the embodiment of the McCarthy era, brought in on the cheap from Gillingham and then exposed by the demands of the Premiership. He allowed a simple pass to dribble under his foot on debut against Charlton; he conceded a corner from the halfway line against Newcastle; he was unexpectedly superb against Fulham. He was a curious mix of the graceful and the gormless, and was relished as such, a cult right-back in the fine tradition of John Kay, Dariusz Kubicki, and Chris Makin. Fans accepted him because he was clearly trying, and it wasn't his fault if he wasn't good enough. Except, it turns out, he is good enough, just not at full-back.

Gregory wasn't the only one asking the question of how Keane had wrought such a transformation. It wasn't just that Nosworthy had suddenly learned how to defend; it was that he was also bringing the ball out from the back and passing it around. Against QPR he had initiated the move that led to the first goal, and had laid in David Connolly with a mortar that dropped on to his toe from 60 yards back having reached an altitude of about 40 feet.

McCarthy, in fairness, had tried without success to transform him into a centre-back. 'Nuggsy has gone and played at centre-half, which he never would for me,' he said after Wolves' defeat at the Stadium of Light. 'He never fancied it, in spite of my protestations. Maybe Roy's got more ability to coerce somebody to play out of position.' Maybe he's just got more authority, full-stop.

'I kind of ran away from the situation when Mick asked me,' Nosworthy admitted. 'Obviously I've got playing centre-half right now and wouldn't swap it for the world, but a lot of people had said it wasn't my position and it hadn't worked out when I'd played there in the past. I played the role a few times in pre-season games and even though I had a nightmare in one particular game in North America, I knew I could do better and I'm proving it now.

'I have to concentrate a lot more at centre-half and organise people around me and I think that's brought my game on a lot. It also gives me great confidence knowing the fans are behind me now; they've given me the support to prove what a good player I am. At the start of the season I saw myself purely as a right-back but after how things have gone at centre-half, I'm ready just to call myself a defender. I've come round to the role of playing centre-half. I'm beginning to see myself as a defender who hasn't got a specific position. Playing at centre-half could not have gone any better for me.'

Keane, as ever when praising players, spoke of Nosworthy's 'attitude'. 'Nyron summed up the attitude of the whole team in terms of the way the season went,' he said. 'He adjusted to a new position. When I got here, he was not even training with the first team. I was sussing out different players, but when he got his chance, he took it. He was good as gold. Nyron has been as consistent as anybody.'

Nosworthy was just as complimentary about his manager. 'The gaffer keeps everyone on their toes,' he said. 'He has an aura about him. You respect him and when he comes in the room it goes quiet. It's like when you were a kid and your dad or granddad was around. You sit there and wait for him to talk, and then you answer. He has that natural affect on people. He always wants to do better, push the boundaries, and that's a good thing. Everyone had raised their game. He's definitely pushed me along. He'll tell you what he wants and, if you're not doing it, he lets you know. The gaffer keeps everyone on their toes by watching them and making sure they don't take their foot off the pedal. And he's got us much more organised than before.

'He's calm, calm, calm, calm. It's surprised me because he was very fiery as a player but he's relaxed all the time now, even if we're not doing well. His team talks are very calm and he's brought that quality out in the players so we go on the pitch confident. He doesn't say a lot but, when he does speak, he usually gets his point across without raising his voice.'

So consistent was Nosworthy that he even pipped his centre-back partner Jonny Evans to the Player of the Year award, the fact that the two came top of the poll suggesting just how desperately Sunderland had needed strengthening at the back. 'I honestly think he was man-of-the-match in most of the games we've played,' Evans said. 'I've had a lot of praise but it's been great for me. All I've had to do is pick up the pieces after Nyron most of the time.'

What really endeared Nosworthy to fans was his evident enjoyment of it all, and as he pranced jubilantly around the Kenilworth Road pitch at the end of the season, bare-chested but wearing his pork-pie hat, his feeling for the club was clear. There can have been few players so obviously delighted by a terrace song. There had been a couple of uninspired attempts, but it was when the PA at Ninian Park played the Amy Winehouse song 'Rehab' that his chant was born: 'They tried to take the ball off Nyron, but he said, "no, no no."'

'It's a massive compliment and it feels real nice,' he said. 'I've never had a song before and it makes me feel great. The first time my family heard it, they were buzzing about it. They were ringing me up and singing it down the line. It's a great thing because it makes me feel appreciated and helps bring the best out of me.'

Impressive as Nosworthy was at Cardiff, he was never better than in that QPR game, as a 14th win in 16 games returned Sunderland to the top of the table. That meant that a win at Colchester the following Saturday would ensure promotion if Derby lost at Luton the night before, or if Birmingham lost to both Leicester on the intervening Tuesday and Wolves the following Sunday. Not that Keane was too bothered about that. 'I haven't got a clue,' he said when asked about the various permutations. 'No matter what happens next week we will be trying to win, no matter where, no matter what the situation is. That's what we're trying to do at this football club – continue to win football matches. Along the way, things will fall into place. But I'm not looking too far ahead.'

With three games of the season remaining, others might have been content to retrench, to conserve tired limbs in readiness for the challenge ahead. Not Keane. The Wednesday after the victory over QPR, the players arrived at training to be told they were getting on a coach to Swaledale for a mountain-biking session, the latest in a series of outward bounds adventures he had prepared for his players. This, he said, was 'mental freshening' of the sort in which Brian Clough used to indulge at Nottingham Forest. 'There's some rough terrain out there so, yes, you do think about what might happen if one falls off,' Keane said, 'but, thank God, they all got through, nobody got injured. The goalkeeping coach getting a puncture was the one real incident. We've got to be careful about the danger side of things and the insurance, but we've got a few more things like this planned. You can't just put footballers on the golf course all the time; we like to keep testing them and challenging them in different environments.

'I gave the lads a challenge and it was a very difficult challenge – four hours on a mountain bike is not easy. We were in four teams of ten and every team wanted to win. I find out who the leaders are, who likes to be in control, who the real winners are. We've done a lot of this stuff over the last seven months and you find out a lot about your players through different challenges. The lads are comfortable with a football at their feet but throw them on a mountain bike or into a white-water raft and you see another side of them, some good, some maybe not so good. We like to keep them guessing and give them surprises. They only knew we were going to Swaledale two minutes before we left. You'd be surprised who comes to the fore, there were one or two I thought wouldn't enjoy it, but did. And it means they look forward to getting back training here and getting a feel for the ball again.'

There was, though, to be a glitch. After all the talk of belief, all the goals plucked from nowhere just when they were most needed, all the talk of a relentless, inevitable rise, there was a stutter. It came at Colchester, who would finish the season with the joint second-best home record in the division, and this time it was Sunderland conceding the late goals. They fell behind in first-half injury-time as possession was squandered cheaply on the left, leading to a free-kick in a wide position. Kevin Watson swung it in, and Wayne Brown was unmarked to head into the top corner. Sunderland seemed to have got away with it as that goal was cancelled out nine minutes after half-time. Leadbitter, having been laid in by Whitehead, was denied only by the snaking boot of the goalkeeper Dean Gerken, but when Murphy returned the ball into the middle, Dwight Yorke was able to guide a header through a clutch of bodies on the line.

Sunderland's policy all season had been not to settle for

what they had, and as they pressed again in search of a winner, they were caught on the break. They seemed to have got sufficient men back to cover as Colchester countered with eight minutes remaining, but Richard Garcia lost Evans with an adroit turn, and guided his shot into the bottom corner. Seven minutes later, as Sunderland sought an equaliser, Colchester got a third as Cureton tucked away a penalty after being sent sprawling as he cut across Whitehead. 'We've lost a game and it hurts,' said Ward. 'Any defeat is unpleasant, regardless of whether you've had a good run as we have. Throughout this run we've emphasised that the hard work lies ahead. Losing at Colchester doesn't change the fact that our aim is to win the next two games. This is the time for fans and players to maintain their belief because our destiny is still in our own hands, and that's the way we want it to stay.'

It was, though, a little less in their own hands. Three wins from their final three games would have secured for Sunderland the Championship; now they knew that winning their last two would secure promotion, but they also needed Birmingham to drop points if they were going to take the title. In the reaction to the defeat, though, the difference Keane had made could clearly be seen. There was no panic; most fans expected Sunderland to get the two wins they needed. Only Keane spoke of caution. 'Sometimes,' he said, 'the final step is the biggest.'

Saturday, 21 April, Championship

Colchester United	3-1	Sunderland
Brown 45		Yorke 55
Garcia 82		
Cureton 89 (pen)		

Colchester: Gerken, Duguid, Baldwin, Brown, Barker, Garcia, Watson, Izzet, Jackson (Ephraim 35), Iwelumo (Guy 76), Cureton
Subs Not Used: Davison, White, McLeod
Sunderland: Ward, Whitehead, Evans, Nosworthy, D Collins, Edwards, Leadbitter (S

Elliott 85), Yorke, Murphy (Stokes 73), John (Wallace 60), Connolly
Subs Not Used: Fulop, L Miller
Ref: L Probert (Gloucestershire)
Booked: Cureton, Duguid (Colchester); Murphy, Yorke (Sunderland)
Att: 6,042
League position: 1

It was, though, a little less in their own hands. Three wins from their final three games would have secured for Sunderland the Championship; now they knew that winning their last two would secure promotion, but they needed Birmingham to drop points if they were going to take the title. 'Sometimes,' Keane said, 'the final step is the biggest.'

Victoria Hall, my gran's funeral, the Norman and German assaults, the cholera epidemic and Jack Crawford, Sid James: death has been a constant theme. That was not the original intention: the book was supposed to be triumphant, not ele-giac. I worried it had become overly morbid, and wondered if it was inevitable given the way coming home tends to cast the mind back, but the more I thought about it, the more I realised that football and death have always gone hand in hand.

So many fans wanted their ashes scattered on the Roker Park pitch that the club had to ban the practice because it was dam-aging the grass. Wander around the Stadium of Light looking at the bricks fans have paid to have inscribed with personal messages, and a significant number are in memory of friends or family members. Even the Cup final hymn, 'Abide with me', written by Francis Lyte as he lay dying of tuberculosis, is a deathbed meditation: 'Heaven's morning breaks, and earth's vain shadows flee;/In life, in death, O Lord, abide with me.'

Empty grounds I find eerie, perhaps because the sense of still-ness is so alien that it seems somehow more intense, a reminder that no matter how lively a life, it still ends in silence. Yet, in that silence, if you're in the right mood, the roars seem to echo down the generations. Bobby from Chas's Cabs tapped into it immedi-ately. He could still hear it, even though Roker Park is long gone.

I'm not sure why football should have this effect, why it should so often conjure up the ghosts of its past, but I suspect it is because it is the one great remaining communal rite, a truth – oddly, given how much they have done to change the game – reflected in the titles of Sky's coverage as a black and white shot of fans fades to a colour shot of modern fans. The clothes and the stadium and the football might be different, but the emotion, the act of supporting, remains the same. Going to a match is a ritual passed on from generation to generation. Now that heavy industry has gone – hideous the conditions may at times have been, but there was a certain masculine pride that could be taken from it, as is suggested by Charley Hurley's obsession with the coal-blackened hands of miners – it is the one thing that still unites Sunderland.

A colliery wheel sits atop Sunderland's badge, and there is a replica of a similar wheel at the north-west corner of the Stadium of Light. That, admittedly, is in its most immediate sense a reflection of the fact that the stadium is built on an old mine site, but it surely invokes more generally the city's industrial heritage.

Just across the car park, outside the main entrance, there is another statue. In bronze, it depicts a family of the thirties – standing behind two children, a mother holds up the arm of a flat-capped father as though she were a boxing referee and he had just won a title bout. His face creased by the hardships of life, he holds aloft a sphere made of three interlocking hoops.

A plaque in the plinth makes the point overtly: 'All generations come together at the Stadium of Light,' it reads. 'A love of "The Lads" has bonded together supporters for more than 125 years and will for many more years in the future ... Supporters who have passed away have their support carried on by today's fans, just as the supporters of today will have their support continued through family and friends.'

Perhaps this is characteristic of late phase one: football not as an expression of provincial industrial pride, but as a reminder of it.

ENDGAME

What is it in the soul of a fan that demands not merely victory, but victory in a certain style? It was a view expressed in the 1998-99 season when Sunderland accumulated a then-record 105 points, seventeen clear of their nearest challengers. When they won at home to Birmingham on the final day – thanks to a highly dubious Kevin Phillips goal, not given offside, it seemed, only because the linesman was flagging for a foul on halfway and had been caught behind play when the referee waved an advantage – it meant they had beaten every team in the division at least once. After the agonies of the play-off final defeat to Charlton the previous season, there was a sense of relief about it, as though the relaxed nature of the final weeks was some kind of pay-back after the tension of a year earlier, but there was also a feeling that it had been a bit too easy. There was a bizarre affection for the ground-out 2-1 win over Wolves, when victory was snatched only with a Niall Quinn toe-poke in a last-minute goalmouth scramble. It turned out that being 2-0 up at half-time and cruising can become boring.

There had been nothing boring about 2006-07, but it had lacked an epic, a game of such extraordinary twists and turns that people would still be speaking of it decades into the future

– an equivalent of the 3-2 win over Huddersfield in 1995-96, when Patrick Stewart did the half-time draw and Michael Bridges came off the bench to score twice in the final quarter-hour, or the Kieran Brady-inspired 4-3 win over West Ham in 1989-90. It did come, and at the most dramatic moment possible.

With two games of the season remaining, Sunderland trailed Birmingham by a point, with Derby a point further back. They faced Burnley on the Friday, with Birmingham playing Sheffield Wednesday the following day, and Derby were away at Crystal Palace on the Sunday. Given Sunderland's goal-difference was significantly superior to Derby's, that meant that if Sunderland won and Derby didn't, promotion would be secured.

Billy Davies, the Derby manager, seemed almost to have given up hope of winning automatic promotion. At a press conference on the Friday morning, he glumly reviewed the club's injury situation and commented that he would at least have Michael Johnson back 'for the play-offs'. There was a pause, as journalists gave him the opportunity to add 'if we're in them' or a similar modifier, but it never came.

His belief in Sunderland seemed justified as they set about Burnley with a verve and a swagger. David Connolly had already had a goal ruled out for offside when, after 14 minutes, his low cross from the right was turned in by Daryl Murphy. When a penalty was then awarded as Connolly stumbled over Wayne Thomas as he stooped to head clear, it seemed that the game could become a procession. The Burnley keeper Brian Jensen, though, at full-stretch low to his right, pushed Connolly's spot-kick away, and doubt began to loom.

The law of the ex has rarely felt so immutable. There on the touchline as Burnley's manager was Steve Cotterill, a desperate failure in his time on Wearside as Howard Wilkinson's assistant, and there at centre-forward was Andy Gray, whose 22 appearances at Sunderland had brought a single goal. Six minutes before half-time, Wade Elliott got away from Danny Collins, Eric Djemba-Djemba played him in, and as Elliott made the most of minimal contact from Darren Ward, the referee Trevor Kettle gave another penalty. Gray, inevitably, sent Ward the wrong way to equalise.

That was bad enough, but worse was to follow five minutes after half-time as Elliott, allowed to advance through midfield, sliced a drive from 30 yards into the top corner. On the bench, Keane flicked his gum twice around his lips, and gave a little jerk of the head as he turned his gaze from the scorer's celebrations to the centre-circle, but remained otherwise impassive. Horror gripped the Stadium of Light; 44,000 people can never have been so silent. Surely not now, not this late. Minds went back to 1998, and the 2-0 defeat at Ipswich on the penultimate weekend that ended up costing Sunderland automatic promotion. Some even recalled 1963 and the final-day defeat to Chelsea.

The anguish did not last long. Four minutes later, a diagonal ball from Liam Miller found Carlos Edwards cutting in from the right. He beat Jon Harley and was on the verge of rounding Jensen when the keeper clattered him. The first two penalties might have been soft; this one was cast-iron. Jensen made no protest, merely pursed his lips ruefully and hoped the card would not be red. Bafflingly, there was no card at all.

Connolly stepped up again. Television cameras found a fan in an away shirt who, unable to watch, turned his back on the pitch. Only when he heard the roar, only after his fist had almost involuntarily reacted to the noise, only after Connolly had confidently clipped his penalty high inside the left-hand post, did he dare turn round. That was guts. That was the character Keane had spoken of so often, the character he must have seen in Connolly. A few days later it was pointed out to Keane that Connolly had had a lot of clubs, the implication clearly being that he was seen as unreliable. 'Maybe he just hasn't had the right manager,' came Keane's response. Maybe he hasn't.

'When they took the lead you think, "bloody hell!"' said Connolly. 'I think Dean Whitehead fancied the second penalty and rightly so. But I think you have to show some responsibility and that's why you're at a club like this; that's why you get paid and that's why the fans come to watch you. You have to have that stupidity, bravery, whatever you want to call it; that's why you're there and that's why you play the game. If you didn't have that bravery then you'd have to question why you're out there. Penalties are pressure, but I wouldn't have been able to sleep at night if I'd shied away from taking the second one.' Had Danny Dichio, you wondered, slept after the play-off final in 1998?

Connolly grabbed the ball from the net. Given there were still 36 minutes remaining, it was a largely pointless gesture, but the message was clear; this was a game Sunderland were determined to win. They did, but the vital goal did not arrive until the 80th minute. It was suitably magnificent. It began with Danny Collins dispossessing Gray in his own box. He turned the ball out towards the touchline where Tobias Hysen showed admirable composure to keep the ball in play and feed it down the line. With one touch Grant Leadbitter helped it on for Daryl Murphy, who advanced infield from halfway. This was the sort of slick, intelligent passing Sunderland had produced in patches all season, the spells when the thought of competing in the Premiership seemed so obviously a realistic goal. And then came the moment of individual brilliance.

Murphy pushed the ball on for Edwards, who skipped in from the right and, finding space as Joey Gudjonsson was a fraction slow to close him down, arrowed a drive from 25 yards into the top corner. Struck almost entirely without spin, the logo stayed perfectly still and the ball's trajectory was unnaturally straight as it flew on the diagonal across Jensen and into the net no more than three inches below the bar. Fans behind the line of the shot were on their feet almost as soon as it left Edwards's boot; the North Stand erupted not as one, but as a wave rippling back from those whose view gave them fractionally advanced warning.

By the bench Keane skipped forward a few steps and clenched a fist undemonstratively by his side, as though this were merely confirmation of what he'd been expecting all along. Up in the stand, though, Quinn's joy was unconstrained. Arms spread, fists beating, he looked to the heavens, his face suffused with what can only be described as ecstasy. 'That performance summed up our season,' Keane said. 'We gave away one or two soft goals, but the players showed great character, determination and desire. That last goal was a fitting way to win any game.'

He had particular words of praise not for Edwards, not for Connolly, nor even Murphy, who had led the line superbly, but for the captain, Dean Whitehead. 'He tackles, he's brave and he's honest,' Keane said. 'He does a lot of stuff that goes unnoticed, but not by me.'

Friday, 27 April, Championship

Sunderland	**3-2**	**Burnley**
Murphy 14		Gray 39 (pen)
Connolly 54 (pen)		Elliott 50
Edwards 80		

Sunderland: Ward, Simpson, Nosworthy, Evans, D Collins, Edwards, Whitehead, L Miller (Leadbitter 73), Stokes (Hysen 71), Murphy, Connolly (John 86)

Subs Not Used: Fulop, Yorke
Burnley: Jensen, Duff, Thomas, Caldwell, Harley, Elliott (Spicer 73), Djemba-Djemba,
  McCann (Gudjonsson 29), Jones (Akinbiyi 58), Gray, McVeigh
Subs Not Used: Coyne, Coughlan
Ref: T M Kettle (Rutland)
Booked: L Miller, Edwards (Sunderland); Duff, Djemba-Djemba, Gudjonsson (Burnley)
Att: 44,448
League position: 1

Birmingham beat Sheffield Wednesday 2-0 the following day to return to the top of the table, and so, nervously, everybody's attention switched to Selhurst Park. Well, not quite everybody's. Keane had initially said that he saw Sunday as a family day, so would probably be at the cinema watching the new *Simpsons* film. As it turned out, he had the release dates wrong, and, with it not due out for another two months, he went for yet another walk with Triggs. The labrador, it seemed, had become to Keane what the white cat was to Blofeld.

Again Sunderland were dislocated from their fate, but this time their eyes were on Selhurst Park rather than reaching desperately out from it, this time Crystal Palace were on their side, and this time they got the right result. Derby, as though infected by Davies's pessimism, were sluggish, verging on the lacklustre and Palace were comfortable 2-0 winners, their goals, appropriately enough, coming from Clinton Morrison and Mark Kennedy, both Republic of Ireland internationals. And so, ten years after being relegated at Selhurst Park by events elsewhere, Sunderland, this time themselves elsewhere, were promoted there.

The city council, well-versed in the protocol of promotion, offered a parade and civic reception but, neglecting all precedent, the club turned them down. There was some grumbling, a sense that Keane had taken his downbeat approach a step too far – although he did suggest that he might drive the bus as a way of staying out of the limelight – but for many Quinn's explanation made sense. 'We are immensely grateful to the city council for their very kind offer,' he said. 'However, we feel that this is only the beginning of our journey. Everyone is rightly proud of the team, but we feel that we have simply got the club back to where we should be – back among football's elite. We recognise there is still a long way to go ... We hope that fans will understand our reasons for this and don't think we're spoiling the party. This is a statement of our intent – we're not content with what has been achieved so far and this is when the hard work really starts ... Everyone is now focusing on next season and beyond and trying to achieve sustained success for our football club.'

The old Sunderland had been so in need of opportunities to celebrate that they'd had a parade after losing in the FA Cup final in 1992. The new Sunderland didn't even celebrate promotion because they believed there would be far greater triumphs ahead. Nothing could better have summed up the developments of 15 years. Nobody would be allowed to think that this was enough of an achievement; there would be no lapsing into the comfort zone. It was all part of Keane's overall desire to ditch the 'happy camper' mentality.

Certainly nobody could have accused him of excessive glee that week. Although the players were given the Wednesday and Thursday of the final week of the season off, it was essentially business as usual at the training ground.

Keane, meanwhile, carried on with characteristic grumpiness. Was he enjoying management? 'Not really,' he said. 'At this time of my life, it feels like the right thing to be doing. I can understand that sort of stuff when other managers come out and say it's like an addiction. Winning, especially. Winning. That's addictive.' Never enjoy, only succeed.

*

The success was spreading. The effect of a successful team on productivity in the city's workplaces has long been noted, but the link-up between Sunderland and Ireland had begun to effect people way beyond football's usual confines. Quinn is popular because he sees the bigger picture. Nobody can mistake his motives. He is not at Sunderland to make money for himself. He is not even there necessarily to win trophies; he is there because he can make a difference. One of *ALS*'s range of T-shirts quotes a passage from Quinn's autobiography: 'I learned my trade at Arsenal, became a footballer at Manchester City, but Sunderland got under my skin. It hurt me deeply to leave. I love Sunderland.' He was not talking merely about the club.

That was clear enough from the donation of his testimonial money to the hospital, but it is clear in his every action. He can list redundancy figures from across the city: 140 jobs gone at a laundry, 790 at the last two glass-blowing firms, 600 at Fujitsu, 670 at Groves Cranes, 600 at Vaux Breweries ... 'At this club, in this region,' he said, 'there is a moral responsibility. The club is the biggest symbol of identity for Sunderland people. What I have to make sure is we strike a balance between being affordable and making sure we can compete.'

In the modern world of football, when people barely bat an eyelid at paying £8 for a slice of pizza and there is nobody who does not acknowledge the importance of keeping the corporate sector happy, it is easy to be cynical. 'If I was offered Chelsea for one pound I wouldn't take it because I can bring nothing to it,' Quinn said in an interview in *The Guardian*. 'But I think I can bring something here because I relate to these people. I hung around with ex-miners when I came here and I still do – they've come over to see me in Ireland. When I first came to England [in 1983] I saw these miners getting the shit kicked out of them by all these cops. It struck a chord with me and, when I came up here, I began to find out more. There was a bitter aftertaste and it helped me find out the real spirit of the region, the real problems, the real pleasures. And it's different here: it's not London, it's not Manchester, not Liverpool, it's Sunderland. It's an incredible place, I know that. These are real people, it's real football. There's a warmth here that this football club has to use. We feel it's starting to work.'

It is, and not just on the field. As early as October, the local tourist board was reporting an increase in visitors, largely because of the Roy Keane factor. 'There are a lot of people coming to the area mentioning his name – he is a real pull for the city,' said Carol Walsh, from Sunderland's tourist information centre. 'They are initially coming to see the football, but then are wanting to stay and wanting to know where to eat and where to visit to make a weekend of it.'

The majority of those, naturally, are from Ireland. Accordingly to Drumaville shareholder Charlie Chawke, the Quinn-Keane axis at Sunderland is the biggest thing to happen to Irish football since they qualified for Italia 90 under Jack Charlton. 'Roy Keane has made it more successful and the whole country is gone mad on supporting Sunderland,' he said in an interview in *Business Limerick*. 'The support from Ireland is so big that Ryanair have shown an interest in running direct match flights from Dublin and Shannon. Ryanair are taking us seriously now and Aer Arann are getting involved with the club.' Extra flights are being laid on. Hotels and guest houses, previously dormant in the winter, are finding themselves booked up months in advance on match weekends, and there is Irish investment in property in the area. At the end of 2006, Sunderland City Council sent a delegation to Dublin as part of the Visit Britain initiative. 'We had a big poster of Roy on our stand. It seemed to attract more attention than anything else at the expo,' said Susan Wear, head of corporate communications at the council. 'We got ninety applications from travel agents to come and have a look at the area, much more than we would normally expect.'

Aer Arann sponsored Sunderland's summer tour of Ireland in 2007, and, in that final week of the season, it was announced that the Irish bookmakers Boylesports would take over shirt sponsorship from Reg Vardy, as well providing in-stadium betting for the next four years.

As Quinn had said, the difficulty is striking the balance between success on the field and being a community service. A parade, perhaps, would have raised interest and, in the short-term, generated revenue for a small number of businesses – burger vans, pubs on the route, merchandise stalls, for instance – but a decision was taken that embracing the Championship as success would damage the long-term interests of the club. So, for the fans at least, the celebration rolled on unreleased to Luton, a venue nobody would choose for a party. At Tranmere in 1996, Sunderland had taken three sides of the ground as they celebrated the title – and Newcastle squandering a 12-point lead in the Premiership – but there would be none of that in 2007. The capacity at Luton is a paltry 10,500, and Sunderland were given just 1,800 of that, although many more finagled their way in. Not that Keane was thinking about celebrating anyway. Predictably, he wanted the title as well as promotion. Given Sunderland's previous three promotions had come as champions, that would have been understandable from anybody, but from Keane, it was all part of the relentlessness, of his eternal hunger. This, after all, was a man who, speaking of his fear of the 'comfort zone' – a fear of losing the fear of losing – had been highly critical of his Manchester United team-mates for losing the last two games of the 2001-02 season, after the league had already been secured. 'Winning promotion was the priority, but we'll be taking the Luton game very seriously,' Keane said. 'We want to go and finish the job.'

And finish it they did. The comparisons might have become irritating, but the similarity to Keegan's first full season at Newcastle were hard to ignore. His side had left the division with a 7-1 demolition of Leicester, and Sunderland signed off with a similarly emphatic farewell, winning 5-0. This wasn't just a joyous release as, with promotion secured, the players relaxed and the goals flew in, this was two fingers raised over the shoulder at the rest of the division, unequivocal proof that Sunderland were too good for the Championship. Back in 1999, after clinching promotion with a 5-2 win at Bury, Sunderland players had ripped down a sponsors' hoarding at Gigg Lane, smashing it as they chanted 'Goodbye to the Nationwide.' The sentiment was little different this time round, but a 5-0 win was a more dignified way of expressing it.

Still, whatever Sunderland did, they were reliant on Preston, who had lost six of their previous seven games, avoiding defeat against Birmingham. The best Sunderland could realistically hope for, it was generally believed in the build-up, was for a draw at Deepdale, which meant beating Luton by two would be enough to lift them above Birmingham. That part of the equation was completed within six minutes. First Anthony Stokes, darting in from the left, reacted first to reach a loose ball after Daryl Murphy's attempt to flick-on his initial pass had been blocked. Then Murphy, gathering a clever volleyed jab from Carlos Edwards, belted in a 25-yard drive.

As on so many other final days, the attention shifted from what was happening on the pitch, to what was happening on the radios and mobile phones. At Tranmere, 11 years earlier, with the title already secured, the focus had turned to events back in the Northeast, where Manchester United needed only a point to complete their comeback and claim the Premiership title, and that point was only needed if Newcastle beat Tottenham at home. Sunderland, playing appallingly, were one down to a Kenny Irons goal by the time the Premiership fixtures kicked off. About ten minutes later, Tranmere were awarded a penalty. Nobody really cared. Then, as John Aldridge put the ball on the spot, three sides of the ground rose as one, saluting David May's goal for United at the Riverside. Aldridge, bewildered, shrugged and tucked in the penalty. In the stands, the cheering went on: Newcastle's laughable collapse was confirmed.

There continued to be no news from Deepdale, which was, in a sense, good news, and at half-time Preston against Birmingham remained goalless. Sunderland added a third a minute into the second half, Grant Leadbitter laying in Stokes to cross for Murphy to knock in, and by the time Ross Wallace lashed in a fourth with 12 minutes remaining, it had long been clear that the only thing that could stop Sunderland was a goal for Birmingham. Gary McSheffrey probably twice should have scored it, but he didn't, and the championship was confirmed five minutes from time. Just as David Connolly was glancing in a Grant Leadbitter free-kick at Luton, the news broke that Simon Whaley had put Preston ahead against Birmingham.

Sunday, 2 May, Championship

Luton Town	0-5	Sunderland
		Stokes 4
		Murphy 6, 46

Wallace 77
Connolly 86

Luton: Brill, Keane, Coyne, Barnett, Emanuel, O'Leary (Langley 55), Spring, Heikkinen,
Bell (Brkovic 60), Andrew, Idrizaj
Subs Not Used: Perrett, Boyd, Talbot
Sunderland: Fulop, Wright, Nosworthy, Evans, D Collins, Edwards (Wallace 75),
Whitehead (Connolly 57), Yorke, Leadbitter, Stokes, Murphy (John 57)
Subs Not Used: Varga, L Miller
Ref: L Mason (Lancashire)
Booked: Coyne, Idrizaj, Keane, Brkovic (Luton); Stokes, Evans, D Collins (Sunderland)
Att: 10,260
League position: 1

Keane, under intense pressure, finally admitted 'I've enjoyed it'
and that 'I've had worse days', but even as his players frolicked
on the pitch, he was thinking about 'being back in on
Tuesday', and a series of meetings to sort out financing for the
season ahead. 'Niall and the board are the team behind the
team,' he said. 'Niall and the board do not interfere, and that
is why it has worked. It would not have done otherwise. It is
nice to go up as champions, but there is a massive challenge
ahead. I will meet Niall and the board next week, and we will
look at what kind of money is available.'

Always meticulous, always looking ahead, this was Keane's
'Law of Accumulation' in action. People spoke of a revolution,
but Keane's impact came not as one great upheaval. There was
no one gesture or idea than enacted the change, rather it was
the combination of a thousand little things. There had been an
overhaul of the playing staff, of course, but that aside there
were few radical differences. There was a greater sense of discipline, of authority from the top, of fitness and direction and
desire. Sunderland had come to retain possession better than
for several years, but was that not simply a function of the
greater confidence given them by Keane's charisma and the
impression he gave of being always in control? It came back, in

the end, to the attribute of which Keane had spoken more than any other: attitude. There was simply a greater belief and sense of purpose about Sunderland than there had been for almost a decade, which had combined with Drumaville's investment to generate a force that, in Championship terms, was irresistible.

Most of all, though, there was Keane and his relentlessness. He wanted no parade, he took no time off to celebrate, he simply got on with shaping the squad for the season ahead, goaded always by his desire for more success.

Never the comfort zone, always the fear.

I carried on under the bridges, where the banks are supported by brick ramparts that once formed part of the shipyards. A fading graffito proclaims that 'ELVIS LIVES', which back in September 2006 would have seemed vaguely more plausible than the smaller slogan next to it: 'SAFC CHAMPIONS'. A brick chute – once, I imagine, used to drop coal down from the colliery to the river – cuts through the tangled grass to my right. The Stadium of Light, I know, is up there somewhere, but even though I can be no more than 60 or 70 yards from it, the steepness of the bank means I cannot see it. Across the river stands the vast shed of the Liebherr Crane plant, the one great factory still based this high up the river. A man passes on a bike, a dog running behind him. 'Eeeh,' he calls amiably over his shoulder, noting my laptop bag and camera, 'yer laden there, son.' I smile and nod and the dog, after paying me a second's notice, trots on. I don't want to fall into any clichés here, but that wouldn't have happened in London.

Behind the West Stand, beyond the car park where the land

falls sharply towards the river, somewhere nobody would go without a specific reason, is a series of sculptures by Graeme Hopper, figures done in the style of the artist LS Lowry, who visited the city regularly from the early fifties until his death in 1976. I had visited them when they were first installed ten years ago, and, as time had gone by, had come to equate them with Sisyphus, the Greek hero who dared to challenge the gods and was punished by being forced perpetually to roll a rock up a hill, only for it to tumble down before he could reach the summit. In my mind, though, largely because I couldn't believe anybody involved with a yo-yo club would ever go for such aptly depressing symbolism, these were mineworkers, pushing a cart up the bank. I had even wondered whether seeing a reference to Sisyphus was an affectation, a *post hoc* search for meaning on my part. But no, as I got to the bottom of the bank that morning, not only was the Sisyphean spirit apparent, but it was explicit. These weren't miners pushing a cart, although they clearly nod to the miners who once worked the site: they were weird silver stickmen in three groups, each straining to push an enormous silver polyhedron – manifestly a rock – up the bank.

In *De Rerum Natura*, Lucretius argues that the classical idea of hell and the various torments inflicted on unfortunates therein are metaphors for the frustrations of everyday life. Tantalus, who in his version of the myth was bound beneath a boulder that threatens perpetually to fall, represents for Lucretius those oppressed by a fear of the gods (in whom he didn't believe). Tityos, having his liver ripped out constantly by birds of prey, stands for those tortured by love, anxiety, or other passion. Cerberus and the Furies are, for him, embodiments of agents of retribution, feared needlessly by all. Lucretius, following Epicurus, believes all men should try to attain a state of *ataraxia*, a detached and balanced state of mind in which pain is neither feared nor pleasure pursued. (The Josh Hartnett character in the Paul McGuigan film *Lucky Number Slevin* claims to have a condition called *ataraxia* when the Lucy Liu character asks him how he remains so calm despite two different gang bosses threatening him.)

Ataraxia is the exact opposite of fandom. It is precisely the feeling of caring, come what may, however often the stone goes crashing back down the hill again, that makes supporting a club worthwhile, that binds the city together, one generation to the next. It is the numbness brought on by the endless defeats of 2005-06 that Keane has managed to cast aside, and that is why the version of *Hey Jude* used to salute him, with all its exhortations to 'let her into your heart', to 'let her under your skin', is so appropriate. Quinn used that same phrase of Sunderland getting under his skin; for fans, Keane allowed the club back there. After the shellshock of the previous season, he has taught the city to care again.

Alone, at the top of the bank, sat a single figure, gazing over the heads of his companions towards the Liebherr plant. He is clearly a man apart. There is a sense that he is somehow above the toil of the others, that he has perhaps even succeeded in the task, although his rock is nowhere to be seen. What is most striking, though, is his posture, for as he squats there, aloof, commanding, he resembles nothing so much as that photograph of Roy Keane perching on a ball among the saplings at the side of the training pitch.

APPEARANCES

	LEAGUE		FA CUP		LEAGUE CUP	
	App	Gl	App	Gl	App	Gl
Ben Alnwick	11 (0)	0	0 (0)	0	1 (0)	0
Chris Brown	10 (6)	3	0 (0)	0	0 (0)	0
Steve Caldwell	11 (0)	0	0 (0)	0	0 (0)	0
Trevor Carson	0 (0)	0	0 (0)	0	0 (0)	0
Clive Clarke	2 (2)	0	0 (0)	0	0 (0)	0
Danny Collins	36 (2)	0	0 (1)	0	0 (1)	0
Neill Collins	6 (1)	1	0 (0)	0	1 (0)	0
David Connolly	30 (6)	13	1 (0)	0	0 (0)	0
Kenny Cunningham	11 (0)	0	0 (0)	0	1 (0)	0
Rory Delap	6 (0)	0	0 (0)	0	1 (0)	0
Carlos Edwards	15 (0)	5	0 (1)	0	0 (0)	0
Robbie Elliott	7 (0)	0	0 (0)	0	1 (0)	0
Stephen Elliott	15 (9)	5	1 (0)	0	1 (0)	0
Jonny Evans	18 (0)	1	1 (0)	0	0 (0)	0
Martin Fulop	5 (0)	0	0 (0)	0	0 (0)	0
Peter Hartley	0 (1)	0	0 (0)	0	0 (0)	0
Tobias Hysen	15 (11)	4	1 (0)	0	0 (0)	0
Stern John	10 (5)	4	0 (0)	0	0 (0)	0
Graham Kavanagh	10 (4)	1	0 (0)	0	0 (0)	0
Kevin Kyle	0 (2)	0	0 (0)	0	0 (0)	0
Liam Lawrence	10 (2)	0	0 (0)	0	0 (1)	0
Grant Leadbitter	24 (20)	7	1 (0)	0	1 (0)	1
Liam Miller	24 (6)	2	1 (0)	0	0 (0)	0
Tommy Miller	3 (1)	0	0 (0)	0	0 (0)	0
Daryl Murphy	27 (11)	10	1 (0)	0	1 (0)	0
Nyron Nosworthy	27 (2)	0	0 (0)	0	0 (0)	0
Lewin Nyatanga	9 (2)	0	0 (0)	0	0 (0)	0
Arnau Riera	0 (1)	0	0 (0)	0	1 (0)	1
Danny Simpson	13 (1)	0	0 (0)	0	0 (0)	0
Jon Stead	1 (4)	1	0 (0)	0	0 (1)	0
Anthony Stokes	7 (7)	2	0 (0)	0	0 (0)	0
Stanislav Varga	20 (0)	1	1 (0)	0	0 (0)	0
Ross Wallace	20 (12)	6	1 (0)	0	0 (0)	0
Darren Ward	30 (0)	0	1 (0)	0	0 (0)	0
Dean Whitehead	43 (2)	4	1 (0)	0	1 (0)	0
Stephen Wright	2 (1)	0	0 (0)	0	1 (0)	0
Dwight Yorke	28 (4)	5	0 (1)	0	0 (0)	0

BIBLIOGRAPHY

Yearbooks and Almanacks
Rothmans Football Yearbooks
SkySports Football Yearbooks

Brett, Alan and Andrew Clark, *Newcastle v Sunderland: A History of a Great Football Rivalry* (Northeast Press, 1995)

Clough, Brian, *Clough: the Autobiography* (Partridge, 1993)

Corfe, Tom, *Sunderland: a Short History* (Albion, 1973)

Dykes, Garth and Doug Lamming, *All the Lads: A Complete Who's Who of Sunderland AFC* (Sunderland AFC, 2000)

Garrick, Frank, *Raich Carter: The Biography* (SportsBooks, 2003)

Hetherington, Paul, *Sunderland Greats* (John Donald, 1989)

Howey, Martin and David Bond, *Meet me in the Roker End: A Revealing Look at Sunderland's Football History* (Vertical Editions, 2004)

Hudson, John and Paul Callaghan (eds), *Sunderland AFC: The Official History* (Sunderland AFC, 1999)

Keane, Roy, *Keane: The Autobiography* (Penguin 2003, first published Michael Joseph 2002)

Kirtley, Mel, *50 Post-War Seasons of Sunderland AFC* (Wearside Books, 1996)

Quinn, Niall, *Niall Quinn: The Autobiography* (Headline, 2002)

Simmons, Bill and Bob Graham, *The History of Sunderland AFC 1879-1986* (Mayfair, 1986)

Sinclair, Neil T., *Sunderland: City and People since 1945* (Breedon, 2004)

Smith, J.W. and T.S. Holden, *Where Ships are Born, Sunderland, 1346-1946: A history of shipbuilding on the River Wear* (Thomas Reed, 1946)

Talbot, Bryan, *Alice in Sunderland: An Entertainment* (Jonathan Cape, 2007)

Newspapers and magazines

A Love Supreme
Business Limerick
The Daily Mail
The Daily Mirror
The Evening Chronicle
The Financial Times
FourFourTwo
The Guardian
The Independent
The Independent on Sunday
Ireland on Sunday
The Irish Examiner
The Irish Times

The Journal
The Mail on Sunday
The News of the World
The Northern Echo
The Observer
The Sun
The Sunday Mirror
The Sunday Telegraph
The Sunday Times
Sunderland Echo
The Telegraph
The Times

Websites

www.fifa.com
www.rsssf.com
www.safc.com
www.since1888.co.uk
www.soccerbase.com
www.uefa.com